THE LIFE AND TIMES OF HENRY MONNIER 1799–1877

The Life and Times of HENRY MONNIER *1799–1877*

EDITH MELCHER

HARVARD UNIVERSITY PRESS
Cambridge, Massachusetts
1950

PRINTED IN THE UNITED STATES OF AMERICA

LONDON—GEOFFREY CUMBERLEGE—OXFORD UNIVERSITY PRESS

To the memory of Marcelle Pardé, who taught at Bryn Mawr College from 1922 to 1929 and was Directrice du Lycée de Jeunes Filles of Dijon when she died in the German concentration camp of Ravensbruck in January 1945.

PREFACE

Henry Monnier was an artist, an actor, a writer, and that elusive phenomenon known as a humorist. His comic and satiric prints belong to the period of Daumier and, although he has never attained and does not deserve first place among French comic artists, the number of his admirers has grown and the market value of his work has increased in the twentieth century, during the years when Daumier's greatness has been receiving due recognition. As an actor Monnier is almost forgotten today, but between 1830 and 1860 he was considered one of the most original and amusing of French character actors; as a mimic and monologuist, both amateur and professional, he invented a realistic technique which his contemporaries judged as approaching perfection, preceding by some fifty years many of the ideas carried out by Antoine in the Théâtre Libre. In the history of nineteenth-century literature, Monnier is usually labeled a "predecessor" of the Realistic movement. A contemporary and friend of Balzac, he specialized in scenes and types of lower-middle-class society, which he presented with a mingling of photographic exactness and Romantic irony. As a humorist he possessed all the Romanticist's sense of the ridiculousness of human nature, and he had a consummate skill in hoaxes and practical jokes.

It is the aim of this book to romanticize Monnier as little as possible, for whatever role he chose to play, it was never that of the Romantic hero. The story of his life reflects the times in which he lived: Monnier might almost be called a symbol of the nineteenth century. Victor Hugo, whose life spanned nearly the same period as his, was deeply conscious of his mission as *écho sonore* of the century born with him. Yet perhaps Monnier, who was not a great artist, whose varied talents seldom lifted him above second-rate achievement, is more truly representative of that diversified era. Some twenty years ago Professor Eunice Morgan Schenck, of Bryn Mawr College, first called to my attention the extraordinary fidelity with which Monnier reproduced in the *Mémoires de Monsieur Joseph Prudhomme* the ideas, tastes, and sentiments of the average

Frenchman of his time. As I have continued to study Monnier's work and career, I have found that he reflects not only trends in caricature, dramatic art, and literature, but also the social, economic, and political history of the Restoration, the July Monarchy, and the Second Empire. He knew personally most of the Romanticists, the artists, actors, and writers of his own generation, but succeeding generations found also in him some congenial trait, some talent to be admired, so that he is connected with the Bohemian group from which grew the Realists of the mid-century, with the neo-Romanticists of the Second Empire, and even to some extent with the Naturalists.

Monnier's influence on Balzac's study of the *bourgeoisie* and the resemblances betweeen Monnier's and Flaubert's observations of that class would suffice in themselves to preserve his literary work from the oblivion to which its defects might have condemned it, but he has in his own right another title to fame. The average Frenchman today may not know the creator of Monsieur Joseph Prudhomme, but Prudhomme has become a permanent type, whose physical traits and humorous aphorisms are as familiar as those of any national figure. The history of Prudhomme is the history of the middle classes, and a study of his mentality, morality, and philosophy contributes to an understanding of the traits which determined the course of French life between 1789 and 1940.

In writing in English a book whose sources are chiefly French, I have had to decide whether it is desirable to quote extensively in the foreign language. It has seemed to me preferable to use English translations whenever possible, except in the quotation of poetry. In the notes, however, I have kept the French in some cases where the effect would have been lost in translation.

Those more readable notes which enrich the meaning of the text appear as footnotes, while the more purely bibliographical and documentary references are given at the back of the book.

It gives me pleasure to express here my deep gratitude to the following friends whose help in criticizing and correcting the manuscript of this book has been continually heartening and stimulating: Professors Andrée Bruel and René de Messières of Wellesley College, Eunice Morgan Schenck of Bryn Mawr College, Henri Peyre of Yale University; Dr. Anne Cutting Jones. I wish to thank also the publishers for permission to quote from the following books: Gertrude Stein, *Paris France*, Scribner's; T. S. Eliot, *Selected Essays 1917–1932*, Harcourt Brace; Egon Friedell, *A Cultural History of the Modern Age*, Knopf; S. M. Waxman, *Antoine and the Théâtre Libre*, Harvard University Press. I am grateful to Professor William A. Jackson of the Houghton Library, Harvard University, for obtaining permission for me to use the Monnier letters in the Gentili di Giuseppe Collection, deposited in that library, and to Mrs. Raphael Salem, owner of the letters, for granting the permission. I am indebted to M. Paul Touzet of Paris for many of the illustrations used in the book, notably for photographs of works by Monnier in the Jean Thesmar Collection.

CONTENTS

ILLUSTRATIONS

"La Fuite de l'amour."

Water-color drawing. Collection Jean Thesmar, Paris. Photograph R. David, Paris.

"Jean Iroux" (1838).

Drawing. From Marie, Henry Monnier.

Madame Henry Monnier (1837).

Drawing. From Marie, Henry Monnier.

"Les Voituriers" (1833).

Water-color drawing. Photograph R. David, Paris.

"L'Huître et les plaideurs" (1866).

Wash drawing. Photograph R. David, Paris.

"La Salle d'attente."

Water-color drawing. Photograph R. David, Paris. Marie (p. 223) lists "Salon d'attente" (14 figures), "L'Attente" (7 figures), "L'Attente" (10 figures), all dated 1869, and (p. 230) "L'Attente," with 4 figures, not dated.

"Ecole des orphelins, Amsterdam" (1864).

Water-color drawing. Collection Jean Thesmar, Paris. Photograph R. David, Paris. Dated 1845 in Champfleury, Henry Monnier, *p. 315.*

THE LIFE AND TIMES OF HENRY MONNIER 1799–1877

I

1799–1815: CHILDHOOD THE FIRST EMPIRE

I was born in Paris," wrote Henry Monnier, "at 31 rue de la Madeleine, faubourg Saint-Honoré, of poor but honest parents, just a year after the proclamation of the Empire, and I saw enough of the Empire to have remained entirely faithful to that regime." [1]

In this apparently simple statement several points must be examined. When it was written, Monnier was a middle-aged actor enjoying considerable success in Paris. His loyalty to the Napoleonic regime was no doubt sincere enough, but he may have felt that a politic reminder of it in 1855 was in accord with popular taste. When he knocked a few years from his true age, he was merely following professional tradition, unless with tongue in cheek he was deliberately parodying the famous line, *Ce siècle avait deux ans*, which has served so conveniently to fix the date of Victor Hugo's birth. The style of Monnier's autobiographical statement does suggest a humorous intention, for who would use that phrase about the poor but honest parents, unless he wished to make fun of the sentimental novels whose heroes always recalled the humble start of their brilliant careers?

As a matter of fact, Monnier was born in 1799, as the records of the parish church of Saint-Roch attest: "19 *prairial an* VII [June 7, 1799]—Henry* Bonaventure Monnier, son of Jean-Pierre-Etienne Bonaventure Monnier, *employé*, and of Guilberte Perrier, his spouse, dwelling at rue de la Madeleine, no. 1382." [2] His father belonged to that genteel section of the petty *bourgeoisie*, the civil servants, whose numbers, increasing enormously during Napoleon's reign, were to weigh more and more heavily on the French state until they formed the overgrown body of *fonctionnaires* that proved so burdensome to the Third Republic. It is safe to assume that Jean Monnier's position

* His given name is occasionally found incorrectly spelled *Henri.*

as an employee at the Ministry of Finances led him to support Napoleon and to encourage similar enthusiasm in his son. Henry was too young during the Consulate to understand the gradual approach of dictatorship, as Bonaparte's increasing power assured the country that the disorderly inefficiency of the Directory was ended.

Monnier's father was progressive enough to have his son vaccinated, in spite of maternal fears of that alarming practice, which was just beginning to be followed in Paris. If we may believe Monnier's most important literary work, the *Mémoires de Monsieur Joseph Prudhomme*, many of whose details are unquestionably autobiographical, the little boy had the measles, although Providence preserved him from the whooping cough. In 1803 he was probably taken to see the fireworks at the Tuileries, a favorite entertainment of the Parisians, who rejoiced at its revival in that year. In 1803 also he could have witnessed the intimidating spectacle of the first steamboat on the Seine, one of Robert Fulton's experiments. And it is to be hoped that he caught a glimpse of the male elephant which was moved through the streets from the Jardin des Capucines to join the female elephant at the Jardin des Plantes, a ceremony of such scientific interest that it was attended by the Minister of the Interior and several members of the Institute.

A few years after the establishment of the Lycée Bonaparte in 1803, Henry was admitted as a pupil there. In the *Mémoires* he describes how proudly he exchanged baby dress for trousers, with buttons fastening them to his jacket and a pocket for the large handkerchief pinned to the trousers so that it would not be lost; and how he carried a large lunch basket, doubly proud that his mother soon allowed him to go to school unaccompanied. With the sense of independent individuality, he began to develop an unruliness which became a lifelong resistance to discipline.

It is not surprising that the boy was rather a problem, both to his parents and to his masters. The atmosphere of those years was too turbulent to encourage quiet devotion to the traditional program of dead languages or mathematical theory. Boys were destined to become soldiers and physical development was emphasized at the expense of study. The schools were organized on a military pattern; the pupils in uniform marched to classes to the rhythm of a drum.

While such training gave Henry Monnier no lasting inclination for army life, its militaristic pageantry certainly did little to keep his mind on his books. He was probably not greatly exaggerating the deficiencies of his education when he stated later: "I left the Lycée Bonaparte knowing Latin very badly, little Greek, no mathematics at all, not a speck of geography; writing French sadly enough and spelling fairly correctly." He might have added that he had discovered a gift for caricature, which he turned against some of his schoolmasters whose personal eccentricities or political views aroused his animosity.

He kept not too unpleasant memories of his school days, however, for he wrote in middle life a rather sentimental sketch of some of his teachers, and described the schoolyard as a peaceful spot where he had learned to appreciate simple and gentle things. In another sketch he recalled his boyish devotion to the driver of the coach in which he traveled from Paris to Magny-en-Vexin when he went to spend his holidays at his uncle's house in the village of Parnes. *Le père Alexandre*, with his green velvet coat, stout hobnailed boots, and venerable otterskin cap, was a Dickensian figure doomed to disappear along with his lumbering vehicle when the railroad came to replace the stagecoach.[3]

The world of which Henry Monnier was growing conscious was dominated by the glittering, all-conquering name of Napoleon. The establishment of the Empire at the end of 1804 was accompanied by lavish celebrations: the Parisians danced in the streets, tried their skill at the popular sport of climbing a greased pole, gaped to their heart's content at fireworks and brilliant parades. Then dawned the wonderful year 1805, which brought ever brighter glory to France and its hero, and culminated in the intoxicating triumph of Austerlitz. During that year of victories there was plenty for a boy to do and see. In February the Carnival was revived, with the traditional celebration of the *Boeuf gras* that had not been held for fifteen years. If the spirit of revelry was more military and nationalistic in character than it had once been, the children were aware only of the exciting fun. They were always ready for a parade, and the streets of Paris were rarely without the tramp of marching feet and the glitter of uniforms.

What would a boy have known or cared about the other side of this display? The hollow luxury of court life, the lavish spending of soldiers' pay, the feverish thirst for diversion, these were the façade of prosperity; but behind, there was unemployment, there were the tears of young men's mothers, there was the human need for rest and peace, and a growing realization that the ideals for which the Revolution had been fought were betrayed and cast aside by the Emperor. Henry Monnier must have heard the criticisms which the middle class expressed freely enough when the time came for the divorce of Josephine. She had given the Empire whatever beauty or grace it had, and her departure marked the beginning of a more somber period.

The show still went on, however. A boy like Henry Monnier, unaware of such significant literary happenings as the condemnation by Napoleon in 1807 of Madame de Staël's *Corinne* or its defense by Chateaubriand, was likely to amuse himself with the comic prints displayed in the booksellers' windows: Carle Vernet's "Incroyables" and "Merveilleuses," Debucourt's animated scenes of elegant society at Frascati's or in the gardens of the Palais Royal, Boilly's caricatures of Parisian types. Or he might even wander into the Musée Napoléon to see the Dutch and Flemish paintings sent to Paris among the booty from the wars and so get his first glimpse of the kind of realistic genre painting that he was to produce himself many years later. Public entertainment was abundant. When an imperial order closed many of the theaters, there were shows of trained dogs or trained fleas, horse races on the Champ de Mars, or the balloon ascensions which were a favorite pastime. And the boulevards were becoming more and more the place to go for free, open-air diversion of all kinds, from the efforts of barkers to attract curious idlers into spending a few pennies to the ever changing spectacle of the passing crowds.

The *Mémoires de Monsieur Joseph Prudhomme* give a charming account of the delights which could lure a school boy to the public gardens and boulevards of Paris during the Empire. The favorite haunt of small truants was the Jardin des Capucines, rendezvous of all kinds of acrobats and freaks: tightrope dancers, a robust lady who suspended herself between two chairs by her heels and neck and invited five or six youths to climb up on her while she sang a popular romance, a wild woman who ate pebbles and live chickens. The Franconi brothers opened their first circus there. Robertson, the great magician, performed incredible sleight-of-hand feats. It was there that Henry Monnier learned to distinguish reality from the make-believe of the theater. He said later that the experience was a sad one, as disillusionment always is. It concerned a certain royal prince, native of a savage land where a language was spoken incomprehensible to Europeans. Fascinated by the feathered headdress and painted face of this impressive personage, the boy used to spend hours before the trestle where the prince appeared, in the hope that one day some learned person would be able to speak to him in his native Caribbean. At last there came a response to the customary invitation to advance and ask his royal highness a question. A young man stepped up, said he was entirely familiar with the language, and had some important news to give the prince. Thereupon he began a flow of weird and meaningless sounds which threw the "noble savage" and his announcer into a state of alarmed embarrassment, to the mocking delight, of course, of the crowd. So Monnier witnessed his first practical joke, the sort of trick which he himself was to carry to an extraordinary degree of perfection.

After that the Jardin des Capucines lost something of its charm, and was gradually displaced in the boy's affections by the Boulevard du Temple, a quarter celebrated for quacks and vendors of all sorts. Here a quavery little old street singer, who called himself the "modern Ossian," touched the heart with plaintive refrains which he accompanied by thin chords of an Irish harp. Farther on, a vendor of soap and toothpaste performed his egg dance with amazing agility before seizing some embarrassed victim among the spectators to exemplify the filth that only his products could remove. Song sheets were sold by the *Grand Turc*, magnificent in red, with a three-foot turban and two black-faced followers. The *grimacier*, peculiarly characteristic of the period, astonished by his grotesque grimaces which, Monnier affirmed, he could change as often as seventeen times in five minutes by actual count. Before the theaters were reached, an apple tart might be bought, piping hot, from a vendor who made them in a portable oven, or a cake from the most famous of all the singers of the boulevard, *la belle Madeleine*.

It was the custom then to attract business to the legitimate theaters of the boulevard by stationing in front of them a clown or mountebank who did tricks or exchanged repartee with the crowd in a continuous display of improvised wit. Sometimes the acts of these performers were more famous than the plays to which they tried to draw the public. Henry Monnier remembered well two of these *parodistes*, the celebrated team of Bobèche and Galimafré, who began their long career at the door of the Théâtre des Pygmées and were later associated with the Théâtre des Délassements Comiques and the Théâtre de la Gaîté. Galimafré was long and thin, and punctuated with a foolish laugh his silly, blundering remarks, puns, and slangy witticisms in various forms of patois. He could be jolly, noisy, vulgar, or pompous with a solemn self-satisfaction which turned him into a kind of majestic Pantaloon.* Quite different was Bobèche, who was handsome, blond, of medium height, and pleasantly plump. Bobèche was very careful of his costume, which consisted of a red jacket, a gray three-cornered hat, yellow pants, blue stockings, a black tie, and a red wig. He too played the clown, but with an unbridled tongue and caustic wit which more than once brought the police to warn him that Napoleon did not tolerate mockery and criticism even from so lowly a source. From this comedian, whom legitimate actors as famous as Monvel or Talma admired and respected, Henry Monnier may have had an early lesson in the comic effects to be obtained by a dead-pan expression and an air of imperturbable coolness, for similar impassive detachment was to characterize his own acting.

Monnier must have reveled in the gala days of 1810 and 1811, celebrating the arrival of the new Empress. There were free performances in the theaters, as well as outdoor pageants and pantomimes, accompanied by a distribution of wine and food, endless dancing, and display of fireworks. Everyone was singing the songs of an obscure clerk named Béranger, whose mingling of gaiety, sentimentality, and political appropriateness won him immediate and increasing popularity. Another song writer, Désaugiers, composer of *vaudevilles* and farces, struck the public fancy with his types of lower-middle-class society, such as Monsieur and Madame Denis, who became for a time symbols of the Paris *bourgeoisie*.

* English "gallimaufry": heterogeneous mixture, medley (Concise Oxford Dictionary).

The *roi de Rome* was born on a mild spring day in 1811, so warm that the classroom windows could be left open, the better to listen for the twenty-two-gun salute which would announce the birth of an heir and the founding of a dynasty. What greater treat for a schoolboy celebrating with his parents and all Paris, than to be taken to a real play? And what better indication of the state of the popular mind at that momentous period in French history than the fact that, just as all America crowded to see Walt Disney's *Snow White* in 1938, while global forces were preparing to shatter the civilized world, in 1811 the great success was Désaugiers' *Petite Cendrillon, ou la chatte merveilleuse?* It had four hundred performances at the Variétés, and brought new laurels to the veteran actor Brunet, who at the age of forty-five enchanted audiences with his performance of little Cinderella. We can only guess that Henry Monnier saw that play, but it is interesting to speculate on the bits of technical knowledge his observant eyes may have noted there, to be stored away until the time came for his own impersonation of female roles.

Monnier entered his teens in the somber year 1812. Paris suffered a food shortage that year and increasing unemployment. The months of the campaign, the weeks of the retreat from Moscow, were a time of anxiety growing almost to panic as rumors of disaster reached the people who waited so long without official news. Feeling ran high as the upper and middle classes expressed more and more openly their royalist or republican sympathies. The working class remained loyal to Napoleon, even when the brunt of the suffering fell on it, and it furnished the last pathetic regiment of youngsters, scarcely older than Henry Monnier, sacrificed in a desperate effort to turn the tide of defeat.

There was still amusement, to be sure, for those who could enjoy it. An active boy could climb the winding stairs inside the Colonne Vendôme, for the thrill of coming into the bright light high above the paving stones and face to face with the immense and awe-inspiring statue of the Emperor himself. Or he could follow the returning troops, not victorious these, but ragged and ill or wounded, all the more heroic for the tales they might be coaxed to tell of courage and endurance. While the city waited for the return of Napoleon, it took up one of those silly fads which occasionally sweep a whole populace. This was the game of *diabolo,* in which a top was tossed into the air by a string tied to two sticks. All Paris learned to *faire ronfler le diable*, as numerous prints of the time bear witness.

In 1813 such diversion was offered as the coming and going of foreign emissaries, who drove to the great gates of the Carrousel to seek treaties of peace or alliance with the Emperor. There was a flash of gaiety at Carnival time, but the people soon slipped back into a weary and somber dullness unlike the usual animation of Paris, as though they sensed the uncertainty of the future.

To very young Frenchmen the restoration of the Bourbons in 1814 was not a return to a familiar regime, but the sudden resurrection of a name which meant only bygone history. As the allied armies approached Paris, the atmosphere of the city was half sinister, half comical. Crowds of refugees who had fled before the troops thronged the streets, carrying under their arms their one treasured possession, the long loaves of black bread they had been able to bake before their flight. On the boulevards the Gallic spirit burst out in a contest of jokes and puns which accompanied speculation on the fate of France. It was said, for instance, that the allied sovereigns would enter the city by the *barrière du Trône*, that Napoleon would leave by the *barrière d'Enfer*. The advance force of huge Cossacks who were helping the newly organized National Guard to keep order in the streets were the objects of curiosity and a thousand witticisms. But the password of the gamins who climbed every lamppost and tree along the route the soldiers were to follow was: "The Bourbons? Don't know 'em!" [4]

Youth has its own ways of arriving at political convictions. The generation which had never known any other loyalty than to Napoleon, which took for granted that the last of the Bourbon pretenders had disappeared when the Duc d'Enghien was put to death—otherwise why should they have shot him?—that generation was at the self-confident age which rejects everything new, especially if detrimental to its idols, when it was confronted for the first time with the name of Louis XVIII. Let one of Monnier's contemporaries express the reaction:

> Oh! how awkward and cheerless that number eighteen coupled with a proper noun appeared to us, when we heard it for the first time! No, it wasn't possible that the poetic name of *Napoléon premier* should disappear from the

language, to give the honors to *Louis dix-huit!* Thus did we reason, great politicians that we were, who didn't even know that there still existed a Bourbon![5]

Although the term "liberal" was beginning to be used, it had not yet the force of the rallying cry it was to become before and after 1830. It seems to have been given political significance for the first time in 1815, in a publication called the *Censeur*, in which the word was used as an adjective, soon to be adopted as a noun. Tremendous discussion was aroused by an article "De l'impossibilité d'établir un gouvernement représentatif sous un chef militaire et particulièrement sous Napoléon Bonaparte."[6] Such a republican theory was quite incomprehensible to those for whom the First Republic was as dead as the Bourbons. Most of them remained, like Monnier, loyal to the regime symbolized by the name of Napoleon.

II

GOVERNMENT SERVICE

Henry Monnier left school at sixteen, in the year when the world of his childhood came to an end with the exile of Napoleon. To a whole generation of young men the Bourbon Restoration meant the destruction of their plans and hopes for a future of glorious activity in the service of the Emperor. They had grown up in an atmosphere of excitement and tension. Now that the current of existence was beginning to move in a new tempo, it was not easy for them to find an occupation which would satisfy the idealism and restlessness of youth.

The Monnier family had a small property at Les Godebins, a hamlet on a hillside in the Vexin region on the border of Normandy. It had belonged to Henry's grandfather, who had been a cooper in the nearby village of Parnes and was still living there with something of the austere simplicity he had inherited from his peasant ancestors. For a short time Monnier worked as a clerk for his uncle, the notary of Parnes, with whom he had spent his holidays as a schoolboy. But such a job, in an office which probably followed the semipaternalistic pattern of the period, could not give the boy the discipline or training he needed.

A one-act comedy of manners called "L'Intérieur de l'étude," by Scribe and Dupin, gives some idea of what a notary's office was like in those days. It shows the imposing desk of the head clerk, the tables where his subordinates were supposed to spend their time writing, the shelves filled with files and records, the stove which was the social center of the office. If Monnier's uncle was as old-fashioned as his conservative distrust of such modern notions as vaccination would seem to indicate, his clerks may have, as in the days before the Revolution, shivered without a fire except in the coldest months of the winter, and been obliged to satisfy their hunger on a meager noon meal of soup and boiled meat, "garnished with parsley on holidays!" [1] And they probably made up for their discomfort by playing practical jokes and composing *vaudevilles* when they should have been attending to business. Although such a clerkship was respectable enough, especially in a provincial district where the notary enjoyed nearly as much prestige as the doctor and the *curé*, Henry decided very soon to return to Paris and follow his father's example by entering government service.

At that time the bureaucratic system in France was beginning to assume the characteristics which were to distinguish it for more than a hundred years. Under the *Ancien Régime* a system of administrative offices had grown up, depending directly on the authority of the King or of ministers delegated by him. During the Consulate and Empire administrative activity was completely centralized in Paris. The Napoleonic system was based on the subordination of the individual, not to a personal authority but to the State, so completely that all initiative and personal responsibility were taken away; activity depended on superior direction, unauthorized experiments and deviation from normal routine were discouraged.

This was the nature of the administrative organization when the Bourbons returned to the throne. Unofficially it may be said to have enjoyed certain amenities due to the peculiarly *nouveau riche* character of the imperial government, which bestowed its favors without restrictions of a long-established social and political hierarchy. Personal ambition worked for the furthering of private ends, inevitably, in ways not provided for by the system and not easily controlled. Or in the words of the cynical Bixiou who appears in several of Balzac's novels:

> Empresses, queens, princesses, the wives of marshals in that happy time, had their caprices. All those fine ladies had the ambition of noble souls; they loved to give their protection. Thus one might fill a high position for twenty-five years; one might be auditor to the council of state, or *maître des requêtes*, and bring in his reports to the Emperor while amusing himself with his august family. Pleasure and work went on together.[2]

The establishment of a constitutional monarchy had two important effects on the civil service. The State was no longer either a flesh-and-blood ruler sustained by divine privilege or an idealized abstraction of revolutionary philosophy, but a parliament, a council of ministers, subject to the fluctuations of electoral whim, a body which seldom kept its identity long enough to emerge from anonymity. "Today the State is everyone," said Bixiou. "Now everybody is not concerned with anybody. To serve everyone is to serve no one. No one is interested in anyone. A clerk lives between two negations." [3] And the consequences of being a servant of the public appeared to be, in the majority of cases, an encouragement to become your own servant and to get what you could for yourself, since your employer was too indifferent to consider your individual needs.

In the second place, it became more and more a policy of the government to increase the number of federal employees, as pressure was brought to bear by electors seeking places for protégés or younger sons. As the numbers increased, the salaries were diminished in an attempt to appease the so-called liberals, who wanted to encourage private industry and attacked the budget on the ground that the civil service was a leech on the veins of the taxpayer. The civil servants, victims of political compromise, were paid a pittance which many of them made little pretense of earning and which their whole energies were absorbed in augmenting by promotion.

Henry Monnier was given the position of *surnuméraire* in the bookkeeping department of the Ministry of Justice. This meant that he received no regular salary at first, but made himself useful by doing whatever jobs were assigned to him, for which he was tipped according to the generosity of the official for whom he performed them. The institution of supernumerary was peculiarly characteristic of the system at that time. According to Balzac, the species was divided into two varieties: the rich young man, cousin or nephew of a cabinet minister, deputy, or peer, whose family desired for him an administrative career and whose advancement would be facilitated by influence from above rather than by native ability; and the poor young man, whose mother's sole ambition was to see her meager pension as widow of a government employee supplemented by her son's success in serving his country as his father had done. It was of the latter that Balzac wrote: "The supernumerary bears the same relation to the administration that the choir-boy does to the church, that the child of the regiment does to the regiment, that the ballet-girl does to the theatre: something naïve, frank—a being blinded by illusions." [4]

To judge from the rather bitter sympathy with which both Balzac and Monnier have presented this individual, he must have been a kind of scapegoat on whom fell the burden of all the tasks which everyone else could avoid, and whose youthful candor and ardor were soon dimmed by realization of the true nature of the system which he was in a particularly good position to observe from within and below.

> Evidently the position of supernumerary bears the same relation to the government as that of the novice to religious orders [wrote Balzac]. They are on trial, and this trial is harsh. The state discovers how many of them can bear hunger, thirst, and indigence without succumbing; how many can bear incessant work without becoming disgusted; whose temperament will accept this horrible existence, or, if you like, the disease of government life. From this point of view, the position of supernumerary, far from being an infamous device of the government to obtain work gratis, should become a useful institution.[5]

Monnier's apprenticeship was not so painful as that of Balzac's orphan, whose every nerve must be strained to work his way as soon as possible into a regular appointment. The initial stage usually lasted at least two years, but Henry was promoted after two months to the lowest rung of the administrative ladder, the position of *expéditionnaire,* or copy clerk. In his autobiography he ascribes the rapidity of this advancement to his fine penmanship, an accomplishment which probably gave him the idea of making Monsieur Prudhomme a professor of penmanship and inventing for him a flowery signature which adorned some of Monnier's books and many of his drawings.[6] As further proof of the official importance given to an art so purely mechanical in nature, there is an anecdote told by Alexandre Dumas, who had an experience comparable to Monnier's when he too, as a young man, was seeking his first job. He had gone for advice to an influential friend, General Foy. He was obliged to confess his complete ignorance of almost everything, mathematics, Latin, Greek, and the general, with all the good will in the world, was beginning to despair of finding anything he could do, when they remembered his beautiful handwriting. "We are saved!" cried the general. They would place him as supernumerary, in the hope that his fine hand would win him the position of *expéditionnaire!*[7]

This dullest of occupations had the virtue of leaving the copyist's mind free to busy itself as it chose. That is perhaps why the *expéditionnaires* often dabbled in versemaking, novel-writing, or the turning out of *vaudevilles* for the second-rate theaters. To the names of Monnier, Balzac, Dumas, can be added others of their contemporaries whose latent talents began to ripen in the uncongenial routine of the office work they were soon to abandon. While Monnier was discovering at the Ministry of Justice the creative gifts which were to give him a distinguished place among the young artists of the Restoration, H. de Latouche, years later one of his best friends, was employed at the Ministry of Finance, where he had as a colleague the future Romantic poet, Emile Deschamps. Latouche once wrote an amusing sonnet in which he reminded Deschamps of those early days and added to the list of famous *expéditionnaires* the name of the poet Béranger.*

The personnel of the government bureaus reflected in the early years of the Restoration the confusion and hodgepodge of the whole of French society. At the head of the various offices were men who owed their posts to their personal connection with cabinet ministers and who were more concerned with their own importance and social activities than with the official duties of their subordinates. The latter, rigidly classified in a descending hierarchy of clerkships, in-

* Quand nous étions tous deux plus jeunes, et . . . commis,
Vous du terrible fisc un agent débonnaire,
Et moi, pour les péchés que plus tard j'ai commis,
Du bon Français de Nante humble pensionnaire,
Nous avions du copiste un talent ordinaire;
Au rang des plumitifs on nous avait admis.
Un seul écrivait mieux: l'expéditionnaire
Avait nom Béranger; nous nous étions soumis.
Maintenant qu'on vous cite homme de goût, de style,
Vous griffonnez ainsi qu'un procureur hostile:
On dirait du foyer le quinteux animal.
Laissez l'hiéroglyphe aux courbes insensées;
Pitié pour notre ardeur à saisir vos pensées;
Comment diable écrit-on et si bien et si mal?

Henri Girard, *Emile Deschamps* (Paris, 1921), p. 66; quoted in Frédéric Ségu, *H. de Latouche* (Paris, 1931), p. 62. For the benefit of students of calligraphy who believe that creative ability is indicated by poor handwriting, it might be mentioned that Monnier did not always practice the talent with which he began his career, for his handwriting in later years became extremely difficult, almost illegible enough to deserve the reproach addressed here to Deschamps.

cluded all kinds of people, from stewards of great estates whose masters had emigrated during the Revolution, to retired opera singers. Petty merchants ruined by the hard times of the Empire, defrocked monks, younger sons who would have gone into the army a few years earlier, had all managed to obtain the sinecure of a position for which the only essential qualification seemed to be the favor of someone higher up. As a change in cabinet usually brought about a shift all down the line, and as the government even then had a tendency to change fairly often, the bureaucrats spent most of their time in speculative gossip or active cabal to secure and preserve that favor. Being in a position where they had to please all the others, the poor supernumeraries naturally did most of the actual work. Even the *expéditionnaires* soon mastered the art of appearing to be industriously occupied while in reality they delegated whatever had to be done to the few conscientious souls who applied themselves to their duties.

There were some of these, of course, in every bureau. Such a one is Monsieur Dumont, the head clerk in Monnier's "Scènes de la vie bureaucratique." Aiming at nothing more than to keep his modest position, he has developed to perfection the technique of agreeing with everyone in authority, and remains from one regime to the next a permanent fixture in the office, where his kind heart and sense of justice make him the mentor and defender of less experienced underlings. There is also the *expéditionnaire*, appropriately named Bellemain, in a one-act comedy, "L'Intérieur d'un bureau," by Scribe, Imbert, and Varner. He is the type of solemn and dependable automaton whose existence runs smoothly in a routine from which he has not swerved in twenty years. With his younger colleagues Bellemain can be pompously patronizing:

> Look, young man, you see that desk and that armchair. Twenty years ago today I installed myself there bag and baggage, I mean to say with my pocket knife, my pens, and my umbrella . . . There it is as a witness, it is still the same one. From that time on, employees, *sous-chefs, chefs,* and directors, how many of them I have seen come and go; how many letters announcing reductions in salary, discontinuance of services, and permanent dismissals, this hand has copied. Everything has been changed or overthrown . . . everything except my armchair, which, in spite of these continual oscillations, is still on its feet, as I am on mine. It is still there, fixed to the floor, stationary, immobile,

and I do as it does: I do not advance, but I remain where I am, and that is something.[8]

When he is threatened with dismissal for having copied automatically among other papers on his desk an impertinent song about the director of the division, a crime of *lèse-majesté* of which he is entirely innocent, he addresses his superior in a tone of respectful dignity: "I shall call to your attention the fact, sir, that it is I, Belle-main, *expéditionnaire*, twelve hundred francs salary: that can never be dismissed." [9]

There must have been in every government office someone like the faithful Belle-main. In Balzac's *Les Employés* there is Phellion, *commis-rédacteur*, proud of his position as servant of the government and reverencing the Powers, as distinguished from political ideas and parties, which he scorns. Faithful and hard-working, he follows the pattern of those functionaries who have maintained the continuity of the French State through the revolutions of a hundred and fifty years by refusing to let political opinions interfere with loyalty to their job. Phellion is a simple-minded fellow, like Belle-main, whose serious devotion to duty makes him a born victim of his more humorous associates.

It is regrettably in the category of the pranksters that Henry Monnier must be placed. The bureaucratic atmosphere fostered the spirit of mischief which had made him a refractory schoolboy. From such harmless tricks as a surreptitious exchange of hats or umbrellas, to the more dangerous sport of disseminating false rumors or malicious gossip, Monnier could run the gamut with a success all the greater because of his outward appearance of almost priggish solemnity. He soon gained a reputation for extraordinary variety and ingenuity in suiting his tricks to the intended victims, whom he studied until he had discovered the way in which they would be most vulnerable.

In more than one trait Monnier was like Balzac's Bixiou, whose description of the imperial system has been quoted. Like Bixiou, Monnier had an unmistakable physical resemblance to the early portraits of Napoleon. Like Bixiou, he combined great inventiveness in the matter of practical jokes with skill in mimicry. He also possessed Bixiou's talent for the drawing of caricatures, and although he had not yet had any training in art, he certainly had a natural gift for composition and line, and the visual memory of the artist.

In one important respect, however, Monnier differed from Bixiou. The latter, said Balzac, was so clever and made himself so useful to his superiors that they kept him on, in spite of his flippant attitude and constant foolery. In a way perhaps they did not dare dismiss him, for his caustic eye had seen too much and his pen was too bold. Monnier was less valuable to the Ministry. He wrote later that he gave up the position because he felt that his fine penmanship would prevent his advancement, marking him as it did for the perfect copyist. But there were difficulties also with his immediate superior, one Monsieur Petit, a clerk of the conscientious school, whose dignified belief in the sacrosanct character of administrative formulas could not brook Monnier's total absence of respect. Frank mockery was not bearable in a milieu where outward decorum must be preserved, whatever the inner sentiments. As Champfleury wrote in his life of Monnier: "What a pest this Monnier was in such a world! A wag with no sense of good conduct! A bad fellow worker who makes fun of his colleagues, who shortens the days of his chief! No *esprit de corps*, still less sense of decorum! For there is decorum in sitting in front of a desk, even if it be only to sharpen a pen all day long." [10]

Monnier was already beginning to consider the possibility of following a very different career. One day he chanced to meet in the Louvre an old school friend, who persuaded him to take up the study of art and thereby join the group of young men who, even if they were often ragged and hungry, had the satisfaction of thinking themselves superior to the middle-class world of *bonnetiers* and *épiciers* who were not "in the arts." So at the age of eighteen Henry Monnier was enrolled in the studio of Girodet, although he continued his work at the Ministry for two years longer. Now that his glove was so to speak flung down, many of his fellow employees must have looked on him as a member of the enemy camp, for an art student was then, as he is traditionally even today, a thorn in the flesh of conventional society.

The most important result of Monnier's four years in government service was the accumulation in his memory of a collection of human types which he utilized later as subjects for lithographs and literary sketches. In the album of lithographs called *Mœurs administratives* (1828), he represented the hierarchy of a government bureau, from the janitors up to the *chef de division*, and the daily routine, from the gossip around the stove between eight and nine in the morning, through the series of social calls and official inspections, the leisurely luncheon hours, the complimentary call of ceremony upon a newly appointed cabinet minister, to the departure with greatcoats, top hats, and umbrellas at four in the afternoon.[11] The "Scènes de la vie bureaucratique" and a series of "Scènes de la France administrative," which form the literary counterpart of the *Mœurs administratives*, complete the record of Monnier's first-hand observation of the civil service.[12] It is quite possible also as Champfleury suggests, that Monnier found in Monsieur Petit, the very *chef de bureau* whose days he helped to shorten, a preliminary model for Joseph Prudhomme. He could have taken here the dignified solemnity, the pompous speech, and the reliance on clichés, which were to characterize later his famous incarnation of the bourgeois.[13] By an odd and unexplained trick of circumstance, Monsieur Petit was to reappear in Monnier's life at the very time when Prudhomme was entering upon one of his most significant phases.

III

MONNIER AS AN ART STUDENT THE INTRODUCTION OF LITHOGRAPHY

Henry Monnier began his formal education in art at Girodet's studio in 1817. He remained there only a few months, however, and then entered the studio of Gros, whose pupil he was for about two years. While his contact with these famous artists was too brief to have much influence on his own style, it was of capital significance in showing him that his talents lay elsewhere than in classical painting; and a fortuitous external circumstance, the introduction into France of the process of lithography, helped to guide him into the field of art in which he was to distinguish himself.

Though not an old man, Girodet was near the end of his life when Monnier studied under him. His great work was done: "Le Sommeil d'Endymion," the famous "Atala au tombeau," "Palémon et Sylvie," "Le Déluge," had done their part toward strengthening the romantic current which flowed from the stormy crags and haunted forests of Ossian, through the melancholy landscapes of Joseph Vernet and Léopold Robert and the passionate pages of *Atala* and *René*. From Girodet a young artist might learn, not the realistic portrayal of life as it is, but suggestive handling of masses and shadows which evoke the world of legend and myth. Monnier kept the memory of a gentle and generous master, whom he represented in the *Mémoires de Monsieur Joseph Prudhomme* as adored by his pupils. They respected his susceptible vanity as an atrocious violin player and amateur translator of the classics, and learned to their surprise that he could on occasion hold his own against their lively tricks. On the day when they had bribed a grotesquely misshapen old Auvergnat to pose in place of the regular model, Girodet had contemplated him long and seriously, made a round of the studio to criticize the students' work with his usual gravity, and departed without any indication of noticing anything abnormal, so the young men had to admit that the joke was on them.

What Monnier wanted at that period of his life was to learn to paint great historical scenes, like the canvases on which David, Gros, Gérard had recorded with epic vigor the life of Napoleon. Diversely talented as he was, he did not possess the gift of self-knowledge, and so could not foresee that his work was to be of such a different character that his early ambition seems almost laughable. It was natural enough, no doubt, that when he felt within himself a rather sudden conviction of his artistic vocation, he should turn first to the kind of art which all his life had been the most esteemed, and to the artists who had received high honors from the idol of his boyhood. If he did not realize that the genre was dead, that the historical painter belongs to a period when great deeds are being performed, when the taste of the public is for grandeur in life as well as in art, this lack of critical perception is perhaps an indication that the newer currents were not yet flowing strongly enough for Monnier to be affected by them. For the man of genius makes his own current, which sweeps before it whatever obstacles it encounters, but the man whose talents are limited and varied must often wait to be guided by the mood or fashion of the moment, which he then in turn may dominate or mold according to the degree of his ability. That is why Monnier represents again and again a touchstone by which to measure the varying and complex movements of his time.

Jacques Louis David, official artist of the Revolution and the Empire, had been exiled at the return of the Bourbons, but he had left his studio in charge of his disciple and rival, Baron Gros, who still held a place of great honor among the master artists of Paris. The classical tradition consecrated by David was maintained out of respect for him, and the students were set to copying the antique, or the statues by Michelangelo from the tomb of the Medici, which Gros himself had drawn in Florence. But Gros was a master of color and composition as well as drawing, and his prestige as the painter of "Bonaparte au pont d'Arcole," "Les Pestiférés de Jaffa," the "Champ de bataille d'Eylau," brought crowds of young men eager to learn from him how to represent the human form in action, how to combine more realistic warmth and vitality with the rigorous laws of neo-classical design. As most of these students, like Monnier, had grown up under the charm of Napoleon, they must have rejoiced to find in the very person of the master a relic of the stiff ceremoniousness, the military flavor of the Empire. For Gros is said to have kept all his life the *pantalon collant* and the high boots which were fashionable when he and David were sharing and enhancing the Emperor's glory.

Such a symbolic clinging to the past was doubly dangerous when it was combined with intransigent insistence on conformity to traditional precepts. Gros' star was setting fast. His distinguished successor in the domain of historical painting, Delacroix, was the severest critic of his later work, which became more and more old-fashioned as the time demanded a truth and reality whose roots were in the direct observation of life. Of the group which worked under Gros between 1816 and 1822, the lucky ones were those whose talents were so completely different from his that he could only allow them to follow without interference their own line of development. The pupils on whom he tried to impose rules which interfered with their individual freedom of expression showed their ingratitude later by attacking him in caricatures, and worse still, allowed him to sink into that melancholy state of loneliness which comes to those who have outlived their fame and from which he found escape by suicide in 1835.

Like several of the others, Henry Monnier soon substituted the new process of lithography for painting in oils, but he possessed all his life a skill in portraiture which he may well have learned from Gros. And the great colorist may also have given him the interest in color which distinguished Monnier's work as a lithographer. It is unfortunate that their personal relations were spoiled by Monnier's undisciplined sense of humor, which made him constantly resist the authority of his superiors. But the friendships he formed with his comrades reveal one of his salient traits, the ability to dominate a group by the charm of his originality.

Most of the artists of the Romantic school passed through Gros' studio, and many of them were connected with it while Monnier was there. Horace Vernet already had a studio of his own, in close and friendly intercourse with the group surrounding Gros, to whom he sent young Eugène Lami for training in the technique of composition. Delacroix was connected a few years later with the group as a result of his intimate friendship with the gifted young Englishman, Bonington. In spite of his British air of reserve, Bonington was generally liked by his comrades, and his enthusiastic study of the use of water colors undoubtedly influenced Henry Monnier as it did Delacroix and Lami. In its delicacy and perfection of execution, his work resembled especially Lami's, whose engravings and lithographs of social manners had an aristocratic grace that Monnier's work never possessed.* Lami, who began by painting military scenes with the encouragement of Horace Vernet, and ended in the highest circles as a kind of official court painter for Louis-Philippe, seems an odd friend for Henry Monnier, who was destined to stand for posterity as the interpreter of the working classes and the *bourgeoisie*.

The same might be said of their comrades, Camille Roqueplan and Paul Delaroche, who were to belong in the full frenzied swing of Romantic painting while Monnier soon abandoned the "gothic troubadour" style for the representation of daily reality. Delaroche, with whom Lami lived for a time in the house where Balzac set up his printing shop, took his work more seriously than did some of the others, perhaps because he was temperamentally more somber. Alexandre Dumas said that his was one of those unfortunate natures unable to reconcile themselves to the divergence between their ambition and their talent. And there, curiously enough, is perhaps a resemblance with Monnier. For just as Delaroche regretted always that he had missed the career of statesman and diplomat, so Monnier, professional humorist, never in later life completely abandoned the desire to write a tragedy for the Théâtre-Français. How often that aspiration to be other than they were reappeared in the creative artists of the nineteenth century, as it always does during a period when the dominant traits of human nature are romantic!

Delaroche illustrated in his work another trait characteristic of his time, in his manner of presenting a subject such as the little

* Bonington had been studying for some time under Gros when one day the latter entered the studio and addressed his pupils: "You do not pay enough attention to color, gentlemen; color, however, is poetry, charm, life, and there is no work of art without life. In my walks I see in the dealers' windows certain water colors and paintings brimming with light. Go to see them and study them, it's superb! It's signed Badington–Bounington, I don't know exactly what. In any case, gentlemen, that man is a master!" During this speech Bonington hung his head and blushed, not daring to say a word. (Jean Gigoux, *Causeries sur les artistes de mon temps*, Paris, 1885, pp. 249–250.)

princes in the Tower with the most minute attention to the realistic details of local color. He devoted laborious research to the study of costumes, draperies, colors, just as Dumas *père* and Victor Hugo strove to satisfy the curiosity of their contemporaries by giving to their dramas accurate historical settings. In tracing the evolution of realism through the first half of the nineteenth century, it is interesting to note how it gradually approached everyday reality, seeking to represent the unknown or the exotic by turning to the Middle Ages or to distant lands, then refreshing jaded curiosity by substituting for the genuine Mohicans of the primeval forests a study of the Mohicans of Paris, the underworld which seemed to respectable society as picturesque as any Romantic subject. Although the Romanticists were not yet ready to conceive of realism as the representation of the daily commonplace, they learned the faithful reproduction of external details, and Henry Monnier's choice of material marked a bridge between their realism and that of the Realistic school of the mid-century. In 1820, when neither "Romanticism" nor "Realism" was clearly defined, one could scarcely be distinguished from the other.

In the group of *rapins* who were Monnier's comrades at the studio of Gros, the outstanding figure was that of Charlet. Some ten years older than the others, tall and striking in appearance, with the massive head of one of his own grenadiers, he was easily the leader. Not only did he excel in his chosen field of half-humorous, half-sentimental drawings of the soldiers and common folk of the Empire, of which he was, like his friend Horace Vernet, an ardent admirer, and which he constantly contrasted with the retrogressive mediocrity of the Restoration; he also took first place in the perpetrating of practical jokes, puns, and gags, the traditional pastime of the art students of the Left Bank. Seconded by his fellow artist, Hippolyte Bellangé, who held up his end in the constant guying and foolery, Charlet seems to have been responsible for an atmosphere of disorder which concealed whatever genuine respect or affection the students felt for their master.

Such was the company in which Henry Monnier found himself as he crossed the threshold of that world of art and artists in which for better or for worse he was destined to live. Feeling within him the divine spark, aspiring to follow in the footsteps of the great artists of the Empire, he must have given the impression of youthful ardor which Bonington conveyed in a water-color portrait of him in 1824. Here his fair hair is in wind-blown Byronic disorder, his clear-cut features, so suggestive of Bonaparte at the same age, have an expression at once pensive and mocking, and he holds an open album in the pose of the artist interrupted at his work. In spite of the conventionality of the pose, the head has both nobility and charm, and it is easy to imagine how cordially Monnier was welcomed among those young men, who would appreciate both the liveliness of his features and their classic beauty. But the unique place he made for himself among his comrades was due at first, not to his talent as an artist, for he had not yet learned to express himself in that domain, but to his gift of improvising and acting comic sketches. With the encouragement of Charlet, who recognized in him a kindred spirit, his serious intentions evaporated in the animation of the studio, to be replaced by that immoderate and unrestrained love of mischief which was one of his dominant traits.

No sooner would Gros leave the studio than the students would thrust into Henry's hand a pointer or riding whip, with the cry, "Come on, entertain us!" [1] Then while the others worked before their easels, he would mount to the model's platform and amuse them by inventing scenes in which his slim, vigorous young form would impersonate various types familiar to his audience and droll because of the impeccable veracity with which he could reproduce their gestures, voices, and tricks of speech. Some of these sketches he wrote down later, at the instigation of his friends, and thus began the long series of *Scènes populaires* which, with the *Mémoires de Monsieur Joseph Prudhomme*, are his chief title to literary fame. It is quite probable that the most famous of the *Scènes populaires*, such as the "Roman chez la portière," "La Cour d'assises," and "Un Voyage en diligence," were acted by Monnier at least ten years before they were published. No one knows how many other scenes became celebrated in the studios without ever being written down, although Monnier's admirers made an attempt later to collect and edit them.

A vivid impression of the tumult which habitually reigned in the studio is given in a chapter of the *Mémoires de Monsieur Joseph*

Prudhomme describing the initiation of a newcomer.[2] Except for a few serious workers, the *rapins* are a noisy group, bursting frequently into the choruses of popular songs, exchanging rapid repartee full of stock expressions of which they are inordinately fond, such as the reply, whenever anyone asks for one of them: "He is dead!" There is a punster, of course, who is fined every time he makes a play on words. And there is a comedian, who assumes an air of pompous gravity as he declines to provide entertainment:

> No, gentlemen; I wish to work, I am very weary of being, at my age, a burden to my family. At the cost of the most noble sacrifices they keep alive in me that fire which they believed to be divine and which is burning out in empty smoke . . . My poor father still considers you my brothers and my friends; he hopes, in his blindness, that you will lead me back to the right path; he is mistaken!

The new student, received with scarcely veiled impertinence is put through an initiation of singing, dancing, and answering embarrassing questions, according to the principle that "it is useful and necessary that the newcomers should have to undergo the trials and tortures which we all endured when we arrived." After this has gone on for some time, interrupted by intervals of attention to work only when the model can not be persuaded to rest, it is easy to agree with the *rapin* who says of his comrades: "They're all *farceurs!*"[3]

Even the gravest chroniclers of social and political history can profit by a study of the humor of a period, for fun is a reaction, a means of escape, the *revers de la médaille* which may give some unexpected or indirect revelation of the springs of more serious activity. Particular traits must not be pedantically overemphasized, however, at the expense of general significance. Henry Monnier and his comrades were art students, a double guarantee of freedom from conventional restraint and tendency toward youthful wildness. Many of them, sons of respectable middle-class families, had known the dull routine of clerks in a government office or small business house, and were experiencing for the first time the chance to match their wits and talents with those of congenial contemporaries. While some of their quips and pranks have an ageless familiarity, the gusto with which they enjoyed them seems peculiar to the post-Revolutionary era in France.

The need for the childish kinds of relaxation which had made the boulevards a perpetual fair and circus during the Empire led to a similar development of private entertainment. The vogue of amateur theatricals invaded even the most modest homes, where the master's bedroom was turned into a theater and the mistress satisfied a secret desire to wear masculine clothes by playing the role of the young hero. In wealthy houses professional actors added luster to the performances and there were sometimes impersonators paid to amuse and mystify the guests by their clowning and practical jokes. The *grimacier* of the boulevards found his way too into the salons, where he gave programs of comic faces, a curious forerunner of the art of the monologue which began to develop during the Restoration with such performances as Henry Monnier's improvisations. During the very years when the tears of Werther, the yearnings of René, and the passions of Lord Byron were thrilling romantic souls, there was a vigorous revival of the universal pastime of punning. The walls of a room might be painted with inscriptions whose comic or mocking significance could be discovered only by penetrating search. In certain Restoration engravings the head of Napoleon was concealed in the leafy branches of a tree, or careful observation might transform an idyllic landscape into a picture of lovers' embrace. As for the play on words, that favorite French pastime since the days of Maître Pathelin* attained among the wits of Monnier's generation, if not its greatest subtlety, at least exceptional lustiness.

The name of the unfortunate Gros offered a temptation too strong to resist. Even his dignified fellow artist, Baron Gérard, left to posterity a famous *bon mot* inspired by the colossal figures in the paintings at the library of Sainte-Geneviève: "Oui, c'est plus *gros* que nature." [4] Is it surprising then that Monnier, with the budding reputation of a humorist to foster, sought every opportunity to torment the master? According to Nestor Roqueplan, the brother of Henry's comrade Camille, he specialized in the words *groseille* and *groseillier*, which he worked into a dozen ingenious combinations.[5] Now Gros had an irascible temper and was always quick to take offense. As a result of the various ways in which Monnier succeeded in suggesting the resemblance to a gooseberry, he found himself one

* The artful cheat in the fifteenth-century farce, *L'Avocat Pathelin.*

day shown the door, in a scene which caused no little comment in artistic circles, and which reflects only discredit on Monnier. There were hurt feelings on both sides, the master reproaching his pupil for lack of appreciation, the young man bitter at what he considered the unjust severity of an expulsion which meant the end of his connection with the school of the Beaux-Arts. About 1822 he found himself completely adrift, having relinquished his government position and realizing that no studio in Paris would accept him because of his reputation as a mischief-maker.

What Monnier would have produced had he remained with Gros it is, of course, impossible to say, but it is harmless to speculate that he might have painted landscapes and genre pictures in a manner suggestive of the Flemish. But his break with the world of high art has an almost symbolic significance, coinciding as it did with the rise of a new form of popular and commercial art which revolutionized caricature and illustration. This was the introduction into France of the process of lithography, which Charlet, Bellangé, Monnier, Raffet, Grandville, Gavarni, Daumier, and many others were to develop as a means of satisfying a great public demand and earning a living which for the artist is precarious at best.

The process of lithography had been invented in 1798 by a native of Prague, Aloys Senefelder, who was at that time in Munich experimenting in a cheap method of printing music. He found that by drawing with a fatty crayon or with special ink on a flat stone, it was possible to take advantage of the repulsion of water from grease to obtain an impression of the drawing on paper. Hitherto artists had had to depend on the engraver to reproduce their works, either by the tedious and costly means of steel or copper plates, or the cheaper but rather crude use of wood. Now they could make their own reproductions, rapidly and inexpensively, with much more fluency of line and delicacy of finish than could be obtained in wood-engraving. The use of the new method soon spread to Berlin, to Vienna, to London, and in the early days of the Empire, to Paris, where it was taken up as an amateur fad by the Duc de Montpensier and even some of Napoleon's officers. In 1816 Lasteyrie established the Lithographie du Roi et de son Altesse Royale, and the new art entered upon a bitter and mortal struggle with copper engraving.

Within ten years the triumph of lithography was celebrated in the words of a popular song:

Vive la lithographie!
C'est une rage partout:
Grand, petit, laide, jolie,
Le crayon retrace tout.
Nos boulevards tout du long
A présent sont un salon
Où, sans même avoir posé,
Chacun se trouve exposé . . .[6]

The success of lithography brought to a climax the popularity of a mode for which the lithographs themselves contain abundant evidence. Many of them represent scenes before the windows of the printsellers. Fashionable young ladies and their escorts are shown crowding before the shop of Martinet, rue du Coq; in Charlet's charming "Seriez-vous sensible?" a soldier addresses his question to a young servant girl gazing raptly at the prints the merchant has hung outside his door. Later Daumier studied the faces of print collectors as they eagerly leafed through albums of lithographs, and Monnier included in his series of the *Boutiques de Paris* a scene in an elegant shop where prints were displayed before aristocratic clients, in a modernized and popularized version of Watteau's "Enseigne de Gersaint." It must have been before some such shop on the quai Voltaire that the hero of Balzac's *Peau de chagrin* paused in his project of suicide to observe a stylish young woman paying several gold pieces for albums of lithographs.[7]

It is no exaggeration to say that thousands of lithographs were published between 1815 and 1830, and that they form an illustrated encyclopedia of the manners, the modes, the tastes, and the sentiments of the Restoration. Being chiefly popular in appeal, they usually represent the middle and lower classes, their clothes and their pleasures, their loves and their vices, the tragicomic incidents of their daily lives, forming thus a pictorial bridge between the realistic theories of Diderot and the works of Champfleury, Duranty, Courbet, and the other Realists, thirty or forty years later. From single prints presenting separate subjects, the artists passed to a series of pictures telling a story, such as the *Histoire d'une épingle racontée par elle-*

même, by Gérard-Fontallard, or the comic sequences by the prolific Victor Adam, whose *Plaisirs de Paris* were comparable to a German series, the *Fliegende Blätter*, by Meggendorfer. Soon the story was made more dramatic by the addition of a caption, often in the form of a brief comic or sentimental dialogue, and the artists who could best combine pictures and words achieved the greatest success. A specialist in scenes of tender gallantry was Jean Scheffer, forerunner of Gavarni and Forain. Bellangé was one of the first to make good-natured fun of the National Guard, that institution which was to be so often satirized during the monarchy of Louis-Philippe. Charlet, one of the earliest lithographers to win celebrity and considered one of the greatest in France, made the printed text and the picture equally important, using the genre to express his Bonapartist loyalty, to attack with Voltairian irony the clericalism of the Bourbon regime, and to portray sympathetically the lives of the common people. But the two artists who seem to point the way most clearly to the work of Henry Monnier are Gaudissart, whose scenes of family life have been compared to Monnier's, and Pigal, whose humorous studies of the lower middle class and the proletariat bear such titles as "Scènes de société," "Scènes familières," and "Scènes populaires," and combine laughable situations with captions in which popular language is reproduced as faithfully as possible.

After 1820 the popularity of lithographs in series took the form of a craze for humorous albums devoted to various subjects, and prepared often by several artists working in collaboration. Thus there appeared as early as 1820 an album devoted to the adventures of a hunchback, predecessor of the infamous Mayeux; in 1823 a curious *Album comique de pathologie pittoresque*, to which Pigal and Bellangé contributed; for several years after that a set of *Albums lithographiques*, published by Englemann; in 1824 a series called *Les Contretems*, recalling Rowlandson's *Miseries of Human Life* and suggestive of Monnier's later *Petites misères humaines;* and in 1827 an *Album parisien*. And so Henry Monnier was following the fashion when he published between 1827 and 1830 his *Mœurs parisiennes*, *Mœurs administratives*, *Grisettes*, *Jadis et aujourd'hui*, and other series, with a success which brought him in those few years the fame he has never lost among nineteenth-century artists.

IV

ENGLAND

When the quarrel with Gros cast Henry Monnier out of the sheltered respectability of a famous Paris studio, he was an unknown young man of twenty-two or twenty-three whose immediate problem was to decide what to do with himself now that he had no regular employment or means of livelihood. Lithography interested him and seemed to offer a quicker and more certain success than any other kind of art, but his early attempts at it, chiefly sketches of actors and actresses in costume, were fumbling and heavy. The technique of color printing had advanced much farther in England than in France, and it may have been the publication in Paris of prints by English comic artists such as Rowlandson and Cruikshank which gave Monnier the idea of going to England to study their methods.

Such a decision was, after all, quite natural. The cultural intercourse between the two countries, interrupted by the Revolution and the Napoleonic wars, had been renewed even before Waterloo by the return to France of *émigrés* who imported many English fashions. As early as 1814 Stendhal had observed gloomily how English in taste and temperament the French were becoming; he prophesied the ruin of literature and art if English influence imposed on France that lamentable love of politics which was incompatible with the cult of beauty. There sounded, indeed, a warning for Monnier and his generation, and the century which was born with them! The love of politics, the cult of ugliness—whether the one sprang from the other and both from English soil, or whether they were separate emanations from the causes and consequences of the Revolution, the two currents flow unmistakably through the century, leaving their mark on men of letters, Hugo, Balzac, Baudelaire, Flaubert, on artists, Daumier and all the satirists, on the middle-class citizen, Monsieur Prudhomme, and necessarily on Henry Monnier, who represented so faithfully the man of letters, the artist, and the middle-class citizen of France.

He may have reached England as early as 1822. A letter dated June 25, 1825, showed that he was in London then, quite at home in the city and in contact with various fellow countrymen.[1] For there was a whole group of young French artists in close and frequent contact with their comrades across the Channel. The tradition had been started, perhaps, by Géricault, whose enthusiasm for the realism in contemporary English art was probably augmented by the favorable reception given to his "Radeau de la Méduse," which he had exhibited in London in 1820 after its failure to win approval at the Paris Salon of 1819. Following his example, Horace Vernet had taken up English customs, and was largely responsible for the introduction into France of the terms and traditions of the turf and the ultrasnobbish sport of horse racing, which culminated in Paris with the organization of the Jockey Club. In return, Bonington was only one of the numerous English artists who studied in Paris. Painters like the Fielding brothers and James Harding, who happened to be friends of Monnier, introduced English methods of using water colors and prepared the way for the wave of admiration which brought to a climax at the Salon of 1824 the appreciation of English art.

So strong was the impression made by the works of Bonington, Thales and Copley Fielding, Constable, Lawrence, and other artists of the English school, that French painters began to flock to London. As Delacroix wrote in his journal and letters of that period, there was a triple attraction in a country which was not only the home of so many distinguished artists, but also the land of Shakespeare and Byron, besides being the center of masculine elegance in dress and manners. Delacroix was there in 1825 with Bonington, and a short time later Eugène Lami came to join Monnier in his study of color printing. As a *habitué* of the capital, Monnier was able to initiate his friend into the particularities of British ways and traits, which he undoubtedly interpreted with animation and Gallic frankness, and to give him the practical advantages of his connections among publishers and printsellers. It was probably through him, for instance, that a contract was arranged with the fashionable print dealer Colnaghi, for a book of travel scenes which Monnier and Lami were to illustrate in collaboration. This was the *Voyage en*

Angleterre, at which they worked in 1826 and 1827, and which was published in London and Paris in 1829.

It may have been preparation for the publication of this book which caused Monnier to return to London in 1828. By that time he must have realized that success for him lay in Paris rather than in England, and the nostalgic tone of a letter he wrote while he was there indicates that there were personal reasons, although not entirely disassociated from his work, which made London seem dull: "English girls are very pretty, but where are those naughty figures, those charming little faces, that would arouse the dead? I hunt everywhere for *grisettes*, for *lingères*, etc. However, we shall see them again before we die . . ." [2]

The relatively small number of his lithographs published between 1825 and 1827 by various London editors indicates clearly enough that Monnier was not very successful in obtaining the popular favor and editorial support which would have established his reputation.[3] That some of his ideas were not acceptable to the publishers is of course to be expected. He planned one elaborate series of prints, for instance, on which he and his friends apparently based great hopes, for Balzac referred to it several years later as the unknown masterpiece which was destined to establish Henry's fame as a satiric artist. The subject was the career of a young man in Paris, the sowing of his wild oats in various scenes of debauchery and vice, the inevitable duel, illness, and disillusionment, and the final return to respectability through literary success, crowned by matrimonial happiness. A letter in which Monnier outlined this *Vie d'un jeune homme à Paris* throws interesting light on his method of making the more obscene parts of it palatable: "It seems to me necessary to present a young man who, in the midst of all his adventures, is always fashionable and in good form, and to compose very short, clever titles." [4] This conception of an elegant man about town, whose lack of a sense of moral values is counterbalanced by his wit and his consciousness of social decorum, has an almost Byronic tinge, might have been inspired by Hogarth's *Rake's Progress* or by Mérimée, and suggests at the same time certain aspects of the *dandysme* which was to be perfected by Baudelaire. Had such a personage ever seen the light of day, the public might well have wondered what kind of cynical sophistication had guided the young artist's pencil.

As a matter of fact, the description would not have been entirely inapplicable to Monnier himself at the age of twenty-seven or twenty-eight, if the testimony of an observant contemporary can be believed: "With his aquiline nose, his firm, pointed chin, thin lips and caustic expression, with glasses concealing a mocking eye, Monsieur Henri Monnier himself jokingly finds his portrait in the profile of a cabriolet; a shrewd and witty artist, he sees society in the form of epigrams, and reproduces its absurdities in the most pungent guise." [5]

The resemblance to Napoleon must have been a great source of satisfaction to Monnier, whose smoothly shaven cheeks and carefully waved short hair showed the meticulous regard for his appearance that had given him the reputation of being what the Restoration called a young *fashionable*. It is easy to imagine a well-cut blue frock coat, open to disclose the flowered or brocaded vest, a close-fitting *pantalon à sous-pied* revealing shapely legs and descending to elegant boots, matched by the perfection of kid gloves and a hat of the latest form.[6] Such was the young man who, beneath a worldly exterior, brought to London in the 1820's that aura of devil-may-care impertinence, sharpened by a keen eye, a biting tongue, and fingers skillful at translating both eye and tongue, which was the peculiar charm of the Parisian artist.

There can be no doubt that he made friends, as he did always, and more quickly than foreigners habitually do on their arrival in the English capital. They liked his gaiety, so very French! His originality may have shocked them at times, but it was always entertaining. There was, for instance, the evening when he and Lami had been invited to the theater by English friends. At the end of the first act, Henry disappeared, to reappear as the curtain went up, among the supers on the stage. He had met old acquaintances backstage, where his passion for the theater had drawn him, and had hastily daubed on a bit of make-up so that he could walk on with them and continue his conversation, not thinking for a moment that his hosts might disapprove of his unconventional behavior. No one else could have carried off with Monnier's composure a prank which shocked even his fellow countryman.

In the artist George Cruikshank, Henry found a kindred spirit. Seven years older than he, Cruikshank was in a period of prolific activity, adding to his wide reputation as a humorist and political cartoonist a talent for illustration which was beginning to give him a position of importance in that field, and a power of realistic observation which he showed in his studies of the life of London's lower classes. It was probably his *Diorama anglais ou Promenades pittoresques à Londres*, published in Paris in 1823, which had contributed to Monnier's decision to study English methods of color printing, and may very well have influenced him too in the direction of comic studies of manners. Cruikshank's penchant for the fantastic and the grotesque was so different from Monnier's manner, however, that he could not have left more than a passing imprint on the latter's style. The two young artists would have been drawn together rather by their common inclination to view life as a series of funny or ironic situations.

But there was more than their art to make them congenial. Since Cruikshank's subjects of the early twenties do not show the tendency toward moral reform that characterize his later work, particularly in the cause of temperance, it is safe to assume that he was still the convivial youth portrayed by his brother Robert, with a massive head of unruly hair, sparkling blue-gray eyes not unlike Monnier's, and cheerfully disordered clothes. One of his friends described him enthusiastically: "His appearance, his illustrations, his speeches, are all alike—all picturesque, artistic, full of fun, feeling, geniality and quaintness. His seriousness is grotesque and his drollery is profound. He is the prince of caricaturists, and one of the best of men." [7] When to these lively traits were added an ardent love for the stage and the society of actors, a clever talent for acting and mimicry, and a fondness for practical jokes, it seems that Monnier could plausibly have found in him an alter ego. While their comradeship did not develop into lasting friendship, its warmth is shown by the album of *Distractions* which Monnier published in 1832 with the dedication: "To his friend George Cruikshank." [8]

There was another artist whom Monnier may have met in London, whose work he certainly knew, and whose professional kinship with him cannot be overlooked. This was Thomas Rowlandson, who continued to work nearly to the time of his death in 1827. Belonging as he did to the generation of Cruikshank's father Isaac and of that other political caricaturist Gillray, Rowlandson represented the last of the great comic and satiric artists of the eighteenth century, the greatest of whom was Hogarth. They were a full-blooded, hard-hitting group, who represented with gusto the roistering wantonness of a society whose sham, debauchery, and wickedness they sought to counteract by the wholesome remedy of laughter flavored with moralizing. Although Rowlandson moralized somewhat less than did Hogarth, he had the same predilection for the half-realistic, half-satiric portrayal of disreputable human types. These he placed in situations less moralistic, but more realistic than those of *A Harlot's Progress* or *A Rake's Progress*: one or another of those embarrassing or uncomfortable circumstances in which fallible humans find themselves through their own stupidity or the follies of their fellow men.

When Henry Monnier was barely old enough to trot off to school in his first pair of buttoned trousers and Charles Dickens was not yet born, Rowlandson was publishing the *Comforts of Bath*, and *Miseries of Human Life*.* These humorous sketches of contemporary society suggest in their general plan and point of view Monnier's *Esquisses parisiennes* (1827), *Vues de Paris* (1829), and various other works containing groups of scenes connected by a central theme, particularly the *Petites misères humaines*, for which Monnier may have borrowed Rowlandson's title, and its companion work, *Petites félicités humaines* (1829). In 1809 Rowlandson sponsored the first public appearance of the pedagogical Dr. Syntax, a hero whose flesh was too weak for the excellence of his intentions or the strength of his curiosity, which led him into such a multitude of adventures that they filled three books, rhymed in satirical verse by William Combe and illustrated by Rowlandson.[9] The popularity of this work may be judged from the fact that it was translated and

* 1808. Subjects included: following a slow cart on horseback through an endless narrow lane when you are in a hurry; escorting several country cousins on their first visit to London; chasing your hat through a muddy street; squatting on an unsuspecting cat in your chair; dining and passing the whole evening with a party of fox-hunters after they have had what they call "a glorious time," etc. Art Young, *Thomas Rowlandson* (New York, 1938), p. 48. For similar studies of everyday twentieth-century life, compare the work of the American cartoonist Harold T. Webster, especially the *Life's Darkest Moment* series.

published in both Berlin and Paris in 1822, and that Dickens' original conception of the *Pickwick Papers* was a set of incidents and accidents affording subjects, as did the experiences of Dr. Syntax, for comic illustrations. If the tall, thin pedagogue created by the pencil of Rowlandson was thus in a way the forerunner of the plump and benevolent Mr. Pickwick, the latter was to discover in due time that he and Monsieur Joseph Prudhomme were "brothers under the skin." Even if by some unlikely chance Monnier was not familiar with the English editions of Rowlandson's work, he must certainly have seen the French edition, whose publication in 1822 gave it a place among the albums to which Monnier began to contribute a few years later.

It is simple enough to enumerate certain tangible results of Monnier's visits to England; there is no doubt that his technical skill had improved tremendously by 1827. His earlier lithographs seem flat and crude in comparison with those of the *Voyage en Angleterre*, which was the most important work done by him in England. It is interesting not only to observe the progress in the processes of coloring lithographs, but also to compare Monnier's technique with that of his collaborator Lami. The illustrations for this book were drawn boldly in outline on the stone with a pen and then colored by hand from water-color sketches prepared in advance by the artists. The resulting prints had much of the warmth and clearness of the original water colors. Lami's gentle delicacy and grace were invigorated by the more robust and sardonic talent of Monnier, whose contributions to the work show that he was less interested in the elegance of the upper classes than in the activities of the common people going about their daily lives. From the sailors in a seaside port to the butchers and fishmongers of London markets, Monnier reproduced with minute precision all the ugly, unsavory picturesqueness of homely trades and occupations, revealing his talent for seizing upon characteristics of costume, silhouette, gesture, which distinguish the various social types of modern life. In the large street scene which Monnier and Lami did together, it is easy to distinguish between the very different traits of the two artists. The architectural details of the background and the richly liveried carriages in which members of the aristocracy recline have the refinement and grace that characterize the work of Lami, while the sidewalks are filled with rather squat, angular, heavy-set figures, to which Monnier knew so well how to give an unflattering vulgarity suggesting heaviness of intellect.

It is more difficult and dangerous to try to define those intangible influences which offer such strong temptation to the psychologically minded historian. By 1827 Monnier had evidently found the mode of expression and the subject matter which suited his talent. It has been said that he brought back from England the kind of humor which combines the comic with the realistic, unshakable composure with hilarious laughter, and that his own person and manner showed for the rest of his life certain traits which he acquired during his stay in England. Perhaps it would be more prudent to believe simply that the contact with English caricature and London life strengthened characteristics which he had already begun to reveal, and that, encouraged in the direction of the humorous and satiric study of manners, his art attained rapid maturity in an atmosphere which was congenial to him. As for his "British" manner, the sense of humor hiding itself beneath an imperturbable exterior, the air of cool detachment masking cynical mockery, this was perhaps Monnier's contribution to the anglicizing of France which Stendhal had dreaded and which Gertrude Stein expressed in her own disparaging way when she wrote: "England created the nineteenth century." [10]

V

SUCCESS: 1827–1830—ROMANTIC ART THE DEVELOPMENT OF ILLUSTRATION

During the years of traveling back and forth across the Channel, Monnier's headquarters were in Paris, where his bachelor's pot had to be kept boiling on means which must have been at times rather slim. Until 1827 he had been feeling his way in the medium he was learning to use, publishing a comparatively small number of rather timidly executed lithographs. Then in the next three years, as though his talent had ripened suddenly, he produced series after series of prints which form the largest and most celebrated part of his artistic work and give him a distinguished place among the comic and satiric artists of the nineteenth century.

First he tried a genre in which he showed great proficiency at later intervals of his life, the sketching of actors and actresses in the costumes of their roles. He may already have had connections with theatrical people, through his fondness from childhood for playgoing and acting, and profited by these connections to obtain orders for the portraits which it was the fashion to print as frontispieces to the published editions of the plays in which the actors starred. Or it may have been the moderate success of his early efforts at this type of portrait which brought him into personal relationship with the world of the stage. The prints which have survived show that he made only a few lithographs for the Théâtre-Français, the Odéon, the Opéra, and the Opéra-Comique, working more especially for the small theaters of the boulevards: the Gymnase, where he did a series of portraits of the actor Bernard Léon and others in the spectacular melodramas typical of that theater; the Vaudeville, whose company included the celebrated Lepeintre father and son, who remained Monnier's friends; and the Théâtre des Variétés, where Henry himself was to make his debut in 1831. It is evident that these intimate contacts with professional actors gave him a precious opportunity to observe some of the tricks of costume and make-up and the pictorial effect of gesture and facial expression in the delineation of character. And now it is clear how he happened to be so friendly with the actors whose company he joined temporarily that evening in London when his more conservative friend Lami was scandalized to see him appear on the stage.

Although in the beginning Monnier chose that curious unreal world where his models were, nevertheless, living people whose clothes and accessories were intended to suggest a scene or story, he soon turned to the real world about him, as the others were doing who had found in lithography an easy, rapid, and inexpensive means of suiting popular taste. Following a path already well established, Monnier joined the group of satirists whose work forms a social history of the last years of the Restoration. But he quickly won a place among the most important not only of that period but in the history of French art during the whole nineteenth century. For in his special field he may well be ranked second to the giant who towers far above all others, Honoré Daumier.

Monnier's style has certain easily recognizable traits which distinguish his work from that of his contemporaries and give it a uniformity which the casual observer might consider monotonous. There is a conspicuous lack of grace in his personages; they are drawn with heavier lines than the figures of Eugène Lami, for instance, or of Gavarni; they are solidly planted on their feet, their bodies are short and stocky. They are clothed with almost photographic veracity, with minute attention to the details which are appropriate to their social status. But the most remarkable thing about them is the way in which Monnier made them live: the vivacity and variety of their facial expressions, and the precision, appropriateness, and restraint of their gestures, all the more noticeable in contrast with the tendency of the Romantic artists toward florid and violent action. The setting in which the characters appear is presented with the same accuracy of detail. Compared with the caricatures of Traviès or Grandville, or the deadly irony of Daumier's studies of manners, Monnier's work is unmistakably closer to everyday life. It is in the composition of his scenes, however, that he rises above reality to a height of comic art that is peculiarly his own. Where many of the others found in lithography a medium whose facility of execution encouraged spontaneity rather than carefully planned composition, Monnier made of his drawings genre pictures in which the figures are subordinated to the setting as they are in certain seventeenth-century Dutch paintings. Instead of portraying characters and social types by close-up studies of heads or by scenes in which the people are enormous in proportion to the background, as did Daumier, Monnier deliberately shrank the human figures until they live like rather pudgy dwarfs in houses or landscapes that are too big for them. The result is an admirable evocation of that middle-class world Monnier was interpreting, with its petty preoccupations and stunted aspirations, where human dignity seems crushed beneath the stupid materialism of daily living.

From a technical point of view, Monnier's lithographs and the few water colors he attempted during this period show a method that was extremely simple and at the same time painstaking. He used clear, flat colors, heavily outlined, and shaded with crosshatchings done with pen or pencil. His skill lay in the choice and combinations of colors and in the delicacy of the pen work, in both of which traits he may have profited by his study in England and especially his contact with Cruikshank.

Between 1827 and 1830 Monnier produced numerous albums and sets of lithographs recording his observations of Parisian life. Besides the *Mœurs administratives*, in which he presented the bureaucratic world he had known as a government clerk, he ranged from the aristocratic salons of the Faubourg Saint-Germain to the unsavory streets of the populous Saint-Denis quarter. But he seemed to take particular pleasure in choosing scenes of middle-class interiors, the elegant houses of the bankers of the Chaussée d'Antin, the less-assured prosperity of the financiers of the Bourse, or the humbler life of that petty *bourgeoisie* to which Monnier himself belonged. And perhaps because he was still unmarried, and living among students and artists, he studied with unique thoroughness and comprehension the life and character, the simple pleasures and loves, of that most Parisian of females, the *grisette*.[1]

Here he was thoroughly at home in a subject which he evidently knew intimately from personal experience and which was close enough to his heart to have inspired nostalgic longings when he was in London. His young shopgirls and milliner's assistants have a charming good nature and simplicity beneath their pert bonnets, coiffures *en coque*, leg-of-mutton sleeves, and full short skirts. Gone was the modest gray costume which had given the *grisette* her nickname in the eighteenth century. During the Restoration her favorite colors were pink in the summer and blue in the winter, her dress was of *percaline*, *indienne*, or *mérinos* according to the season, and everything about her, from her lightly tripping little feet to the half-impertinent, half-ingenuous glances which she knew so well how to direct, revealed the coquette whose chief pleasures were those of the heart. The meager wages she received were supplemented by other sources of revenue. In Monnier's album can be distinguished the three categories of lovers who were the rule: the weekday *bailleur de fonds*, always well established and therefore necessarily advanced in years; the Sunday *amant de cœur*, a student, clerk, or petty officer, who shared the fun of picnics in the country when the weather was fine, or parties in the *grisette's* attic room; and the official fiancé, whom she planned to marry when he had saved enough money. Such an existence was complicated on the sentimental side, and Monnier represented many a scene of jealousy, suspicion, tenderness suddenly transformed into anger, or accusation melting into forgiveness and reconciliation. But none of the passions was very violent, the lovers' quarrels were soon ended, and the gay, carefree existence went on its good-humored round. Later the *grisette* was to change her nature, as she changed her name, and to lose, in Gavarni's *Lorettes*, the naïveté and *joie de vivre* which make her, in Monnier's work, a symbol of the youthful optimism which the nineteenth century had not yet lost.[2]

Monnier's other work of that period shows varied contacts and experiences, some of them rather unexpected for a young man of no social standing or fortune. How did he happen to be admitted, for instance, to the fashionable salons of the Chaussée d'Antin? He reproduced with a fidelity which must have come from direct observation the somewhat overelaborate toilettes and coiffures of the ladies, and the cutaway frock coats, fancy waistcoats, and stiff stocks of the men of affairs, politicians, and dandies who paid court to them.

That world of big business and banking was far removed from the milieu which young artists usually frequented.

Monnier possessed, however, a charm that opened many doors to him. For the reputation he had made in the studios had grown. As he became more widely known as an artist, he was more and more sought after as a wit, a raconteur, a mimic, and a monologuist. In the rather heterogeneous society of the Restoration, where the impoverished nobility of the *ancien régime* mingled with the upstart peers of the Empire and the new bourgeois aristocracy of money, he was the well-dressed, personable young man who was invited to dinner in order to provide entertainment for the other guests. As one of his contemporaries said, he was at that time a man of the world, much sought after because of his gay and piquant conversation, a lively wit which exercised itself in parody and mimicry, the humor of his stories and of the original scenes which he acted.[3]

Later Monnier became very sensitive about being expected to pay for his dinner by playing the part of professional humorist, and would turn silent and churlish if he suspected his host of such a motive.* In the days of his youthful success, however, he was no doubt less independent about displaying his talents as a comedian. Perhaps he was willing to sacrifice his pride for the sake of the priceless opportunity to observe the people who applauded him, innocently unaware that they were themselves being added to his stock of social types. A born mimic is as great a potential menace as he may be a social asset, and it was probably because Monnier was only moderately malicious that his humorous imitations were relatively innocuous. Although nothing remains of that parlor entertainment except a few enthusiastic contemporary descriptions, and although many of the scenes themselves were never written or published, the studies of manners which form the chief part of Monnier's artistic

* Realizing on one occasion that he was being lionized because the guests thought he was there to amuse them, Monnier devoured an enormous dinner without uttering a word. Later the host asked him to give some of his *Scènes populaires*. "You know it is a thousand francs a scene," Monnier replied solemnly. Then it was suggested that each guest sing something. Whereupon Monnier began in a deep and lugubrious voice a song which was so licentious that they had to stop him. "*Eh bien*," he said with dignity, "since it is impossible to take part in the conversation, I bid you good-evening!" and he departed, never to return. Berthet, "Silhouettes et anecdotes littéraires," *Revue de France*, III, 322 (May 1, 1877).

work between 1827 and 1830 are good-naturedly realistic rather than markedly satiric and it seems likely that good-humored mockery characterized the tongue as well as the pencil of the young man about town.

One of the Paris circles which Monnier frequented he later described in his "Souvenirs d'un enfant de Paris." [4] Near the rue de la Rochefoucauld, where he lived in the 1820's, a new quarter was being built, rue Saint-Lazare, rue de la Tour-des-Dames, rue Bréda. There among the still open fields northwest of the boulevards a colony of actors, men of letters, and artists was established, calling itself pretentiously New Athens. The theatrical members of the group were headed by Talma and Mademoiselle Mars of the Comédie-Française, Lafont of the Vaudeville, and the famous decorator and designer of stage scenery, Ciceri. Horace Vernet had his studio in the rue de la Tour-des-Dames, where his prestige as a painter and what Alexandre Dumas called his d'Artagnan-like charm attracted other artists, Ary Scheffer, Isabey, whose names, like his, are associated with the great years of Romantic painting. The writers of the group were connected chiefly with the theater: Scribe, Bayard, young Eugène Sue, who was beginning to identify himself with some of the more frenzied aspects of the Romantic movement, and Romieu, whose lively youth gave little foretaste of his later dignity as prefect.

Henry Monnier recalled years later the gay parties which attracted many Parisians to the Nouvelle-Athènes. At one masked ball, when the cult of the Middle Ages was at its height, Romieu made a dashing appearance as a troubadour: "The future prefect of Périgueux, Haute Marne, and Indre-et-Loire wore on his head a crenelated velvet cap, the traditional tunic of apricot color girded with satin, yellow boots, then *Son épée et sa harpe Se croisaient sur son cœur*." [5] Another time it was decreed that everyone should wear the white apron and toque of a chef, in which simple disguise could be recognized magistrates, a peer of France, and two princes, who appeared to be having a famously good time, wrote Monnier.

One of the favorite rendezvous of Monnier and his friends was the Café des Cruches, near the Théâtre-Français, where the modern "Athenians" organized their forces to applaud the latest Romantic drama. They gathered there, for instance, before the first performance of Dumas' *Henri III et sa cour* in 1829. And it was there that Monnier may have received additional inspiration for the character of Joseph Prudhomme from the pompous figure of General Beauvais. At any rate he once wrote to Dumas that he had conceived his hero in 1829 at the Café des Cruches.

There has been found a souvenir of those gay times in a watercolor sketch, dated 1827, representing a comic personage, no doubt Monnier himself, in shirttails and long blue stockings but no trousers, with a chef's cap on his head and a long pipe in his mouth, and inscribed in the artist's hand: "My costume for going to lunch henceforth at my friend Romieu's with the Lion and the Tiger." The identity of those carnivorous comrades can only be conjectured. Knowing that Monnier was associated in that very year with the authors of the *Soirées de Neuilly*, for which he did the frontispiece, and that Romieu published a volume of dramatic proverbs and collaborated the next year in the *Scènes contemporaines*, it is a temptation to guess that the Lion may have been Loève-Weimars, and the Tiger, Cavé or Dittmer, or perhaps even Stendhal or Mérimée.[6]

In those years when French Romanticism was at its height, Monnier's friends were all connected with the movement. To understand his place in the history of Romantic art, it is necessary first to put aside the great painters. Monnier is not to be compared with Géricault, Delaroche, or Delacroix. His is a humbler, more democratic position, among those whom Gautier, with apologies for the neologism, called the *illustrateurs*,[7] whose abundant and charming productions enhance so greatly the beauty and value of books published during that period. For the modern art of illustration was in a sense an offshoot of the Romantic movement.

In the eighteenth century, when Classicism was fighting unsuccessfully to maintain its supremacy, interest in the picturesque life of distant lands and past times was stimulated as travelers like Tavernier, Chardin, and Madame de Lambert's friend, the Abbé de Choisy, wrote of their voyages to the Orient, and Montesquieu's Persians brought to Paris the exotic flavor of the seraglio; as Voltaire put into practice on the stage some of the lessons he learned from Shakespeare's historical plays, and French audiences began to realize that costumes and scenery added real enjoyment even to the performance of tragedy; as Diderot and the writers of bourgeois dramas used stage pictures not only as an additional medium by which to convey their meaning, but also as an appeal to the eyes and hearts of the spectators. Then came the flowering of melodrama, child of the Revolution, symbol of the end of the *ancien régime*, symptom of a period when emotions were primitive and simple, when art was cast down from its aristocratic pedestal to dress in proletarian garb, and pleasure was derived from the senses rather than from the intellect. Pixérécourt showed that the time had come to achieve success on the stage with the aid of all the spectacular devices the machinist could contrive, and he stood at the threshold of the Romantic period.

Just as the history of the nineteenth-century theater should begin with melodrama, so the history of Romantic art would be far from complete if it included only the great painters. For the democratic ideas whose fruition had been delayed by the Napoleonic regime were seeking expression in art and literature as well as in government and religion. The desire to visualize in concrete form the physical aspects of people's lives led to the rise of book illustration, which found at the psychological moment a medium essentially democratic in character. Lithography had a liveliness of color and action obvious enough to appeal to popular taste, and was cheap enough to suit anyone's purse.

There is an essential difference between the ornamentation of a text by the addition of pictures—such as the illuminations of medieval manuscripts, or the woodcuts and engravings added to printed books in the form of vignettes, *culs-de-lampe*, and frontispieces, whose subjects depend on the fantasy of the artist or have only general reference to the subject of the book—and the use of pictures to set before the eyes of the reader the scenes which are described by the author. The illustrator becomes the collaborator, the interpreter of the author, and may even, if his talents are superior to those of his colleague, turn the book into a picture book, a collector's item, whose literary virtues are ignored or forgotten. So the artist goes down to posterity as the creator of Dr. Syntax or Snow White, and the author sinks into oblivion.*

* Time will show whether Walt Disney's art is more or less lasting than Rowlandson's; *Snow White* has, of course, a literary past and prestige which put it into a class far different from that of *Dr. Syntax*.

The illustrators of the 1820's and 1830's can be divided into two groups much as can the dramatists of the same period. On the one hand there were those who catered to the public taste which demanded, in the name of truth, a representation of people like themselves, wearing modern dress and living in ordinary houses. On the stage this conception of realism led to a significant change in the old melodrama, which transferred its exaggerated and fantastic action from the spectacular settings Pixérécourt had given it to a simpler, more modern setting intended to reproduce, externally at least, contemporary life. Such plays as Dumas' *Antony* and Vigny's *Chatterton* illustrate that trend. On the other hand there was the desire to escape from everyday life, expressed on the stage by the historical plays of Dumas and Hugo, with their insistence on picturesque local color in scenery and costumes, and in art by illustrations of the historical novels, whose exciting and passionate action, under the influence chiefly of Walter Scott, filled their readers' imagination with the color and romance of the Middle Ages. That Monnier attempted both types of illustration is an indication of his versatility. The relative insignificance of his contribution to fantasy shows again that he was at ease only in the field of everyday reality.

The artists of the "gothic troubadour" school were illustrators in the most exact sense of the term, for they represented pictorially scenes from the latest novel or play, to satisfy public avidity for the additional thrill of seeing in more concrete form the details which had touched the imagination. In their etchings, wood or copper engravings, and lithographs, they represented a world of demons, vampires, corpses with their setting of biers and tombstones, moonlit ruins, and death's heads, and their human counterparts in the shape of black-robed monks, assassins with Mephistophelian beards and sinister gestures, cavaliers in tunics or armor, with all the trappings of medieval chivalry, and the whole embroidered with angels and cherubs, and having as its central personage a lovely female, always in a state of semiswoon, with flowing hair and disordered garments. The lithographs appeared, not only in the published texts, but separately also, in fashion magazines, painted on clocks or powder boxes, on the covers of the albums, called *keepsakes*, which young ladies received for their *fêtes* or *étrennes*, and especially as frontispieces of

until Latouche's intransigent republicanism objected to Nodier's accepting from Louis XVIII an appointment as librarian of the Arsenal. It may be true, as Monnier wrote later in the *Mémoires de Monsieur Joseph Prudhomme*, that a duel would have been fought if Monnier had not persuaded Latouche to a reconciliation.[1]

That was in 1824. Latouche appears to have made Monnier's acquaintance at the Café des Cruches, where so many artists, actors, and writers gathered. Like some of the others, Latouche had been employed in a government office before he turned to writing as a better outlet for energies too often directed to criticism of the existing regime. His early work in journalism had given him the reputation of a rebellious opponent of the Restoration. A witty and malicious pamphlet containing sketches of various deputies had shown him gifted with lively impertinence and humor as well as the power of realistic observation.[2] He had distinguished himself also as the perpetrator of a literary hoax, in publishing the *Dernières lettres de deux amants de Barcelone*, purporting to be genuine love letters translated from the Spanish. And he was probably already Monnier's friend when he fooled the public a second time with the salacious novel *Olivier*, attributed to the respectable pen of the Duchesse de Duras.[3] At the same time Latouche continued to reveal his republican fervor, which brought him into touch with Béranger, to whom he is said to have presented Monnier before the latter was commissioned to illustrate the *Chansons*. And it was through him that Monnier made the acquaintance of Balzac.

Monnier tells the story in the *Mémoires de Monsieur Joseph Prudhomme*.[4] He was staying with Latouche at the latter's country house at Aulnay, in the Vallée-aux-Loups. Latouche was in a particularly pleased mood, because he had invited Balzac to pay him a visit, and expected him that morning. But what was their amazement to see the eccentric guest descend from the stagecoach dressed in what he had evidently chosen as a costume suitable for a sojourn in the country:

> He was clothed in a blouse and wore an oilskin cap. Leather gaiters came up to his knees; a knapsack on top of which was buckled a raincoat burdened his shoulders. He held in his hand a heavy iron-shod stick; beneath his blouse he wore a belt, garnished with two pistols, from the end of which hung a small hatchet. You would have said a pioneer from the United States.

Latouche, who was extremely fastidious about the neatness and cleanliness of his house, was horrified to see his polished floors scratched by hobnailed boots, his delicate porcelain knickknacks touched by a careless hand, and his furniture littered with the accouterments which Balzac soon began unconcernedly to remove from his person. But that was only the beginning. As the host became more and more silent and ceremonious in his manner, addressing his guest as "Monsieur de Balzac" when he could not avoid speaking to him, the latter gave louder and more boisterous expression to his good humor. After dinner they went for a walk. The evening calm of the countryside was shattered by the bursts of laughter and incessant chatter of the massive and energetic young man, whose conversation that day revolved about a grandiose scheme to publish his own novels and establish a company for translating them into all languages. Latouche, who was accustomed to dominate every group by the brilliance of his conversation, was forced into the role of audience. He controlled himself with frigid courtesy, however, until Balzac had gone to his bedroom, with the customary pot of cold coffee to drink during the hours of nocturnal composition. Henry never knew just what happened after that. But the next morning, as he was taking an early stroll, he saw a strange sight: Monsieur de Balzac, bareheaded, in his dressing gown and slippers, running after the *coucou* which transported travelers between Sceaux and Paris, and calling breathlessly to the driver to stop. No knapsack, no gaiters, no iron-shod stick, no pistols. Thus ended Monnier's first encounter with Balzac!

Latouche offers a curious study to the psychologist. Extremely gifted intellectually, original, liberal in his ideas, he was recognized as one of the chief figures in the Romantic movement long before Victor Hugo had organized his group.[5] His prestige as a poet and literary critic, the distinction of his manner, the charm of a very beautiful voice, attracted young writers, who fell quickly under his influence. Among his pupils and disciples were counted Marceline Desbordes-Valmore, Louis Veuillot, George Sand. Sophie Gay's lasting affection for him was one of his rare friendships which did not end on the rocks of misunderstanding and bitterness. For Latouche was a benevolent mentor only so long as his pupils were willing to follow his counsels blindly. He would tolerate no discussion, no criticism, and was abnormally sensitive to any fancied slight.

There was rather tragic frustration in Latouche's failure to fulfill the promises of his early career. His genius, so dazzling in the improvised cleverness of conversation, apparently lacked adequate means of expressing itself in more permanent form. And he was perfectly able to realize, implacable critic that he was, his own inability to achieve the glory which was to come to some of his disciples. His refusal to join the brilliant young writers of the *Muse Française*, his feud with Hugo, his ferocious attacks on the *cénacle de Joseph Delorme*, the animosity he expressed and inspired which made him a *bête noire* of the Romanticists of 1830, all this must have been due, not only to the reasons he gave—that he could not accept the royalist and Catholic sympathies of the official Romantic movement, which he considered a betrayal of the liberal principles for which the preceding generation had fought—but also to the bitterness of jealousy, which prevented him from joining in the comradeship of a literary group convinced of its individual and collective genius.

H. de Latouche seems to have been a kind of post-revolutionary Alceste, modern in his political convictions and possessing a sense of humor which provided some outlet for his misanthropic irritability. Sensitive and passionate by nature, his ideal of friendship was one of such complete devotion that he could not forgive any casual neglect, indelicacy, or forgetfulness. Because he suffered from the imperfections of human nature and the world he was forced to live in, he defended himself by a wall of cynicism, sarcasm, and mockery. Those who could break down that wall or make their way inside it found a tender and generous heart, an ardent and uneasy soul, a temperament essentially melancholy.

Twenty years of friendship with such a man certainly bears witness to Henry Monnier's sweetness of disposition. But what was it that held the two together? Temperamentally they were very different, Monnier resembling much more Balzac in his robust and sometimes rather vulgar sense of humor. Perhaps beneath his gay exterior there lurked enough sense of frustration, however, to enable Monnier to understand and forgive Latouche's bitterness. Henry must certainly have been both sensitive and moody to deserve such a reproof as that expressed in a letter from Léon Gozlan, written evidently during a period of disillusionment: "Your discouragement, my friend, is childish; I have told you a hundred times, you remember too well the small drawbacks in life, and not well enough the benefits it brings, which you have known especially well in your career as painter, writer, and actor." [6]

As Monnier's work shows so little concern with politics, it is difficult to weigh the intangible influence that Latouche's republican ideas may have had on him. Perhaps his first literary work, the *Scènes populaires*, reflected Latouche's preference for the accurate observation of reality. Monnier's talents may well have been directed by a friend fourteen years older than he, whose influence on numerous other young writers was so great. But Henry was evidently not modest enough to admit any such influence. He preferred to let Monsieur Prudhomme explain their relationship in a different way: "For twenty years, I can say that I lived with him in the most complete intimacy. He would let a month or two pass sometimes without seeing me, but soon I would see him return, and I would open my arms to him. 'Prudhomme,' he often said to me, 'the sight of you does me good, your conversation refreshes me, you reconcile me with human kind.' " The passage of the *Mémoires* continues: "An astonishing thing, and one which I can't explain: I have exercised the same influence on most of my great contemporaries, painters, musicians, sculptors, poets, journalists, dramatists, statesmen!" [7]—a *prudhommesque* sentence nevertheless revealing a grain of truth that helps to explain Henry Monnier's place in the turbulent century in which he lived.

The need to laugh at the human race in order to be able to bear it is an outstanding trait revealed again and again in all the Romanticists except perhaps in the giants: Chateaubriand, Lamartine, Vigny, and Victor Hugo. The laughter was not only cynical, ironical, directed as much against the cynic himself as against others, but also intellectual, arising from the conviction that most men were stupid and therefore destined to be the victims of the few superior minds whose favorite pastime was to play upon that stupidity. Just as the history of French Romanticism includes a chapter on the development of caricature into a fine art, so it would be incomplete without mention of the hoaxes and practical jokes perpetrated with skill and energy which raised them sometimes above the level of mere youthful sport. These *mystifications,* not yet used specifically as weapons in the artists' war upon the bourgeois, ranged from literary frauds such as Latouche's *Dernières lettres de deux amants de Barcelone* and his novel *Olivier,* down to the *farces* invented by Romieu and his group to torment unsuspecting shopkeepers and concierges. There is no doubt that Henry Monnier's skill and prestige as a *mystificateur* formed the chief bond with many of his friends.

One of the most celebrated of the hoaxers was Mérimée, who not only offered to the public elaborate and false explanations of the origin of *La Guzla* and *Le Théâtre de Clara Gazul,* but was known to have produced for an autograph collector a cleverly forged signature of Robespierre and to have presented at a ball in the Tuileries the son of Paul and Virginie.[8] It will be shown that Mérimée's connection with the men interested in the writing of *proverbes* and *scènes historiques* brought him into contact with Monnier, and he was also closely connected with H. de Latouche, whom he met frequently at the Abbaye-aux-Bois. Of all the Romanticists, in fact, Mérimée has been said to resemble most closely Latouche, in character, mentality, and temperament. They had the same tendency toward misanthropic melancholy, the same intellectual keenness, which they applied in much the same devastating way to the mortification of their fellow men, even of their friends, who must have felt the same insecurity in associating with each sensitive and difficult nature. The older by thirteen years, Latouche may have exercised on Mérimée as well as on Monnier the influence of his liberal ideas in both politics and literature, and also, perhaps, of his impeccable manner as a cynical man of the world.

In certain ways, however, Mérimée is even more comparable to Monnier. As a conscientious and fairly ambitious functionary of Louis-Philippe, he despised his associates in the Ministry of Commerce and Public Works, described them as *hideux de bassesse,*[9] and like Monnier vented his spleen by drawing clever and merciless caricatures. Mérimée had traveled in England with Delacroix and Delécluze in 1825, and had in his appearance and manner the elegance and reserve which formed part of the current fashion of imitating the British. That self-restraint appears in his work, from which he seems to detach himself in a cold and pitiless notation of accurately observed details, betraying the affectation of his attitude of objectivity only by the selection of material which is often more shockingly scabrous because of the impertinently cynical manner in which it is presented. Monnier was less gifted as a writer, but in his humbler sphere he possessed many of the same characteristics.

Like Latouche, and like Stendhal also, Mérimée suffered from an absence of simplicity that led him always to suspect hidden motives, to be afraid of falling victim to the duplicity of others. This explains no doubt why those three men could understand each other so well, and it is a temptation to deduce from Monnier's friendship with them that he too had an abnormally complicated or sensitive nature. There is little evidence, however, of anything more than a tendency, as he grew older and especially in his theatrical life, to suffer from the persecution complex which so often results from a failure to fulfill personal ambitions.

Stendhal too was a *mystificateur*, in his fondness for pseudonyms, of which he invented almost as many as did Balzac, and in the jokes which he occasionally played in the salons of his most intimate friends. That gossipy and self-satisfied lady, Madame Ancelot, tells for instance how Stendhal reproached her for not inviting him to her Tuesdays, when she was at home only to members of the Academies. Having received the desired invitation, he accepted it on condition that she allow him to come under an assumed name. He had himself announced as "M. César Bombay, fournisseur de l'armée pour les bas et les bonnets de coton," made a long and solemn speech on his patriotic trade of protecting His Majesty's armies from colds in the head, and launched a series of scornful epigrams against artists and men of letters, the uselessness of whose products he contrasted with the value of his cotton nightcaps.[10]

The audacity of this *tour de force* recalls one of Monnier's most successful improvisations, in which his usual mockery of bourgeois credulity took a somewhat macabre turn. After 1830 he used to frequent the Café du Divan, which was on rue Lepelletier, near the offices of the newspaper *Le National* and also near the Opera. The artists and writers connected with the *National,* Balzac, Méry, Gavarni, Gérard de Nerval, Gautier, and others, all regular clients of the Divan, resented the respectable operagoers who often dropped in, unfortunate reminders of the usurpation by the middle class of a privilege formerly reserved for the aristocracy. One evening an impassioned discussion of art was interrupted by the arrival of a solid couple that called for beer and dominoes and began a noisy game. Whereupon Monnier, who was seated next to them, spoke in his deepest and most solemn tones:

> As I was saying to you, gentlemen, there are no useless professions, and I have the most profound scorn for the people who refuse to be my friends. What am I, indeed, if not an essential cog in the social machine? Each time that I have the honor of guillotining a great criminal, I put on silk stockings, a white cravat, I have my hair curled, and I say to myself that I am administering a priestly rite.

The game of dominoes was suspended and the beer remained untasted. Monnier continued:

> They maintain that I bring bad luck, it is false; they declare that contact with me is fatal, don't believe it; they affirm that every time I step on a man's foot, that man infallibly passes through my hands within the year . . . Fiddlesticks, humbug, and nonsense.

A shriek was heard as Monnier stepped on the gentleman's boot under the table, and the intruder, livid with terror, dragged his wife away from the accursed spot.[11]

Although Monnier's *mystification* was more good-humored than gruesome, it may be compared with Nodier's celebrated recital of how he had been guillotined during the Revolution. It was said that he told the tale with such conviction that his listeners found themselves wondering how he had got his head fastened on again. Nodier was a student as well as a producer of the literary hoaxes which flourished during the Restoration and July Monarchy. He described various kinds of literary trickery in his *Questions de littérature légale*, besides collaborating in the spurious *Poésies* of Clothilde de Surville and in the four volumes of *Mémoires et souvenirs d'une femme de qualité sur le Consulat et l'Empire*. One of his associates in the latter work was Lamothe-Langon, who seems, like one of the characters in Balzac's *Peau de chagrin,* to have made a successful business of turning out quantities of the false "memoirs" which were extremely popular between 1830 and 1840. Balzac himself experimented with that genre in the *Mémoires de Sanson*, later published under the title of *Souvenirs d'un paria*, of which the hero and narrator was supposed to be the son of that Sanson who was a famous executioner during the Terror.

The only literary hoax with which Monnier was connected, unless indeed the mingling of personal experiences with fictitious adventures in the *Mémoires de Monsieur Joseph Prudhomme* could be considered as such, is the aforementioned volume, *Les Contes du gay sçavoir* (see Chapter V, above), which Monnier and Bonington illustrated for Ferdinand Langlé. Langlé belonged to a band of gay young men of varied talents, who dabbled in painting, the composing of *vaudevilles*, journalism, novel-writing, while they were officially engaged in studying law or medicine in preparation for a serious career. The headquarters of the group was the house of Langlé's wealthy cousin. Eugène Sue, where Ferdinand had at his disposal a bedroom which he offered generously to any friends who happened to be too poor or too drunk to provide their own night's lodging. The key was hidden in a hole in the wall, a cold supper was always ready on the table, and this nonchalant hospitality was sometimes enjoyed by as many as seven young men in a night. Here perhaps was plotted the raid on the rarest wines of Dr. Sue *père*, traces of which were removed by refilling the bottles with a liquid concocted under the direction of the *vaudevillistes* James Rousseau and Romieu. Here Monnier and Eugène Sue may have devised some of the tricks they played on the unwary bourgeois.

Eugène Sue was the spoiled son of a wealthy family. After giving up the study of medicine, his father's profession, he had been sent first to the army and then to sea, in an effort to occupy his energies in legitimate ways. In the late 1820's he tried journalism and writing *vaudevilles*, and later studied painting, before he discovered that he could win fame and increase his fortune by writing novels. He showed no traces yet either of the snobbery which was to earn him the nickname among old friends of "Sulfate de Quinine" during the period of his popularity in the legitimist salons of the Faubourg Saint-Germain, or of the socialist ideas which afterward closed aristocratic doors to him, giving him far wider and more lasting prestige as author of *Les Mystères de Paris* and other novels which the 1840's found shudderingly realistic. It would be interesting to know at what point in his career he began to plan the fabulous existence which was to bring him added notoriety, when his apartment with its Renaissance furniture, Chinese porcelains, and collection of Oriental arms, dimly lighted by stained glass windows and fragrant with fresh flowers, was the talk of all Paris. But in the years when he and his friends were still sowing belated wild oats, the cult of medievalism and exotic local color had not yet reached its height, and there were other less costly ways to *épater le bourgeois*.*

According to Alexandre Dumas, who was so familiar with the habits and traditions of the group that he must have spent more than one night under Sue's roof, although he took pains to declare that his lack of inventiveness made him merely an amused spectator of their pranks, it was in Langlé's room that Monnier met for the first time the "gayest man in France," the celebrated Romieu.[12] No one seems more typical than he of the postwar generation born with the nineteenth century, which devoted its young manhood to the search for pleasure with a cynical belief in its own superiority and its freedom from responsibility under a regime and in a society for which it had no sympathy, feeling, as Romieu said, that its destiny was to supply documents for those who would later edit the "martyrology of the bourgeois." [13]

It was an amazingly clever generation, with a superficial brilliance all the more striking in the men whose names never reached

* There was, for instance, the wearing of a beard. Sue brought back a magnificent one from his cruises in the navy, before the days when the beard became almost an official symbol of the Romantic revolt. During the Restoration the most celebrated beard was worn by a curiously terrifying and mysterious figure. Chodruc-Duclos, an ardent Royalist and Vendéen who had sacrificed a fortune in opposition to the Revolution and to Napoleon, had expected his reward from the restored Bourbons. Disappointed at being offered what he considered inadequate recompense, he let his beard grow and stalked in rags, a somber and silent Diogenes, through the arches of the Palais-Royal. This personage soon took on legendary qualities as a kind of super-*mystificateur*, frightening to women and children, and recognized by the younger generation of dissatisfied spirits as expressing something of their own Satanic inclinations. Cf. Charles Yriarte, *Paris grotesque ou les Célébrités de la rue* (Paris, 1864): "l'homme à la barbe."

the first rank of importance. Romieu was witty, a brilliant schoolboy, a versatile young man who gave up a military career to write comedies with his friend James Rousseau and made a success which rivaled for a short time that of Scribe himself. Then after the July Revolution, like Mérimée and Stendhal, he accepted from Louis-Philippe a government post, entering upon a not particularly distinguished career as an official in various provincial prefectures. Thus Paris was deprived of a *bon vivant* whose occasional visits to the capital brought a momentary revival of the lively times which had disappeared with Romieu and the Restoration:

> Lorsque Romieu revint du Monomotapa,
> Paris ne soupait plus, et Paris resoupa.[14]

The supper parties which had been a lingering tradition since the eighteenth century and which began to disappear, it was said, with the introduction of the after-dinner cigar,* had been the stage on which Romieu had exercised his skill as a conversationalist and humorist. They provided him with an audience appreciative of his *bons mots*, and eager to hear of his latest *mystification* or *farce*, and to spread the tale to the four corners of Paris. Jokes are funniest when they are told to an appreciative audience, and Romieu's friends collected his with the ardor of connoisseurs, whether they were ridiculous adventures which happened to him or tricks which he played on other people. It would be interesting to know whether Monnier took any direct part in them.

There was, for instance, the story of the *limonadier de la Porte-Saint-Martin*, the proprietor of a well-known and expensive restaurant. Romieu and another playwright named Rougemont had menus printed exactly like those used in the restaurant, but with very moderate prices, and substituted them one day. The ensuing delight of the patrons and confusion over settling the bills ended with an appeal to the police to compromise between the printed prices and what the proprietor claimed as his due. And there was the story of how Romieu and Rousseau were coming home one night from a

* The cigar separated the ladies and the gentlemen, the latter strolling in the street to smoke it. There making other feminine contacts, they spent the evenings in quite a different manner from that of an older, more elegant society. Dumas, *Mes mémoires* (1899), IV, 218.

supper party, when Rousseau fell down dead drunk a few feet from his own door. As Romieu was in no state to carry him the rest of the way, he pounded on the door of a nearby shop until it was opened, bought a *lampion* which he lighted and placed beside his friend before he left him, consoled by the thought that he would not be stepped on by a careless pedestrian: "And now, sleep in peace, son of Epicure; they will not crush thee!" When Rousseau woke the next morning, he found in his outstretched hand several coins dropped by charitable passersby.*

The *farce* of the porter's hair was acted out by Romieu and his band before its fame was increased by its appearance in a popular *vaudeville*. Romieu had discovered a porter who was completely bald, and conceived the cruel trick of stopping at his *loge* to ask for a lock of hair: "Portier, je veux de tes cheveux." Every day for weeks one or another of the young men would appear with the same peculiar request, varying the formula to suit his fancy and giving all kinds of reasons for it, sentimental, artistic, or even political, until the poor victim's constantly renewed rage led him to the verge of insanity.†

And so the tales could go on, for the anecdotes about Romieu did not cease when he attained the dignity of prefect. These few examples suffice, however, to give an idea of what amused *tout Paris* in the 1820's, and especially of the brand of *mystification* in which some of Monnier's close friends specialized. As there will be no need to bring Romieu into the book again, it might be well to mention here another incident, which throws some light on his relationship with Monnier as well as on the latter's personality. There are two versions of the episode, by Dumas and Champfleury, neither of whom can be called a thoroughly reliable historian.[15]

According to Dumas, it happened while Romieu was prefect of

* Sometimes the joke was on Romieu. There was another night when, going home with Eugène Sue, he hurt his leg as he entered the carriage. Full of solicitude, Sue took him to the house, helped him to bed, and dressed his leg with the skill he had acquired in his medical studies. In the morning they discovered it was the other leg that had been injured.

† The complicated plotting of this trick and its cruelty recall the exploits of the Chevaliers de la Désœuvrance, under the leadership of the infamous Maxence Gilet, in Balzac's *La Rabouilleuse*.

Périgord. Passing through Périgueux one day, presumably with a company of actors, Monnier dropped in uninvited on his old friend for lunch. Undaunted by the fact that the prefect was entertaining with great propriety and formality a group of provincial notables, Monnier was as talkative and anecdotal as usual, and charming as he could be when he felt perfectly at ease. While he used the familiar *tu* of their earlier comradeship, Romieu kept addressing him as *vous*, until at last Monnier called the length of the table: "*Ah ça, dis-moi donc, mon cher Romieu, tu me dis vous, et je te dis tu,* do you know that they are going to take you for my servant?"

There is a frank good humor in that story which is lacking in the version told by Champfleury, who reversed the roles, making Monnier too timid in the presence of his important friend to use the familiar address of their younger days. It is a little hard to believe that the artist would have been so humble before a functionary whose official position was in his eyes to be scorned rather than respected. On the other hand, there is evidence to show that Romieu would have preferred to forget the associations of earlier days, which undoubtedly interfered with his efforts to be taken seriously in his professional career. Dumas reproached him for refusing to find a position for his former collaborator and inseparable comrade James Rousseau. And the following letter to Monnier certainly has a rather unpleasant tone of condescension, indicating more willingness to repudiate the follies of the past than cordiality in reviving an old friendship:

Chaumont, 28 September, 1843, Office of the Prefect.

My dear friend,

Thanks a hundred times for your kind remembrance. I have not forgotten you and will always think of you. People both witty and tender-hearted are too rare for one not to be honored by their friendship, and you are one of them.

There are people who believe that one must never grow older than twenty-five, and who are amazed to see success come to a man who knows how to choose a steady career, after having forgotten for a while a serious upbringing, after having momentarily given up influential connections for the foolish and pleasant life of poetry and youth.

These are the people to whom you refer, no doubt, and who do not forgive me. Let them, if they like, it matters little to me.

As for you, my friend, who have wished to sample all the arts, because you are a great artist, you will see me no doubt in Paris or elsewhere. Everywhere, and at all times, I should be happy to remind you of the old days, the time of *grisettes* and songs. We shall not be less gay for being less young, nor more stupid, I hope.

A toi de tout cœur,

G. A. Romieu.[16]

Another friendship which Monnier formed in the last years of the Restoration was with the Marseillais Joseph Méry, satiric poet, journalist, and critic, who was in some ways the most brilliant of them all. Like Monnier, Méry was one of the artists and writers whose living depended entirely upon their talents, instead of belonging to the more worldly group of dilettanti, like Stendhal and Mérimée, or the group of sons of well-to-do families, like Romieu and Sue, who dabbled in bohemianism for the fun of it, with the intention of settling down later to serious work. Méry had come to Paris with the plan of earning his living by playing chess. The publication of some violently anti-royalist verses soon marked him as an enemy of the Restoration, and like other liberals he placed his political hopes in the July Revolution. Meanwhile he was not long in making connections with the newspapers as a literary and dramatic critic, and the extraordinary energy of his personality and verve of his style impressed his contemporaries in much the same way that young Diderot had dazzled Paris when he arrived from the provinces. The comparison is not accidental, but suggests itself again and again, as Méry's encyclopedic store of knowledge, his skill in mathematics, his prodigious memory for music, the fireworks of his gift of improvisation, and the kindness of his heart and loyalty to his friends, show him to have had the versatility of gifts and ardor of temperament of the great philosopher beside whom he is the palest of shades.

As a *mystificateur*, Méry had to his credit some first-class achievements, particularly in the line of poetic and dramatic hoaxes. He once wrote the review of a play which existed only in his imagination, giving the title and subject, and adding verisimilitude to his comments by quoting many of the lines. And the story goes that he reviewed Ponsard's *Lucrèce* without having seen a performance of it, improvising an entire first act which he recited in Madame de Girardin's salon. Nodier was so impressed that he hurried to see the play, but came away disappointed that so many of the best lines had been cut! Méry was always welcome in the salons, for he was an entertainer unequaled by anyone except Monnier.*

Méry had been one of Monnier's first admirers, and had paid tribute to his artistic talents in a quatrain which linked Henry's name with that of the most celebrated engraver of the late Restoration:

> Songe au luxe nouveau de la littérature,
> Fais briller sur le titre et sur la couverture
> Une fraîche vignette en forme d'écusson,
> Dessinée par Monnier et gravée par Thompson! [17]

Years later Henry repaid that friendly gesture in a *mystification* which must have been peculiarly macabre. One of the favorite stories recited by the inimitable Marseillais had been the moving tale of the dog that loved a modiste, in the telling of which he used the full gamut of his southern voice, now sad, now caressing, almost magically seductive as he pronounced the sentence: "You could see plainly that the dog was not happy!" After Méry's death, Monnier retold the story with this same voice, imitating so perfectly its cadences that his listeners had only to close their eyes to believe that Méry himself sat before them. Banville, who witnessed the extraordinary resuscitation, exclaimed as he described it: "It was a horrible pleasure." [18]

As a practical joker, Monnier often indulged in the low type of humor which involves some physical discomfiture of an innocent victim. It was told, for instance, that Henry was walking one day on the boulevards behind an unsuspecting bourgeois whose appearance was for some reason offensive to him. Raising his cane, Monnier brought it down on the poor fellow's head, crushing his top hat about his ears. When the man finally succeeded in extricating himself and turned around indignantly to find his tormentor, he saw Monnier waiting with serious dignity, his cane under his arm. "It came from up there," he said, indicating a window above them, and went calmly on his way.

* One of his stunts, for instance, was to have the lights lowered and begin a ghost story, with piano accompaniment, adding horror to suspense until half the ladies swooned from fright.

Monnier's appearance of solid respectability and authoritative dignity was often the foundation of his jokes. One day he entered a public toilet behind whose doors could be seen the feet of various patrons. In his most resonant tones Monnier called: "In the name of the law, let everyone appear at once!" Out came alarmed and embarrassed heads, which he scrutinized solemnly and slowly, then he said: "Very well, you may continue." *

No doubt Monnier's share in the *farces* and *mystifications* that he and his friends enjoyed so much contributed to the stock of human types and comic situations which composed his repertory of monologues and scenes. As a mimic and monologuist he was unsurpassed, from the days when he had amused his fellow *rapins* to the early years of the July Monarchy, when he was as welcome in respectable salons as in the studios of his artist friends. A letter from Madame Delphine Gay Girardin to the wealthy man about town, amateur poet, and journalist, Count Jules de Rességuier, indicates that Monnier was sometimes invited to read from the *Scènes populaires*, and it is interesting to note that on this particular occasion he was considered fit entertainment for no less distinguished a guest than Lamartine.† He was at his best, however, in the studios, whose more bohemian atmosphere welcomed *charges* of a Rabelaisian realism which made them sometimes unfit either for public performance or for publication.

Before the invention of the sound film furnished a means of recording an actor's art in permanent form, no sketch or description or photograph could preserve it adequately for the imagination of

* He was often responsible for creating predicaments which furnished him with material for his study of human nature. The public omnibuses were a rich field for such experiments. One of Monnier's tricks was to slip an extra coin into the handful of change being passed back from the conductor to a passenger, and then to watch the latter's struggle between cupidity and the fear of being found out; or if the passenger was a woman, to slip in a bit of paper, purporting to be a declaration of love, and to watch the conflict between outraged propriety and feminine coquetry. It is doubtful whether such fooling can be said to rise above the level of childish pranks, even if it supplies an artist with subject matter.

† "Henry Monnier is to recite for us this evening one of his proverbs, real Téniers scenes; M. Lamartine will be with us, in a very select group, and you and Mme. de Rességuier would be very kind if you came informally to enjoy this bit of nonsense." Paul Lafond, *L'Aube romantique; Jules de Rességuier et ses amis* (Paris, 1910), p. 207, *lettre* cxxxvii.

posterity. Thus the quality of Monnier's talent can be appreciated only indirectly, through the testimony of a few of his contemporaries, who tried to set down their impressions of the scenes they heard him give. To them he was unique, a perfect mimic gifted with originality and charm, whose observations went below the surface and added to his gaiety the spice of irony. "He has some bitterness in his heart," wrote Jal, "as observers always have when they do not stop at the surface and go to the bottom of things; but this bitterness does not poison his gaiety; it merely underlines it, makes it ironic, gives it significance and energy, in short poeticizes it." [19]

The critic Jules Janin described the evening when he had the pleasure of hearing Monnier for the first time: the half-darkened studio, the silence falling gradually as Monnier took his place on a chair in the middle of the group, crossed his arms, bent his head with eyes nearly closed and began to speak.

> His composure was admirable; he invented innumerable dramas. The action took place wherever was fitting, in high society or low, respectable or not. Everything answered his purpose, street or crossroads, shop or drawing-room, guardhouse or backstairs, and along the way he encountered so many laughable simpletons, so many choice absurdities, so many exquisite and salty witticisms; the pleasure was so great and so complete in following him in his comic meditations, and that excellent tone, varied, natural, free, those burlesqued sketches, passionate cries, side-splitting metaphors, those emotions in the heart and on the voice, that very lewdness itself, veiled in wit or quite naked when it made the play more effective, that we all, and we were a large and diversified group, spent the most delightful evening of drama that you could hear and see . . . [20]

Elie Berthet, with whom Monnier was to collaborate later in two novels, told of another method he sometimes used in giving his scenes. Instead of sitting before his friends, he would remain behind a screen, producing an effect of numerous personalities by varying his voice and accent. That was the way he did his famous "Voyage en diligence," for instance, imitating now an Englishman's insular French, now the truisms of Monsieur Prudhomme, a lady's insistence on her right to travel with her little dog, or the coachman's philosophical calm which carried him through the vicissitudes of the journey.[21]

Charles Monselet, in his *Lorgnette littéraire*, has best expressed a nostalgic regret for something which Monnier's contemporaries evidently felt as the supreme expression of his personal originality, finer than any of the written scenes which survived their creator:

What is not known of Henry Monnier is more valuable, perhaps, than what is known; what he recites is often superior to what he puts into writing. For example: *La Diligence de Lyon, La Pierreuse, Monsieur Prudhomme à Cythère, Les Officiers*. But what will become of these inimitable recitations after he has gone? What memory will preserve them? . . . You and I shall be there to say: I have seen him, I have heard him; I have seen those features marked, as if by strange irony, with a resemblance to Napoleon; I have heard that voice which seemed to come from the bedizened belly of a grandiloquent Polichinelle; I have smiled, I have roared with laughter, I have shuddered at those onomatopoeias, at those gestures, those looks, those words which nothing recalls to mind and which are like nothing else. That is what we shall say, you and I, to an incredulous generation. But after you? but after me? [22]

It is indeed difficult to define the elusive spirit of the fun of a century ago. But certain characteristics of it are fairly clear, and distinguish it as essentially French. There seems to have been very little obscenity for its own sake, although there was no prudish avoidance of it when it happened to suit the subject. There was often insistence on certain physical aspects of human existence, but without the kind of rough-and-tumble boisterousness which plays so definite a part in English or especially American humor. On the contrary, the dominant trait, as has been shown before, was an intellectual mockery based on the conviction that the mocker enjoyed a certain superiority over less gifted mortals, but this mockery was often sharpened by the ironic perception that the mocker himself was as fallible as the rest of mankind.

"Do not be surprised to see simple people believe without reasoning," wrote Pascal,[23] and it was perhaps in protest against the essential impossibility of bringing human actions into conformity with the laws of pure reason that the art of *mystification* reached such a high degree of complicated perfection in France. The word itself was invented in the eighteenth century by the philosophers of the Enlightenment, who used it to signify "the traps into which one makes a simple and credulous man fall whom one wishes to chaff." [24] But there are many examples to be found before that time. Molière's comedies are full of them: Monsieur de Pourceaugnac and Monsieur Jourdain illustrate perfectly the hoaxing of a credulous victim.

The fondness for such practical joking reached even the most aristocratic circles. Saint-Simon tells in his *Mémoires* of a masked ball at Marly, during which the Prince de Conti offered a mask to an old courtier who was beyond the dancing age but not beyond being flattered by the attentions of so distinguished a prince. The mask represented an immense pair of antlers, which the gentleman wore in complacent oblivion of their appropriateness and the open secret of his wife's unfaithfulness.[25]

Some of the celebrated *Mystifications du petit Poinsinet* in the eighteenth century were even less elevated in character. In Poinsinet the practical jokers had found the ideal victim, for he was a grotesque little man with delusions of importance and a naïve susceptibility which made him fall into every snare that was spread for him. While his friends held out to him the tempting hope that he would some day gain membership in their Mockers' Club, they made him its chief victim. They sent him a false dentist, who pulled a tooth before Poinsinet discovered the trick; they persuaded him that he had killed an officer of the musketeers and must hide from the police; they sent him on an innocent errand to the house of a lady whose jealous husband thought he had caught her *en flagrant délit*. The climax came when they convinced him that he had been rendered invisible by a great magician, and the poor creature was shoved about heartlessly and even led to appear stark naked in the belief that no one could see him. The tricks played by Romieu and Monnier seem mild enough in comparison.

The literary hoaxes so dear to the Romanticists had their predecessors also in the eighteenth century. Voltaire tells in his *Correspondance* how one day several *beaux esprits* were scornfully criticizing the fables of Lamotte, which had just been published as a contribution to the quarrel of the Ancients and Moderns, and which they compared most unfavorably with the fables of La Fontaine. Thereupon Voltaire told them that a new edition of La Fontaine was about to appear, containing some unpublished fables which had just been discovered, one of which he proceeded to recite to them. His audience was delighted. Never would Lamotte achieve such style, such grace, such *finesse!* You could recognize La Fontaine in every word! Needless to add that the fable was by Lamotte.[26] There was also the episode, comparable to Nodier's recital of being guillotined and worthy of some of Monnier's best efforts, of an actor who recounted at a dinner party the story of *Tartuffe* as though it had really happened. Imagine the indignation and anger of his hearers as they protested against a social menace like Molière's great hypocrite!

In the feverish search for amusement after the Revolution a new wave of popularity gave to the *mystificateurs* the professional character of paid entertainers. Their presence was announced in invitations to a *fête* or *soirée*, and the guests must have spent uneasy moments wondering which of them would be the victim of the evening. During the Directory and the Consulate the most famous of these *mystificateurs* was a certain Musson, who reached the height of his career as protégé of the Empress Josephine. How strange it is to picture that unhappy lady in the abandonment of Malmaison, spending her time arranging pots of water where they could fall on the head of a passerby, or having the beds unscrewed so that they would spill out the members of her household! And what must have been the temperament of the man who devoted his talents to such foolery?

Musson appears in the *Mémoires de Monsieur Joseph Prudhomme*, for Monnier's hero, like little Poinsinet, had something in his pompous dignity and in the gullible stupidity of his countenance which offered an irresistible target to *farceurs*. After pretending to be a foreign potentate who conferred on Prudhomme the title of baron and chevalier of the order of the Blue Pigeon, the great *mystificateur*, who was also a painter, became his friend, and dropped the external mask to reveal the soul of the man. Could Monnier have been thinking of himself when he wrote: "Like all jokers, Musson was profoundly sad"? And was Musson's revolt against the kind of life he led expressing perhaps Monnier's personal feeling, as in 1857 he looked back on his own role as an entertainer of *tout Paris?* Musson had been confessing to Prudhomme his discouragement:

"The life I lead is horrible, my dear friend; my social successes make me blush sometimes. What am I really, now?"

"A famous man."

"A wretched clown. Society welcomes me because I amuse it, that's all; it lets me take part in its pleasures, on condition that I play my role of *histrion*.

I spend my evenings in the most brilliant salons of Paris, and my days in this studio, where I often shiver for lack of a load of wood. I find luxury at other people's houses; poverty awaits me in my own. I am a painter, and each portrait is ordered out of charity, I can see; my jokes are paid for, and even then, if only everyone paid me!"[27]

There is a note of bitter sincerity in these words, revealing more than Monnier probably intended of his own paradoxical life, the promising talents which never quite overcame the struggle against poverty, the gaiety and cleverness which left so little trace, the immense popularity which brought so few real friends. For the observer of society whose pen and tongue reveal the truth with ironic and often heartless clarity can make men laugh, but they may feel afraid to trust themselves completely to his sense of humor lest the joke be on them.

VII

1830: THE DEVELOPMENT OF CARICATURE

The revolution of July 1830 was an explosion of the liberal forces which had been gathering strength during the Restoration. Republicans and Bonapartists, momentarily reconciled by their common hatred of the Bourbons, saw in Louis-Philippe an acceptable compromise which offered to the nation renewed hope of realizing at last the ideals so long delayed by the reactionary and bigoted regime of the Restoration. In literature and the arts, it was as though the first fervor of this hope burst out in a great wave of creative energy, so that the Romantic movement, which had been gaining momentum as it experimented with new techniques and clarified its theories, suddenly reached the full climax of its genius.

With the triumph of *Hernani* Romantic drama entered upon a decade of success. Lamartine's *Harmonies poétiques et religieuses*, and in 1831 Victor Hugo's *Feuilles d'automne*, showed that lyric poetry had reached full maturity, while *Notre Dame de Paris* marked the apogee of the historical novel. Musset's *Contes d'Espagne et d'Italie* appeared in 1830. Balzac, who had had his first success a year before with *Les Chouans*, completed a volume of *Scènes de la vie privée* in 1830, began *La Peau de chagrin*, and announced plans for various dramatic works. Young Théophile Gautier published his first volume of poetry. Michelet was professor of ancient, medieval, and modern history at the Ecole Normale. Lamennais founded his liberal Catholic paper, with its optimistic title *L'Avenir*, as if to represent all the hopes springing up on the threshold of a new era. Berlioz began the *Symphonie fantastique* which was to express the passion and turbulence and idealistic longings of his generation. The Romantic painters, with Delacroix as their leader, had already triumphed over the Neoclassic school. In the more modest domain of engraving and lithography, the illustrators had been exploring the medieval and the macabre, as well as the picturesque reality of everyday life.

It remained for the comic artists to profit in a peculiarly Romantic way by the sudden freedom of the press which followed the *Trois Glorieuses.*

When Victor Hugo had written in the preface of *Cromwell* that to a modern Christian writer reality consists of the juxtaposition of beauty and ugliness, he gave definitive expression to a theory which has always been demonstrated more or less instinctively in the field of pictorial caricature. Since it is possible to call the art of caricature both romantic and realistic, its great development during the Romantic period in France suggests that it may provide an essential link between Romanticism and Realism. Here too Henry Monnier has his place, which must be taken into consideration in the evaluation of his role in the history of those two movements.

From the Italian verb *caricare,* meaning "to load," and also "to overload," come the French *charger* and *la charge,* with their derived meanings of "exaggeration," "caricature," or "burlesque." It is of course essential in defining caricature to include the overloading, the exaggeration, the straw which could break the camel's back, and the amount of exaggeration may be said to determine the distinction between caricature and mere comic representation. Both the comic artist and the cartoonist must select and bring out in full relief characteristic traits of the subject they wish to present, but the latter is privileged to overemphasize these traits to the point of grotesqueness. This is Hogarth's distinction between "caricature" and "character," the latter being a just portrayal while the former is colored by the personal feelings of the artist.* The subjective nature of caricature is indeed a second important trait, revealing not only the artist's attitude toward society but also his predilection for the grotesque.

There is a third trait, which has been called satanic by Baudelaire and divine by Giraudoux, giving to caricature a philosophic significance that is essentially romantic. In the exaggerated represen-

* "However regular a countenance may be . . . its symmetry is never absolutely perfect. One will always discover in it the hint of an incipient pucker, the suggestion of a possible grimace . . . The caricaturist's art is to seize this sometimes imperceptible movement, and to make it visible to all eyes by magnifying it. He makes his models grimace as they would grimace themselves if they completed their grimace." Bergson, *Le Rire* (7th ed., Paris, Alcan, 1911), p. 26.

tation of man's physical and moral ugliness for the purpose of arousing laughter, the artist expresses his hilarious defiance of man's Creator and revenges upon man his disgust with the human race. At the same time he takes comfort in thus pronouncing judgment upon his fellow men, for in his role of social conscience, as it were, is implied the conviction of his own intellectual and spiritual superiority over the miserable objects of his satire.[1]

The cartoonist seems thus to be an idealist, who seeks escape from the imperfections of the world in which he lives by creating a fantastic world peopled with grotesque beings, or who hopes perhaps to correct some of those imperfections by presenting them with exaggerated cynicism for the social chastisement of laughter. Since of all the graphic arts caricature is the most social, it has been able to flourish only in times when there has been freedom to make fun of social and political organizations, and it has been liveliest during the social and political upheavals of the late eighteenth and the nineteenth centuries.

When Leonardo da Vinci followed through the streets some poor wretch whose misshapen features had attracted his attention, or filled his sketchbooks with the grimacings of madmen, in his search for an ideal ugliness which would complement the ideal beauty he hoped also to discover, he was not concerned with caricature as it has just been defined, but the grotesque held for him the same fascination it exercised on many of the Romanticists. What today would be called social caricature appeared rather in sixteenth-century Flanders, especially in the work of the elder Brueghel. Brueghel's series representing the "Virtues" and the "Sins," his two prints of the "Fat" and the "Thin," have an exaggeration and a satiric humor which make them the forerunners of Hogarth and the other English moralists of the eighteenth and early nineteenth centuries. Flemish comic art seems to have influenced also the imaginative fantasies of Callot, the only important French comic artist before the nineteenth century. Callot is particularly interesting to the student of Henry Monnier, because his etchings of beggars and gypsies show a technique comparable to Monnier's. Like Monnier he used heavy lines, with great economy of detail; he noted carefully the costumes of his personages, and excelled in expressive gestures and the suggestion of movement. This is not so true of his large compositions, such as the "Tentation de Saint-Antoine," whose grotesque buffoonery gives Callot a place among the ancestors of the Romantic *fantaisistes* rather than of the caricaturists.

In the late seventeenth century there began to appear in France occasional attempts at the caricature of manners, but it was in the more liberal air of Holland that religious refugees and freethinkers began to publish drawings, as well as pamphlets and songs, satirizing the reign of Louis XIV and the Regency. The first great examples of modern caricature, however, appeared in England, from Hogarth's strongly moral studies of manners, through the brutal coarseness of Gillray's and Isaac Cruikshank's political cartoons, to the lighter humor of Rowlandson and of Monnier's friend, George Cruikshank.[2]

The revolution of the American colonies, the French Revolution, the Napoleonic wars, furnished ample material for political caricatures on both sides of the English Channel. During the French Revolution, Camille Desmoulins seems to have made the most direct use of cartoons as a political weapon. In his newspaper, *Révolutions de France et de Brabant*, he published as a heading for each number a satiric picture which illustrated the political ideas of the text. There were so many caricatures produced by both Royalists and Republicans, however, that there was even a project of publishing a *Histoire des caricatures de la révolte des Français*, in order to demonstrate the important part they played in amusing and arousing the populace. The makers of these often naïve drawings were not trained artists; their success came from the sincerity of their convictions and the directness of their inspiration rather than from any professional skill. During the Empire political caricature was impossible in France, but the popularity of comic and satiric art was too thoroughly established to dwindle. The artists turned to a study of manners, producing vast numbers of prints whose sometimes Rabelaisian flavor may have influenced the budding sense of humor of Henry Monnier's generation. Its favorite motifs were associated with the coarser manifestations of nature and with overindulgence in eating and drinking.

With the Restoration came a renewal of political attacks, one of which may be worth passing mention for its possible influence on

Monnier's style. A group of Bonapartists established a paper called *Le Nain jaune*, in which they launched a series of caricatures presenting an imaginary *Ordre des Chevaliers de l'Eteignoir.* This order was composed of the Royalists, churchmen, politicians, journalists, who expressed their devotion to the Bourbon cause and their enmity toward its adversaries in a literary style which had something of the high-flown sententiousness that was to characterize later the ineffable sayings of Joseph Prudhomme. Increasingly severe censorship soon silenced the critics of the regime, however, and the further development of political caricature had to wait until a new revolution brought another brief period of unbridled liberty. But the lithographers who reached such heights of excellence in the study of manners toward the end of the Restoration were perfecting an ideal medium for political caricature. As soon as they were no longer restrained, they burst into activity which produced during the early years of the July Monarchy a group of artists whose names form a galaxy in the history of caricature: Gavarni, Bellangé, Traviès, Grandville, Philipon, Monnier, Daumier. Charlet and Raffet had done their best work earlier, creating and preserving in the popular imagination the Napoleonic legend. Monnier's art never surpassed in charm and humor his *Grisettes* and the other great series he had already published. In the fields both of portraiture and of caricature, his drawings continued to show keen and ironic observation, but there was less and less variety in subject matter, as though his originality had exhausted itself between 1827 and 1830.

The immediate effect of the Revolution of July on the artists was twofold: it cut off their means of livelihood, for the public had too much excitement now in its daily life to continue to desire the mildly satiric prints which had been so popular; it created both the need and the opportunity to launch something new. In 1830 appeared the first numbers of *La Silhouette* and *La Caricature*, the two illustrated periodicals which began a comic genre, destined to flourish not only in France, but in England where the venerable *Punch* still sets the tone of British humor, and in America where the *New Yorker* has established a standard worthy of those European predecessors.

The weekly *Silhouette* was one of the early ventures of Emile de Girardin, an ambitious young man who was to win the title of

"Father of Modern Journalism" by founding the first cheap daily paper a few years later. The lithographer Victor Ratier was editor, and he collected as collaborators most of the comic artists, who were only too happy, no doubt, to exercise their talents in a violently liberal magazine devoted to bitter attacks on the fallen Polignac ministry and the bigoted clericalism of the reign of Charles X, and equally enthusiastic defense of the Romantic writers, headed by Victor Hugo and Alexandre Dumas. The artists can be divided into two principal groups: those interested primarily in political subjects, such as Charlet, Raffet, Grandville, Daumier; and those whose names are associated with literary illustration, such as Tony Johannot and Achille Devéria. Philipon did fashion plates. Traviès introduced his famous rascal, Mayeux, symbolizing some of the social deformities and vices of the period. To Henry Monnier fell the honor of contributing the frontispiece of the first volume, and he chose a subject which allied him with the literary rather than with the political cartoonists. His "Songe drôlatique" represents a hungry-looking man in hunting dress, mounted on a nightmarish creature, composite of various beasts, with a grotesquely human face beneath porcupine quills, and wearing rimmed spectacles on its beaklike nose. Around these central figures fly black silhouettes suggesting various themes of Romantic literature. A prefatory article explains that the beast represents official Criticism, bearing on its back the Artist. This work is quite different from Monnier's usual manner and subject matter, suggesting as it does the fantasies of Hoffmann's *Tales* or the grotesque creatures in Callot's "Tentation de Saint-Antoine."

The problem of the artist's place in modern society reappeared in different forms in *La Silhouette*, reflecting one of the increasingly great preoccupations of the Romantic writers and artists. Balzac contributed humorous essays containing semirealistic satire of middleclass types and manners. The war between the artist and the bourgeois, which was to be waged with deepening fury until it reached its climax with Flaubert after the middle of the century, announced itself in skirmishes between the *rapin* who complained that economic necessity forced him to paint the portraits of people who could afford to pay well but who judged the value of the work by the size of the canvas and the amount of pigment spread upon it, and the bourgeois who replied with dignity that such sarcastic condemnation, which might have been justified formerly when the middle class was concerned with nothing except making money, was in bad taste and out of date at present.[3]

After January, 1831, *La Silhouette* ceased to appear, leaving *La Caricature* to fill its place. This was also a weekly publication, founded by the man who, more than any other, was responsible for the development of caricature in France at that period. Charles Philipon is one of the most curious figures in the history of nineteenth-century illustration. He had himself studied art for a year or so in the studio of Gros—where he made friends with Charlet, Decamps, and Bonington, and probably knew Monnier—but he was never very successful as an artist. During the Restoration he had all kinds of practical experience, however, earning his living by designing commercial vignettes and labels, and illustrating penny picture books. Then he decided to start a business of his own, in partnership with his brother-in-law, Aubert. Thus was established at 13 passage Véro-Dodat the famous art shop and publishing house which specialized in comic prints and illustrations.

The first number of *La Caricature* appeared in November, 1830, containing illustrations by such well-known artists as Charlet, Bellangé, Raffet, Grandville, and Monnier, and young Daumier whose fame was just beginning. The text was written entirely by Balzac, who for several months furnished that part of the magazine, until he was joined by the lively and audacious Louis Desnoyers, who was to a considerable degree responsible for the boldly political character which involved the magazine in many legal difficulties and led finally to its suppression in 1835. Monnier's friendly association with Desnoyers, probably begun here, was to continue for many years. After Desnoyers became editor of *Le Siècle* he published some of Monnier's literary sketches, and appears always to have been interested in the vicissitudes of his friend's career.

Philipon scored another popular success with *Le Charivari*, the first daily illustrated publication, begun in 1832 with Desnoyers as editor-in-chief, and such writers as Léon Gozlan, Félix Pyat, Louis Reybaud, Altaroche, on the editorial staff, and as illustrators all the artists associated with the Maison Aubert. Less somberly bitter in tone than *La Caricature*, *Le Charivari* combined political caricature with fashions, travel sketches, satire of manners, current events, literary and dramatic reviews. It published in 1834 Philipon's notorious caricature of Louis-Philippe's head in the shape of a pear, for which suit was brought against the artist, who defended himself so cleverly that the unfortunate monarch was made only more ridiculous and the journal more popular. Daumier published some of his greatest work in *Le Charivari*. Gavarni began the charming sketches of manners, fashions, and theatrical scenes which were to earn him a high place among the artists of the group. Grandville and Traviès revealed their talents for social satire in realistic scenes of contemporary life as well as in caricatures of animals and the further adventures of the hunchbacked and libidinous Mayeux. The range of tone and subject matter of the publication have been well summarized in Friedell's *Cultural History of the Modern Age*, which calls *Le Charivari* "fashion journal, pamphlet, and chronicle in one, a razor-keen, witty, now malicious and now kindly, but never flattering mirror of life." [4]

The freedom of the press, which had been hailed as one of the great reforms of the July Monarchy, unfortunately did not last long. After trying to curb the caricaturists by fines, prison sentences, and official condemnation of various sorts, the government resorted at last to the ultimate weapon, and promulgated in September 1835 a series of laws so severely curbing the liberty of the press that *La Caricature* was suppressed entirely and *Le Charivari* was forced to renounce all political criticism. Turning again to the study of manners, the artists devoted themselves more and more to satiric observation of the great middle class which was becoming constantly more dominant in French life.*

Of all the group of clever and talented satirists associated with Philipon and Aubert during the 1830's, the three destined to most lasting fame were Monnier, Gavarni, and Daumier. Each of these artists has marked his work with the unmistakable character of his personal originality, and yet they possess traits in common which

* *Punch, or The London Charivari*, modeled on the Paris *Charivari*, was founded several years later, with Mark Lemon as editor, and Thackeray and Douglas Jerrold among its contributors. The first issue was that of July 17, 1841.

belong to their period. Monnier and Gavarni employed much the same clear, delicate coloring, in representing the sweep of a woman's skirts, the graceful carriage of her head and arms. Daumier and Monnier used similar tricks of lighting, in their studies of the bourgeois, the functionary, or the magistrate. Gavarni and Daumier represented certain contemporary types with the same merciless cynicism. There is no doubt that Daumier was the greatest artist; Gavarni's work is the pleasantest, arousing the most facile admiration; to appreciate Monnier fully requires perhaps the longest contemplation and most careful comparison with the other two.

Nine years younger than Monnier, Honoré Daumier had prefaced his artistic career by serving as clerk, first in a sheriff's office, then in a bookstore. When he began to study art, Monnier was already ranked as one of the foremost lithographers of the late Restoration; the earliest known lithographs by Daumier date from the agitated days of July 1830. His debt to Philipon was enormous, for the latter recognized his genius and directed it into the path of caricature. In the pages of *La Caricature* and *Le Charivari* they fought side by side against the government which seemed to them to have betrayed again the republican aspirations of the nation. And it was Philipon who conceived the idea of *Les Cent Robert Macaire* which proved to be Daumier's most popular series.

Robert Macaire, brigand, crook, and universal rogue, was a composite creation whose origin went back, apparently, to a second-rate melodrama of the early 1820's, *L'Auberge des Adrets*, in which he appeared as a rascal who arranged that his own son should be accused of a murder he had himself committed.[5] This unsavory role was played by the famous actor, Frédéric Lemaître, who won popular success by turning it into burlesque. Ten years later the play was revived by Lemaître, with the character of Macaire developed and modernized into that of a smooth confidence man who became a banker, with the help of his accomplice Bertrand. Thackeray wrote in his *Paris Sketch Book* that Frédéric Lemaître's Macaire was famous for the picturesque sordidness of his appearance, the philosophical unscrupulousness of his actions, and the high-flown canting knavery of his conversation.[6]

Philipon suggested making this rascal the hero of a series of cartoons for which he would write the titles or legends and Daumier would execute the drawings. As long as they dared, they used Macaire in political satire, and all France rapturously repeated the *Ah, vieux blagueur, va!* of Bertrand, depicted standing in intense admiration before King Macaire, the old *Poire*, a deeper rogue than all his subjects. After repeated prosecution and the September laws of 1835 made it necessary for Macaire and Bertrand to give up politics, they entered into a lively series of private enterprises comparable in some ways with the activities of honest Monsieur Prudhomme. Realizing that the infant profession of journalism was destined to grow into enormous power, they founded newspapers; they joined the National Guard, that supremely bourgeois organization which was particularly important during the July Monarchy; they organized all kinds of commercial ventures, for which they persuaded a gullible public to lend them its savings on the promise of quick and fabulously multiplied returns. In short, they incarnated the type of shrewd and dishonest speculator who fed on the vanity and materialistic greed of the middle classes during the reign of Louis-Philippe. If fastidious souls deplored their existence as an indication of the decadence of French society and official criticism of art and letters disdained to notice them, they delighted the general public, which was not too squeamish to enjoy Daumier's vitriolic satire, and proved again that people will laugh at the most heartless mockery and cozenage of society because they see in the victim always the other man rather than their own folly.

Besides adding Robert Macaire to the permanent gallery of nineteenth-century types, Daumier used the bourgeois as subject of many other studies, giving in such works as "Les Baigneurs" or his "Journée d'un célibataire" an almost epic elevation and vigor to figures previously observed by Monnier and the other comic artists. Daumier also developed personal caricature, publishing in *La Caricature* between 1832 and 1835 burlesqued portraits of the "Membres de la Chambre des Pairs." His most celebrated work in this field is the caricature of Victor Hugo, with huge bulging forehead and a lion's mane of hair, gazing at the comet of 1843. The lithograph bears the famous quatrain, composed by the acid pen of Emile Forgues:

Hugo, lorgnant les voûtes bleues,
Au Seigneur demande tout bas
Pourquoi les astres ont des queues
Quand LES BURGRAVES n'en ont pas.

Baudelaire first gave critical recognition to the greatness of Daumier's art, considering him with Delacroix the most original and among the most important of modern artists. There is certainly an energy and a power in Daumier which make him tower above the gentler talents of Gavarni and Monnier, as the pages of Balzac tower over Monnier's literary work. And just as Balzac fused in the crucible of his creative art certain elements supplied to him by Monnier, so it seems as though Daumier gave supreme fulfillment to an idea expressed by Monnier. In the *Mémoires de Monsieur Joseph Prudhomme* a young *rapin* sounded a new slogan: "The artist must not be content to draw the beautiful, he must also study the ugly; any one of us may be called upon to do the portrait of the bourgeois. *Etudions le laid, messieurs, étudions le laid!*" [7]

Temperamentally Daumier appears to have been quite different from Monnier and Gavarni. Instead of frequenting their gay Bohemian world, he withdrew to the less sociable and more dignified tranquillity of the Ile Saint-Louis, among a group of artists who have left in the chronicles of *tout Paris* no lively anecdotes such as abound in connection with Monnier's friends. He was intimate with Delacroix and later with Corot; Daubigny, Trimolet, Boulard, Barye, Dachaume, belonged to the little colony. At work, he was accustomed to shut himself up in his studio, relying on his amazing visual memory to furnish the details of his subject, even in the case of a portrait, because he hated to work before a model. There is a story, for instance, that he had promised to do the portrait of Monnier, his old comrade of *Caricature* days. When Henry arrived for the sitting, he found that Daumier had completed the portrait in two hours the day before. So excellent was the likeness that Monnier could only exclaim: "Superb! Don't touch it!" [8]

While Daumier brooded over the stupidity, pettifogging, and turpitude of a period when French society seemed to be degenerating into a materialism which destroyed all spiritual ideals, Gavarni preferred to study the brilliant façade of that society, with its gay cynicism and graceful licentiousness. He was perhaps the most sophisticated of the three artists, and the most superficial, but his delicate art has an elegance which continues to give it charm even after his satire of manners has lost much of its contemporary significance.

Like Daumier, he had been influenced by Charles Philipon. Perhaps it was the latter's interest in the development of illustrated fashion magazines which made him urge Gavarni to specialize in the drawing of fashion plates. In *La Caricature* and *Le Charivari*, in *L'Artiste*, which had been established by Arsène Houssaye, in Emile de Girardin's new periodical *La Mode*, and later in the fashion magazines edited by Philipon, *Modes parisiennes*, *Toilette de Paris*, Gavarni developed a new type of illustration. His slender ladies in the stylish leg-of-mutton sleeves and the ribbon-and-lace-trimmed hoop skirts of the 1830's have a lively and natural air which makes the compositions true little scenes of manners. Precise attention to detail of clothes and gestures characterizes all his work, as it does Monnier's, but there is a refinement about Gavarni's personages which gives them a certain kinship with the more genuinely aristocratic society represented in the work of Eugène Lami. In a sense Gavarni scarcely achieved caricature at all, even when his subject was comic. The satiric effect lay less in the pictures themselves than in the humorous captions which accompanied them. In his case, as in Monnier's, the artist composed the text as well as the drawing, and it might be said that Gavarni's humor was more verbal than pictorial.*

A comparison of Henry Monnier with Daumier and Gavarni reveals at once that of the three he remained the closest to observed reality. There is exaggeration in his figures, to be sure, and satire, but they are neither magnified into Dantesque creations suggesting the fire and brimstone of Hell, nor refined into objects of ethereal light-

* On the rare occasions when Gavarni did not compose his own legends, it is rather surprising that he should have chosen as collaborator the intransigent critic of contemporary life and literature, Emile Forgues. Forgues is an interesting example of the close relationship between English and French artistic and intellectual life in the nineteenth century. He translated English works, wrote critical articles on English literature, contributed to the *Revue Britannique*, for which he adopted the pseudonym of Old Nick, and reflected in his style and manner the influence of the British humorists.

ness and grace. He had less imagination, less creative ability; if his work possesses any poetic quality at all, it derives from the fact that his people have their feet solidly planted on the ground, wear sturdy clothes, live in firmly built houses, and sit on real furniture. In that respect he is closer to the Flemish artists than to any of his fellow countrymen.

What was Monnier's part in the political agitation of the 1830's? As one of the artists already celebrated before the Revolution of July, he forms a transition between the lithographers of the Restoration and the caricaturists of the Orleanist monarchy, but his role was not then or ever one of active political importance. In 1830 and 1831 he did produce in *La Caricature* and separately a few works of political significance: a "Victime de l'ancien système," fat and prosperous, puffed up with his own importance; a Talleyrand, shining the boots of the reigning power; a lawyer, who has managed to carry on his practice through all the changes of government and hopes for more changes, to exercise his agility in leaping political fences; a group of black-robed men, presumably Jesuits, whose masks are falling off as they prepare to take their departure.[9] In collaboration with Decamps and others, Monnier contributed to the *Pasquinades*, a series of political lithographs published between December 1830 and February 1831.* While these examples show that Monnier's political ideas were in accord with those of the majority of the Romantic liberals, they seem less indicative of a desire to take an active part in revolution than of his characteristic adaptability to the currents of the time. The caricature is heavy and at times obscure; it is most successful when the artist was content simply to observe and record political types, which he did without the violence of a

* Number 3 of this series bears the famous dialogue between two bourgeois discussing the political tendencies of the period: "Pourquoi, messieurs, pas de République en France?—Parce que la France est trop grande.—Et en Belgique? —Parce qu'elle est trop petite.—Cependant la Hollande a eu des institutions républicaines.—C'est différent, c'est un pays de marécages.—Pourtant la Suisse?— La Suisse est un pays de montagnes.—Mais les Etats-Unis?—C'est un pays maritime. Vous voyez donc bien que la République est impossible." Monsieur Prudhomme made a similar reply to Latouche's efforts to convert him to republican ideas, declaring that a republic was impossible in France, because "la France n'est pas l'Amérique" (*Mémoires*, II, 112). See Champfleury, p. 340; Marie, pp. 256–257.

Grandville or a Daumier and with more good humor than bitterness. But the bourgeois who was at last coming into his own during the reign of Louis-Philippe offered the subject which Monnier chose more and more exclusively, and in which his art attained its deepest satiric power.

Perhaps it might be desirable at this point to try to define Monnier's political convictions. The problem is a delicate one, for it is difficult to distinguish between the ideas expressed with fluent solemnity by Joseph Prudhomme and the genuine beliefs of his creator. Although Prudhomme had been personally disappointed in the Bourbon Restoration, he was constitutionally inclined to accept *l'ordre des choses* and after 1830 settled easily enough into the "left-center" group which represented the opinions of the majority of the citizens.[10] In his autobiographical sketch, Monnier expressed his loyalty to the Napoleonic regime, and the admiration which so many men of his generation kept for the hero of their boyhood. That he never accepted the Restoration may be inferred from his close association with such ardent republicans and antiroyalists as H. de Latouche and Méry, and the fact that he was acceptable to Béranger as an illustrator of the *Chansons*. Still more significant, perhaps, is the parody of La Fontaine's *Fables*, which had taken on a more and more allusive character with the editions of 1830 and 1831, until it even brought to the artist the notoriety of censorial interdiction.[11] It seems reasonable to conclude therefore that Monnier, like most of the artists and writers of his generation, was liberal in sympathies, preferring the July Monarchy to the Bourbon Restoration, but chiefly as a compromise between reactionaries and republicans. In their hearts they still cherished the name of Napoleon as the symbol of a lost greatness France had never regained. As the government of Louis-Philippe became increasingly severe in forbidding all criticism and opposition, and the artists and men of letters saw their momentary hopes of a liberal Utopia fading in the fogs of misunderstanding and suppression, they became as ardent in their attacks against the Orleanist regime as they had been against the Bourbon. Balked in their political warfare, they consoled themselves by finding a symbol of Louis-Philippe and all he represented in the bourgeois, and launched with full force their campaign against him.

How curious it was, and how inevitable, that the Romanticists, with their idealism and their sensitive love of beauty, should have been led through disillusionment, disgust with reality, and the realization that escape from reality was never completely possible, to seek a kind of compensatory torture in the cult of ugliness! *Rien n'est beau que le laid, le laid seul est aimable.*[12] Such was the cry which rallied the spirit of caricature. And that same slogan was to be used reproachfully twenty years later by the critics and opponents of Realism, who saw in the effort to represent life as it is, without artistic elimination or arrangement, little except a dangerous tendency to overemphasize the unpleasant and the sordid. Flaubert is a perfect example of the idealist: he despised the commonplace and mocked the bourgeois, and created a masterpiece of realism out of that scorn and mockery. But twenty-five years before *Madame Bovary* the work of Monnier and his fellow-Romanticists showed that the evolution had already begun.

VIII

SCENES POPULAIRES; THE *PROVERBE* AND THE DEVELOPMENT OF REALISM

As a direct and immediate result of the Revolution of July Henry Monnier was obliged to find a new means of livelihood. His albums of good-natured observation had brought him popularity and he might have continued producing lithographs on similar subjects if the political upheaval of 1830 had not destroyed the market for such studies. In the field of violent political caricature he was obviously not successful; his reputation as an artist seems to have passed its climax. The second of his three gifts promptly won him new fame, however, and a place of clearer significance in the history of the Romantic period in France. He wrote later in his autobiographical sketch that, finding himself momentarily stranded, he seized upon a chance solution of his difficulties: "The Revolution of July, like all the successive ones, left me with nothing to eat. Not knowing which way to turn, I published a book which, overnight, made me a man of letters, an appellation which, after twenty-five years of use, still astonishes me." [1]

It was in the fateful year 1830 that the *Scènes populaires* appeared, containing the first half dozen sketches in dialogue form which were to be the nucleus of Monnier's literary work, growing later into more than a dozen editions published under various titles during the author's life, and until 1890. These had their origin in the comic improvisations that Monnier had been reciting and acting for years in the studios and salons of Paris. After the book's great success was assured, various friends were ready to claim a share in the idea of publishing it. Alphonse Karr, at that time an athletic young man just beginning his bucolic, half-romantic, half-realistic novels, Louis Desnoyers, editor of *La Caricature*, Monnier's later collaborator, Emile de la Bedollière—these may have urged Henry to offer to the public some of the scenes they had so often enjoyed. As journalist and literary critic, H. de Latouche could have given helpful advice during the writing of the book and been influential in having it published. However that may be, Monnier began his career as a "man of letters" with more evidence of conscious method than his casual allusion to it might imply.

The complete title, *Scènes populaires dessinées à la plume,*[2] indicated a deliberate desire to connect his literary and artistic work. Monnier explained this intention in the preface to the first edition:

> The author, a painter himself, has dared to hope that his example would be followed by his *confrères,* that the literary men would come into the studios to learn to prepare a palette, just as the painters would ask the literary men's advice on organizing their ideas . . . In the scenes which he has sketched from life, which he has heard, the author is absolutely nothing but the editor of the deeds and actions of his characters . . . It is his observations, his studies, he is offering, it is with that intention that he has written his book, that his compositions have been lithographed.[3]

This is one of the very few passages in Monnier's work where he made any attempt to formulate his literary theories or explain his intentions. The proposal that the techniques of writing and painting be fused recalls the mingling of the genres with which Diderot had experimented seventy years earlier. There is no indication that Monnier was thinking of Diderot's *Salons* as he wrote his preface, but that he was not unmindful of the eighteenth century is shown by allusions to Hogarth and Greuze, to whom he evidently considered himself comparable because both artists dramatized scenes from everyday life. He suggested that a lacuna in their work would have been filled had they completed the stories by literary texts. Or, as he said of Greuze: "How many noble and touching creations we owe to that great painter of the human heart; but how many delicious pages that admirable genius would have left us, if he had written . . ." [4]

Of the six scenes in the 1830 edition of the *Scènes populaires,* the one which has most pretension to plot is "La Cour d'assises." It deals with the trial of one Jean Iroux, vagabond, accused of having "attempted to commit premeditated murder on the person of the widow Loddé," [5] and finally acquitted after various witnesses have testified against him, the prosecuting attorney has addressed to the jury a masterful speech in which he makes the most of circumstantial evidence, and the lawyer for the defense has shed the traditional crocodile tears instead of answering the arguments of his adversary. Jean Iroux has the peasant inarticulateness of the celebrated Agnelet in the medieval farce of *Maître Pathelin*, without either his slyness or his guilt, traits which have undergone a Romantic transformation into a hoarse and tearful reiteration of his profound innocence and tenderness of heart. Among Monnier's contemporaries Iroux was almost as famous as the bourgeois Joseph Prudhomme, but his fame seems to have been based on a few lithographs and the ephemeral personage whom Monnier created in his spoken scenes, much more than on his appearance in the *Scènes populaires*. He was the *accusé facétieux*,[6] a naïve and disarming version of the original Robert Macaire, a parody of the Romantic criminal as he appeared in Hugo's *Dernier jour d'un condamné*, a bantering Bill Sykes without Dickens' semiphilosophic humor, thumbing his nose with joking cynicism at a law-abiding society. As if to emphasize that defiance, he is confronted in Monnier's play with Monsieur Prudhomme, solid citizen, epitome of respectability. This good professor of penmanship appears as a witness to the inability of the accused, his former pupil, to learn anything, even under his expert instruction. With the pompous manner which is to become one of his distinguishing traits, he interrupts the trial long enough to express to the court his disapproval of the emperor Napoleon and his complete devotion to the existing regime, to "everything which can contribute to our happiness, the King, the constituted authorities, the *gendarmerie et son auguste famille*." [7]

The two scenes called "La Petite fille" and "La Grande dame" complete each other, and could easily be developed into a three-act play, although as they stand they form merely a sequence of sketches of manners. A young artist, Charles, forsakes his loving Fanny for the charms of a lady of doubtful social position and somewhat more doubtful virtue, in whose house he challenges to a duel the official master of the lady's affections. He is wounded, disillusioned, and restored in the end to the forgiving arms of the faithful Fanny. In the presentation of the little *grisette* there is a note of sympathy, almost of tenderness, which is especially conspicuous because one of Monnier's most distinctive traits in his written plays, as in his acting, is his impersonal objectivity. Fanny belongs to the traditionally sentimental milieu which Monnier had presented in his charming album of *Grisettes*, and the reader cannot help feeling that he had a genuinely soft place in his heart for her. The impression is intensified by the contrast between the sincerity of her love scene in Charles's studio and the callousness of the men and women who carry on their intrigues in Madame de Lucy's salon. These represent, not the genuine aristocracy whose manners they imitate, but those middle-class *parvenus* whose sophistication consists of making a mockery of human feelings. Monnier made more explicit here the irony suggested in his lithographs of the salons of the Chaussée d'Antin and of other Parisian groups where he had observed the jumbled and changing society of the Restoration.

The most striking characteristic of the remaining scenes is the total absence of dramatic construction. There is no plot, no conflict, either external or psychological. Each personality is clearly sketched through his own speech and to some extent through the comments of the others, but there is no development of character, nor do the people, with the possible exception of Monsieur Prudhomme, step out of the mold in which their type is cast to become living individuals. Monnier did indeed, as he announced on the title page, sketch from life various groups engaged in their normal activities, of which he preserved a kind of cross section, with almost no posing or arranging by the artist. In other words, he used a technique which the naturalists some fifty years later called the *tranche de vie* and thought they had invented as a reaction to the well-made plays of Scribe, Augier, and Dumas *fils*.

The clearest example of the absence of artificial composition is the famous "Roman chez la portière," for which Monnier, as he wrote in the preface, "braved the smoky atmosphere of the *loge*," [8] to present Madame Desjardins, the *portière*, ancestress of the Paris concierge whose sharp tongue, responsiveness to tips, and insatiable curiosity were as characteristic then as later, as were her fat dog and drunken husband. Here was a figure whose debut in the realm of letters was peculiarly Romantic, one of those picturesque figures who were beginning to be objects of interest because they appealed to a desire either to escape from dull respectability into the more colorful world of the lower classes or to study at close range new elements of a more democratic society. There was as yet little real sympathy with the common people as human individuals, but there was, in literature as well as in art, the realization of a picturesque field of observation. Madame Angot, fishwife turned fine lady, had set a literary style during the Directory and continued for years to tickle popular fancy. Desaugiers' Madame Denis had become nearly as well known during the Empire as her more vulgar predecessor, but she belonged to the petty *bourgeoisie* rather than to the lowest class.

The direct forerunner of Monnier's Madame Desjardins was a *portière* like herself, who had appeared in 1823 in a one-act comedy by Scribe. *La Loge du portier* sets forth the petty intrigues of several middle-class families as witnessed by their servants and the family of the porter. Like Madame Desjardins, the *portière* surpasses her husband in curiosity and a predilection for gossip. As the plot is unraveled with the help of her busy tongue, the other characters join in singing her praises:

> Qui connaît les nouvelles
> De tout notre quartier?
> Par des récits fidèles
> Qui va les publier?
> Qui sait que la lingère
> Passe en cabriolet?
> Qui sait que la laitière
> Met de l'eau dans son lait?
> C'est notre portière
> Qui sait tout, qui voit tout,
> Entend tout, est partout.[9]

This little play shows Scribe's usual ingenuity in weaving the threads of a dramatic situation, however insignificant, and his disregard of the elements of deeper psychological realism. In Monnier's scene, on the contrary, nothing happens, but the people are sketched with complete naturalness. Madame Desjardins and her friends meet of an evening in her *loge* to read aloud. They make little progress with their novel, however, because they are more interested in gossiping about the tenants and commenting on the visitors for whom the door must constantly be opened. It is the realism of the dialogue which is Monnier's most distinguishing trait. He was able to indicate in the written speech the habits of diction peculiar to each character, so accurately that at times the sentences are almost incomprehensible until they are read aloud. Then the language immediately comes alive, and the reader is reminded, if he had forgotten it, that Monnier was a born mimic, and that he recited most of his scenes before he wrote them. Perhaps like Professor Higgins, in Bernard Shaw's *Pygmalion,* he collected samples of popular speech. In that respect he set a standard for realistic dialogue that had not been reached in earlier French literature. In *Don Juan,* for instance, Molière had attempted to indicate by phonetic spelling the patois of the peasants, but for the most part he supplied the turns of speech and left the pronunciation to the skill of the actor. What Monnier carried to perfection was rather the type of notation which had been attempted rather successfully by the popular dramatist of the Restoration, Théodore Leclercq.

In the "Roman chez la portière" there is a glimpse of the round and courteous figure of Monsieur Prudhomme, but he has a longer and more important role in another scene, "Le Dîner bourgeois," where he begins to emerge with some distinctness as the comic type that remains Monnier's greatest creation. His sonorous voice and assured manner dominate the gathering. He is gallant toward the ladies, patronizes the Englishman unlucky enough to have been born on the wrong side of the Channel,* and entertains the guests with a song from the latest sentimental comedy, for Prudhomme adores the theater and prides himself on personal acquaintance with theatrical people.

Very different from the platitudes of this scene is the macabre realism of "L'Exécution." The subject is a public guillotining. Against a background of streets jammed with curious spectators, among whom speculators try to rent points of vantage, attention is focused on the excited and vivid comments of two street urchins, Lolo and Titi, through whose eyes the bloody scene is presented to

* "Ah! monsieur est d'Albion . . . Il n'y a pas de mal à ça, monsieur . . . tous les hommes sont faits pour s'estimer." Reversing the roles in *Our Mutual Friend,* Dickens exaggerated the attitude of condescending superiority in recounting Mr. Podsnap's conversation at dinner with a foreign gentleman.

the shuddering sensibilities of the reader. The creation of a gruesome atmosphere through the use of antithesis and suggestion puts this sketch into the category of horror plays which became in the twentieth century a specialty of the theater of the Grand-Guignol.

Although at least two of the *Scènes populaires* were later arranged for professional production, they were not intended originally to be performed.[10] Being thus independent of the material restrictions of the stage, Monnier could shift the action from place to place with complete disregard of dramatic rules. He might also have availed himself of the privilege of adding expository or descriptive passages which in a published play replace the scenic elements of the stage performance, but he was content to leave such details to the reader's imagination. Only in the "Roman chez la portière" did he take pains to describe the physical appearance and character of the different personages, but it must be remembered that the book was illustrated by the author, so that his drawings made further descriptions unnecessary. There are very few indications of gesture or stage play, and what little action takes place is suggested almost entirely through the dialogue.

The *Scènes populaires* belong in the long series of *proverbes* or *comédies de salon* whose origins can be found in the seventeenth century, when high society enjoyed acting proverbs or charades, and Madame de Maintenon composed little scenes for the edification of the pupils at Saint-Cyr. Becoming increasingly popular in the eighteenth century, amateur theatricals continued to represent much more closely than regular tragedies and comedies the ordinary life of the society that performed and witnessed them. Under the title of *comédies proverbes* or *proverbes dramatiques*, Collé, d'Abancourt, and especially Carmontelle wrote short scenes with little action or plot, dialogue that approached the naturalness of real speech, a kind of rudimentary characterization through the presentation of familiar contemporary types, and occasional humor deriving from the silly things not very intelligent people say quite spontaneously.

Monnier might have created the governess in d'Abancourt's "Le Mariage rompu" who declares that she knows a man whom she has just seen for the first time: "It's one of those faces you don't have to have seen to recognize them. *Cela se devine au premier coup d'oeil.*"[11] Similarly the conversation between two men drinking beer in a café, in Carmontelle's *Les Deux amis*, could almost take its place in Monnier's series called *Diseurs de rien*, and Carmontelle's sketch of the idle life of an eighteenth-century lady, in *L'Après-dînée*, presents high society as realistically as Monnier was to present the lower classes in the *Scènes populaires*.

The fashion of private theatricals was revived during the Empire and the Restoration. After Carmontelle's death in 1806 his comedies were collected and published in a series of editions which testify to their continued vogue. Their simplicity of setting, diminishing as much as possible the artificial barrier between the stage and real life, was continued in the work of Théodore Leclercq, who may be considered Monnier's immediate predecessor. His *Proverbes dramatiques* were tremendously admired for their faithful observation of contemporary society and the good-humored mockery of human foibles which continues to give them a certain gentle charm, although it must be confessed that a modern reader finds their interminable conversation even duller and more pointless than that of Monnier's bourgeois. It has been noted, however, that Leclercq succeeded, in scenes such as *Le Savetier et le financier*, or *Les Paysans*, in transcribing naturalistic speech as Monnier was to do.[12]

All these comedies and *proverbes* had been intended for stage performance, even if only by amateurs and with the most rudimentary setting. In order to understand how Monnier happened to publish the *Scènes populaires* to be read rather than acted, it is necessary to recall the rather curious development during the Restoration of a new genre, the *théâtre livresque*. Influenced by Shakespeare and by the abundant and colorful material on French history which nineteenth-century historians were beginning to provide, Louis Vitet, P.-L. Roederer and his son, and other men began to experiment with new techniques for the presentation of historical material in dramatic form, thus preparing the way for the dramas of Dumas and Hugo. The time was not quite ripe, however, for the successful performance of a Romantic historical play; Shakespeare was hissed in 1822, although he was being read in a new translation which had appeared the preceding year. From a political point of view, moreover, the reign of Louis XVIII was marked by too keen sensitiveness to criticism to allow the free presentation of plays based on periods of French history or on the lives of French kings whose greatness might cast an unfavorable light on the present regime. So the *scènes historiques*, borrowing the realistic technique of the *proverbes*, were written, not as plays whose action must be artificially constructed to create suspense and lead to a climax and dénouement, but as scenes which should present true facts as accurately as the historian could formulate them. The resulting literary work would necessarily have the same formlessness, the same effect of stenographic notation that characterize Henry Monnier's scenes. Realizing more consciously than Monnier seems ever to have done the result of sacrificing art to verity, Vitet chose deliberately to run the risk of boring his reader:

> I have preferred to leave things just as I found them, to introduce into the foreground all the people and all the events as they presented themselves, arranging nothing, and not failing to interrupt the action often by digressions and episodes, just as that happens in real life. I have resigned myself to arousing less keen interest in order to copy with more exactness.[13]

Vitet's *Les Barricades* appeared in 1826, in which year the Roederers published a volume entitled *Comédies, proverbes, parades*, thus suggesting the relationship between the *scènes historiques* and the *proverbe* with its traits of the comedy of manners. In 1827 appeared *Les Soirées de Neuilly*, by "M. de Fongeray," pseudonym of Dittmer and Cavé. The first volume had as a frontispiece a lithograph by Henry Monnier, purporting to be a portrait of the author but in reality a caricature of Stendhal. It is interesting to find Monnier thus associated with Dittmer, Cavé, and Stendhal, all of whom, with Vitet and Mérimée, frequented the salon of Etienne Delécluze.[14]

Like Collé and the other earlier writers of *proverbes*, the authors of the *Soirées de Neuilly* expressed their intention of writing natural dialogue, hinting with a touch of Romantic bravado that they rather hoped to shock their more delicate readers but defending themselves, as the Realists were to do later, with the assertion that their task was to represent as faithfully as possible and not to judge.*

* "L'Auteur au public": "They say the soliders *ont mauvais ton.*–Alas, yes! But what can I do? It is not my fault, it's the fault of the soldiers. . . . Hon-

One scene which definitely suggests comparison with Monnier is "Les Stationnaires," in which two old men recall their memories of the *Ancien Régime*, the Republic, and the Empire. Both subject and dialogue resemble Monnier's "Précis historique de la Révolution, de l'Empire et de la Restauration," the only example in Monnier's work of what might be called a *scène historique*.[15]

In that same year 1827 Monnier's friend Romieu published a volume of *Proverbes romantiques*, whose title seems to indicate a conscious combination of the two genres, the romantic element being the use in certain scenes of historical material, and the more realistic type being represented by other scenes of contemporary social satire. The following year Romieu collaborated with Loève-Weimars and Vanderburch in the first volume of the celebrated *Scènes contemporaines, laissées par feue madame la vicomtesse de Chamilly*. An introduction gave the history of the fictitious Chamilly family, of which a liberal younger member, nephew of the *vicomtesse*, was suspected of being the real author of the book. This elaborate hoax was another product of the group of Romanticists whose political ideas added to the ferment that was preparing the July Revolution and whose theories of dramatic art were far in advance of the practices of the contemporary stage. Monnier did the frontispiece, an illustration of the most famous scene in the book, "Le Tableau du sacre." And the work was printed by Balzac, who had also produced Romieu's *Proverbes romantiques*.[16]

According to a modern biographer, what Balzac admired in the *proverbes* and *scènes* was the direct observation of life, and especially the cynical tendency to insist on the lower, more disagreeable traits of human nature.[17] His own *Scènes de la vie privée*, which began to appear in 1830, show a definite connection with the works which preceded them, not only in the form of the title, but also in the effort to reproduce from contemporary life an accurately described milieu, and in the combination of historical details with a study of social manners.[18] It might be remarked incidentally that

---

estly, when I make a Bonapartist talk, shall I attribute to him the manner of speech of an editor of the *Quotidienne?* . . . I am neither a judge nor a preacher; I try to be a painter." *Soirées de Neuilly, esquisses dramatiques et historiques par M. de Fongeray* (Paris, 1827), I.

Balzac and Monnier had known each other for some time, and that their friendship and professional collaboration were to continue for many years.

Monnier's *Scènes populaires* fall naturally into their place as their antecedents and *raisons d'être* are more clearly understood. That their success was partly due to the fact that readers had enjoyed their predecessors and were therefore ready to give them a warm reception, may perhaps be inferred from the enthusiastic remark of that energetic English traveler, Lady Morgan, who took it upon herself to enlighten her fellow countrymen concerning new currents in French literature: "That rich and amusing class of productions, which by the name of dramas, *scènes féodales*, *scènes historiques*, *scènes populaires*, *romans historiques*, *proverbes*, is so peculiar to the age and nation it illustrates that to mention its existence should be a sufficient stimulus to direct public curiosity to its productions." [19] The tone of Lady Morgan's book is such that her rather snobbish interest in the *proverbes* and *scènes historiques* suggests how works like Monnier's were taken up by the people who prided themselves on their advanced tastes and liberal judgment, and who made a point of admiring what the more conservative public would find incomprehensible or shocking. This might explain Monnier's admission into houses like Delphine Gay's.

There can be no doubt that the *théâtre livresque* prepared the way for the great Romantic dramas of the 1830's. But the *proverbe* was to live on long after the plays of Hugo, Vigny, and Dumas *père* had ceased to please. Even in the early work of Alfred de Musset there are little scenes of this type, which form a transition between the works written to be read, and the professional stage.[20] His *Spectacle dans un fauteuil* was published in 1832, and the next years saw the appearance in the *Revue des deux mondes* of the series of plays collected in 1840 under the title *Comédies et proverbes*. During the Second Empire the traditions of Carmontelle and Leclercq were maintained by Octave Feuillet, author, director, and amateur actor, whose *Scènes et proverbes* were performed in some of the most elegant drawing-rooms of France, and were published in many editions attesting their great success.

The love of amateur theatricals was not a prerogative of the upper classes, however, and it is not in the refined atmosphere of Feuillet's plays that a successor of the *Scènes populaires* must be sought. Monnier's closest imitator was probably his friend Edouard Ourliac, second-rate novelist and journalist, whose ironic wit and lively good spirits made him a kind of Harlequin of the cabarets, until a fit of illness and pious melancholy would give his pale figure more the appearance of Pierrot. His *Proverbes et scènes bourgeoises* appeared in 1868. Some of the scenes, such as "La Jeunesse du temps ou Le Temps de la jeunesse," and "Les Voyages pittoresques," parodied the romanticism of the mid-century. Others like "La Tribu des Charabias," with its *méridional* setting, derived their comic savor from the realistic patois of their dialogue. In "Les Noces d'Eustache Plumet," Ourliac borrowed a milieu and a set of characters which had been peculiarly Monnier's to depict a lower-middle-class Parisian wedding, as Monnier had done some years earlier in "Un Mariage bourgeois à Paris." [21] There are the same stupid conversations among the guests, whose remarks are often identical in the two plays, and Ourliac's addition of a slight plot does little to make his scene more interesting than Monnier's.

Such naturalness was, in theory at least, the goal of the Realists. In 1830 Monnier had achieved it, better, perhaps, than anyone else had done or was destined to do, because he was fortunate enough to have at hand a literary genre which suited him and was clever enough to adapt it to the subject matter he had already mastered.

IX

MONNIER AS AN ACTOR—MORE *SCENES POPULAIRES*—MARRIAGE

After Jules Janin had spent a delightful evening listening to Henry Monnier's monologues, he suggested that such unusual entertainment be made available to a wider audience than the group of friends for whom Monnier acted privately. The decision to try the professional stage was probably influenced by the period of financial difficulty after the July Revolution, for by the early part of 1831 Monnier was preparing his first public appearance. After two months of rehearsals, during which, as he wrote later, he learned "to speak and to walk," [1] he made his debut at the Théâtre du Vaudeville on July 5, 1831, in *La Famille improvisée*, by Duvert, Brazier, and Dupeuty.[2]

In this comedy, Monsieur and Madame Hamelin have arranged a marriage between their daughter and a young man named Adolphe Coquerel. Adolphe has not yet met his fiancée and is reluctant to marry her because he has fallen in love with a girl whom he saw passing in the street. He confesses this predicament to his friend Albert, who has come to the Hamelins' house to attend the wedding. Other guests are expected: Adolphe's relatives. Assuming that the gay and lively Albert is an actor, Monsieur Hamelin asks him to prepare entertainment for them. After Albert has gone out the relatives begin to arrive: Coquerel senior, a retired notary and an old *roué de bonne compagnie;** Monsieur Prudhomme, *membre de l'Institut;* and two cousins, a rustic fellow named Jacques Rousseau and an elderly and loquacious governess, *la mère Pitou.* As these ridiculous personages make successive entries, the girl's parents decide that

* Balzac describes this character: "Ce sieur Croizeau se trouve appartenir à ce genre de petits vieillards que, depuis Henri Monnier, on devrait appeler l'Espèce-Coquerel, tant il en a bien rendu la petite voix, les petites manières, la petite queue, le petit œil de poudre, la petite démarche, les petits airs de tête, le petit ton sec . . ." (*Un Homme d'affaires, Oeuvres complètes,* XVIII, 413).

Adolphe is not so desirable a match as they had thought, and wish to break off the marriage. But the young man has of course realized by this time that Eulalie is the very girl he had seen. A catastrophe is prevented when Albert returns, for he sets matters right by explaining that he had arranged a *mystification,* playing the parts of the four relatives himself in order to furnish the entertainment Monsieur Hamelin had requested.

Such a flimsy plot provided a thread to link the scenes in which the comic characters appeared. Henry Monnier filled not only the role of the young artist Albert, but also the four character parts, a tour de force which he carried through so successfully that it was the theatrical sensation of the season. To add to his fame it was announced in the *Courrier des Théâtres* the next day that he had written the play himself. It is more probable that professional *vaudevillistes* had been asked to furnish the framework of a play which would incorporate some of the character types Monnier had already created, and that Henry composed most of his own lines.

Contemporary testimony is unanimous in describing his success. According to Alexandre Dumas the house on the opening night was brilliant, including artists, writers, actors, high society, "the faubourg Saint-Germain, the Chaussée d'Antin, and the faubourg Saint-Honoré," besides of course the press. To give only a few of the famous names: Horace Vernet, Delacroix, Pradier, Isabey; Chateaubriand, Lamartine, Victor Hugo, Balzac; the actresses Marie Dorval and Mademoiselle Mars; the actors Samson, Frédéric Lemaître, and Perlet, Monnier being immediately compared with him because they both excelled in the realistic presentation of social types.[3] It was an audience prepared to applaud, intrigued by this venture into a new field of the young man whom they all knew as an artist and writer of unusual talent and whom they all liked for his gay skill as an amateur comedian. Nor were they disappointed when he took the stage with the ease of a veteran.

It was indeed phenomenal to appear as a leading actor in a Paris theater with no training at the Conservatory, no lessons in diction or conventional gesture. The secret of Monnier's success seems to have been that he did not try to act with the traditional technique which still dominated the French stage, but based his character portrayals on the detailed observation of costume and facial expression which he used in his lithographs and on the closest possible imitation of voice and gesture. The critics commented repeatedly on the naturalness of his acting, on the truthful accuracy of the types he created, which might have come straight from real life, with all their ridiculous eccentricities. In the first enthusiastic praise there sounded no warning note that perfect mimicry might lack the heightening effect which would turn it into great art. Yet Monnier was never to be recognized as an actor of the first rank. Moreover, his naturalism was ahead of its time; the general public was not yet ready to accept acting so much closer to everyday life than the strutting and fuming of classical tragedy, the bombast of Romantic melodrama, or the stylized comedy of Molière.

In 1831, however, Monnier could not have foreseen the disappointments which were to follow a debut so startlingly brilliant. Ten days after the opening he was still playing to a packed house. In the middle of August he appeared with equal success at a private gathering to celebrate the *fête* of the actress, Madame Darceau, where he gave some new scenes which it was rumored would soon be made into a play for public performance. For several months nothing more was heard of this, until the audiences at the Théâtre du Vaudeville, treated to a series of the *drames noirs* which were a specialty of that theater, began to clamor for another opportunity to laugh at Monnier.

Finally in December 1831 he appeared again, in *Joseph Trubert, ou l'Ouvrier*, by Duvert, Dupeuty, and Saintine. This time the play was so completely worthless that even Monnier's personal success could not prevent its closing almost immediately. Again some months passed, during which there was considerable advance publicity about a new play in which Monnier would reincarnate the most popular of his characters, Joseph Prudhomme. This celebrated personage was given the leading role in *Le Courrier de la malle, ou Monsieur Prudhomme en voyage*, a comedy by Rougemont, de Courcy, and Dupeuty, which was produced at the Vaudeville, April 4, 1832. It was only moderately successful, the general reaction being that again Monnier was superb in an insignificant play. And on the twenty-first of April the *Courrier des Théâtres* announced that

Monnier's engagement at the Vaudeville would expire on July 1, and that he would probably give up the stage and resume his career as an artist in England.

Henry was kept busy during the last weeks of this first season as a professional actor in Paris. At the end of May he appeared in *Le Contrebandier ou le Paquebot de Calais*, an episodic play made to suit his peculiar talents, by Brazier, Carmouche, and de Courcy. Perhaps the well-publicized fact that it was his last appearance contributed to his success this time. On June 30 he gave as a final performance a review of all the parts he had played, before an audience whose enthusiastic enjoyment can be judged from the brief comment in the *Courrier des Théâtres:* "He tired no one but himself." [4]

If Monnier had thought seriously of going back to England, there is no indication that he did so, or that he intended to give up the stage so soon. On the contrary, between 1832 and 1839 he devoted himself almost entirely to acting, limiting his literary activity to preparing a new edition of the *Scènes populaires* and making only occasional lithographs and sketches. Through the dates and places inscribed on these drawings, however, it is possible to trace his nomadic travels after he took to the road to try his fortune in the provinces.

He left Paris in 1832 and so escaped the epidemic of cholera which ravaged the city that year. Probably because he had friends in Brussels, he turned north. At Tournay he inscribed a water color to the Belgian artist Verboekhoven, who had illustrated the second edition of the *Scènes populaires* and was to remain one of his most faithful friends. Monnier reached Liège in September and by October was in Brussels, where his reputation as an artist and the renown of his stage success in Paris apparently made his sojourn profitable, for he seems to have stayed there until early in 1833.

There was another reason for prolonging his stay in Brussels. The Belgian actor Linsel had a daughter, Caroline, who was beginning her career at that time in the tiny Théâtre du Parc, where Monnier saw her. Impressed by her lively but delicate acting and by the grace of her dark, piquant head whose firm modeling had an almost Spanish charm, he proclaimed that her talent would raise her to great heights and set about making her acquaintance. It was not long before they met, common interests gave them a footing of easy friendliness, and Henry realized that his feeling was more than professional admiration. But he did not win her without a vigorous campaign, for she was prejudiced against Parisian artists and their ambiguous intentions. Caroline had been brought up to be an honest girl, ambitious to make as respectable a marriage as her older sisters had done. Monnier enlisted the aid of mutual friends, sent them to her with messages of despair and threats of departure, and finally to her mother with the conventional proposal of marriage. It would be interesting to know whether Caroline was won by the persistence of his wooing, the Napoleon-like arrogance of his handsome head, or the prestige which still promised a career of unusual versatility and brilliance.*

He had to leave her to fill engagements which took him to Lille in February, to Calais, to Le Havre in March, and as far south as Toulon, where he had a curious experience which may have reflected the unusually tender state of his heart, but corresponded at the same time to a very definite trend in contemporary Romanticism.

Whenever he played in Toulon it was his habit to visit the convict prison, where the social pariahs, in their cells or at work in the chain gang, furnished him with material for many sketches which stand out in his work for their keen revelation of character. Except for his obvious attraction toward the ugly or grotesque heads of the more vicious convicts, the artist remained scrupulously objective, handling his romantic subject with unemotional realism. All the more notable then is a water color made in 1833, showing two Arab boys, Suleimann and Ali, one about fourteen, his brother younger. They had been found in Algeria near the body of a murdered soldier, and had been convicted with no further proof of guilt than the supposition that they had killed him in a childish and primitive fit of anger. Their youth and the gentle innocence of their faces impressed Monnier with the injustice of their condemnation. In their portrait he put the naïve melancholy of helpless children who were receiving from him, perhaps, the first kindness since they had been carried away from their sunny land. When he returned to Paris, he tried to

* A miniature dated Le Havre, 1833, shows Monnier very handsome, with large dark eyes and a brow much nobler than Napoleon's, the receding hair not yet having reached the later baldness. Champfleury, p. 185.

interest the authorities in their case. His friend Méry put his warm heart into an appeal, published in the *Revue de Paris* in 1835, that the boys might be educated and not be left to degenerate into hardened criminals. The next year, when Monnier was playing in Brest, he discovered that they had been transferred to the prison there, and twice he received letters from them, pathetic reminders of the momentary kindness he had showed them. Many years later he learned their fate. The younger brother had died, too frail to endure a convict's life. Suleimann had been released at last and had been able to earn an honest living. In 1862 he wrote to Monnier to tell him that he had been appointed to a post in Algeria, and asking permission before he left to present his wife and children to the man whom he still addressed with deepest gratitude as "Sir and father."

This episode confirms in a positive way the impression which is received rather negatively from the rest of Monnier's life, of his essential kindliness and unwillingness to do serious harm to anyone, in spite of his mischievous and often mocking nature. It is interesting too to find him contributing in a small way to the wave of humanitarian sentiment which spread from the doctrines of Saint-Simon, Fourier, Pierre Leroux, and their disciples, and was to rise to its height before the Revolution of 1848. For the most part Monnier's political and social ideas must be deduced from the ostensibly impersonal work of his pen and pencil. The case of Ali and Suleimann is the only direct evidence of an interest in social reforms. Monnier's being in love in 1833 may have had something to do with it.

It was not until January of the next year that he was able to return for any length of time to Brussels. He and Caroline were married on May 21, 1834. Even toward the end the courtship had not gone without storms. At the signing of the marriage contract Monnier learned that Caroline's real name was Péguchet, her father having taken the more musical name of Linsel for professional use. That aroused Henry's sense of humor, and he persisted for several days in calling Caroline "mademoiselle Péguchet," until she retaliated by using the most flowery of his names, "monsieur Bonaventure." Only a few days before the wedding his teasing was the cause of a bitter quarrel, which Caroline recounted many years later to her husband's biographer. The engagement was broken. The tears Caroline shed that night can be imagined. But Henry spent the evening with friends, and had never been gayer or more charming. When she later reproached him for having been so heartless, he replied, "I wanted to forget you that evening, and I succeeded perfectly." [5]

It was no easy responsibility which Caroline Monnier accepted in marrying a man of thirty-five who had chosen a career traditionally free from conventional restraints and whose facile gifts led him restlessly from one art to another until it began to appear that he would be master of none. As a painter or a writer he might have been able to settle down to domestic life in Paris, but as an actor he was doomed to wander. He had begun his career too late in life, without the requisite training to make him acceptable at the Comédie-Française, which would have offered a guarantee of permanent security. And by the time he decided to marry, it was too late also to change the free Bohemian life he had chosen.

For a little while, however, all was rosy. Henry had prepared as a wedding gift for Caroline, in the fashion of the period, a splendid *keepsake*. It was an album bound in morocco leather and ornamented with drawings and water colors by Monnier and his friends. Verboekhoven had decorated the cover; James Harding and Francia contributed landscapes as tributes from England and Calais; Monnier had selected fifty of his own works to offer to his bride. The two weeks of their honeymoon were spent under the hospitable roof of Verboekhoven, who celebrated the event by setting into the Flemish mantel over his fireplace a plaque bearing the names of his two friends and the date of their marriage. Then in the midst of a June storm, Monnier set out with his wife for Paris. Their hopes must have been high and their plans delightful. They were to continue their careers as actors, and Henry would add to their fortune with his pen. While he prepared a new edition of the *Scènes populaires*, Caroline would make her Paris debut and justify his admiration for her dramatic talent.

By the time Monnier began his stage career, the *Scènes populaires* had already been republished twice. A few months after the original edition of 1830, a reprint of the first six scenes appeared in Brussels, enriched by Verboekhoven's etchings.[6] The next year there was a new edition, containing two additional scenes.[7] One of these, "La Victime du corridor," adds little to Monnier's repertory of types or situations, for it takes place on an upper floor of a house whose *loge* might well be kept by Madame Desjardins of the "Roman chez la portière." The milieu is again that of the working class and petty *bourgeoisie,* and the amusement caused by the naturalness of the dialogue is no way increased by the addition of a plot based on the outworn recognition motif. But the other scene is in many respects one of Monnier's most admirable.

It is called "Précis historique de la Révolution, de l'Empire et de la Restauration," and the action takes place in August 1830. An old sergeant, veteran of many campaigns, is mounting guard before the Tuileries, the sight of which reminds him of the various governments he has seen succeed one another. In his own picturesque style he sums up the history of those forty years, to the amazement and admiration of the young recruit who listens to him. The scene is very short, only a little over four pages, thereby escaping one of the great defects of Monnier's peculiar technique. Elsewhere the reader's attention tends to lag because of the length and formlessness of uneventful "slices of life." But the subject of the "Précis" required selection, synthesis, and focus, and Monnier succeeded for once in producing a work of art. At the same time, without spoiling the psychological unity of a narration in which the soldier's point of view is as consistent as his manner of speech, Monnier made the scene a vehicle for biting political satire and for humor which shows what a master of genuine comedy he could be when his gifts were fully utilized.

To the sergeant it is natural that the Napoleonic period should have been the best. With what tenderness he evokes the good old days, when the smart little *farceur* grabbed the cash box and ran things so well, and the soldiers had fine uniforms, and plenty of women, and silver buckles on their shoes: "It was too good, it couldn't last!" Like Joseph Prudhomme, he has remained faithful to that order, and the succeeding regimes have accomplished nothing to shake his loyalty. Can he be expected to admire fat old Louis XVIII in his powdered wig, whose step was anything but military and who humiliated the veterans of the regular army by subordinating them to his newly organized National Guard? The tone of pleasant reminiscence becomes bitter as the sergeant evokes the bigotry, errors, and injustices of the Restoration, the weakness of Charles X being neither better nor worse than the clericalism of his brother. Then came the glorious days of July, when the National Guard was humiliated in its turn and the soldiers of the line helped the Bonapartists and the republican middle class to overthrow the Bourbons. The new regime, which was like a bourgeois taking a walk with his umbrella, seemed to please the nation, everybody shook hands on it, and everything returned to order. But the old sergeant was not born yesterday, and his acceptance of the new order is marked by lukewarm enthusiasm and qualified by a prophetic warning: "It'll all have to be begun over again soon perhaps; let's wait."

While the political satire has now lost much of its savor, the humor of the sketch is more permanent and more universally comprehensible. Monnier handled with deft skill the gamut of comic devices, combining the suggestiveness of understatement with the use of familiar, everyday language to express important and grandiose ideas, or of military jargon to convey non-military ideas.* He obtained other comic effects by repetition and anticlimax, or by the reversal of a normal sequence of thought.† And throughout the scene the description of events of national and continental magnitude in the simplest terms and from the homely point of view of the man in the ranks gives the piquant incongruity of genuine caricature.

Like the handful of political lithographs which Monnier produced in 1830, the "Précis historique" is quite different from most of his work. Primarily an observer of manners, in the new scenes which he continued to publish from time to time, and his later drawings, he devoted himself more and more exclusively to the study of the middle class. If their general character changed, it evolved in

* Understatement: The Tuileries are vacant at present, "que ceux qui y habitaient on les a corrigés"; Louis XVI: "on le fit descendre par les escaliers, plus vite que ça . . . et un matin, là-bas, au bout du jardin, il lui est arrivé l'accident de devenir un gouvernement . . . martyr, qu'on l'appelle." Transposition: The allied coalition against Napoleon, the restoration of the Bourbons: "en v'là de chez nous qui tirent le cordon, ouvrent la porte en manière de suisses, et v'là qu'on met mon gouvernement dedans à la porte." Military jargon: The Revolution: "il y avait donc ici un gouvernement . . . qu'on criait pour le changer, pour qu'il ne voulait pas absolument marcher au pas."

† Repetition: "nous nous couvrions de gloire et de réputation." Reversal: "J'étais simple enfant, et pas comme au jour d'aujourd'hui chevronné, décoré . . . et tout ce qui s'en a *suit*."

the direction of greater social satire, or in other words turned more definitely into caricature.

In 1835 the *Scènes populaires* appeared in a new Belgian edition, considerably augmented.[8] Here was published for the first time the amusing "Voyage en diligence," parts of which had probably been used already in the comedy *Monsieur Prudhomme en voyage*. It was a scene which Monnier had been reciting for years to studio audiences, and a subject rich in humorous possibilities. The idea of representing the embarrassing, dramatic, or comical predicaments in which people could find themselves when they traveled in the uncomfortable public conveyances of the time had appealed also to Balzac, whose "Cour des Messageries Royales" and "Départ d'une diligence" contain some of the types sketched by Monnier and the same atmosphere of uncomfortable confusion which stripped human nature of its pretentiousness and revealed it at its frankest and least alluring.[9] The "Voyage en diligence" is an excellent example of Monnier's skill in suggesting by a brief snatch of dialogue a person's occupation, social status, and character. Monsieur Prudhomme is one of the passengers, and his grandiloquent remarks show him at his most pompous: "As a general rule, gentlemen, when one travels by coach one should always make his will . . . I shall solicit the favor of opening on my side; this concurrence of breaths necessitates the opening of one of the two windows; for it is still important to avoid drafts."[10]

The edition of 1835 contained also a somber scene called "La Garde-malade," foreshadowing the brutal realism of Monnier's later *Bas-fonds de la société*. With cynical irony are contrasted the nurse's cruel indifference to the sufferings of her patient and her sentimental tears as she recalls with a gossipy visitor the misfortunes of the empress Josephine, whose divorce, in her opinion, was the cause of Napoleon's downfall.* The two old cronies are loyal Bonapartists,

* "L'Empereur, comme vous, comme moi, comme tout l'monde, avait fait des bêtises, comme tout l'monde, comme j'en ai fait, comme vous avez pu en faire: mais quand on a l'bonheur d'avoir eune Joséphine, voyez-vous, eune Joséphine, sus le trône, pour épouse, on doit se t'nir tranquille, voilà ce qu'on doit faire, et c'est ce qu'il n'a pas fait" (ed. Dentu, p. 351). As an indication of the prevalence of this point of view, it is interesting to compare Flaubert's *Dictionnaire des idées reçues:* "Divorce. Si Napoléon n'avait pas divorcé, il serait encore sur le trône."

however, in spite of their sympathy for the discarded empress; their dislike of "the Austrian" who supplanted her is mild compared with their hatred and scorn of the Bourbons, and for what a reason! "Me," says Madame Bergeret, "it isn't so much Charles X that I despised, as his brother Louis XVIII. Oh! that fellow now . . . with all my heart. I've never been able to forgive him, and never will forgive him, for massacring the Emperor's coffee-colored horses." [11] A few minutes later the tender-hearted creature refuses to give up her lunch hour to stay with the dying patient.

Monnier included also in that volume the "Scènes de la vie bureaucratique: Intérieurs de bureaux," which, like his album of *Mœurs administratives,* reflected his experiences as a youthful clerk in a government office, and which have already been mentioned in that connection. Another scene, more explicitly moral in tone than most of Monnier's work, belongs clearly to the category of dramatic *proverbes.* This is "Les Bourgeois campagnards, ou Il ne faut pas sauter plus haut que les jambes," which reflects the underlying political and social currents of Louis-Philippe's reign. A newly rich bourgeois couple have retired from business to a sumptuous house in the country. Madame Cibot, a Carlist sympathizer and social climber, tries to attach herself to the poverty-stricken aristocrats of the neighborhood, who exploit her snobbishness. Her husband, formerly a Jacobin and Bonapartist, is only too happy when the social climbing fails and they decide to return to Paris to resume the grocery business.

In the next year, 1836, a fourth Paris edition of the *Scènes populaires,* in two parts, was announced, and the first volume of it appeared, containing all the scenes previously published. The chief interest of that volume lies in the fact that it bore a dedication to Monsieur H. de Latouche, confirming Monnier's indebtedness to his friend for helping him in the selection and composition of the dialogues which had brought him prestige as a man of letters. The second series did not appear until 1839. It bore the title *Nouvelles scènes populaires,* and contained five little plays, somewhat more ambitious in length than the earlier sketches, but similar in technique and realistic atmosphere.[12]

Once more the reader is plunged into the daily lives of various Parisian households. Madame Bidard has her portrait painted as a surprise for her children and gives a big party to celebrate her *fête*.[13] Madame Desherbiers is at home to her friends, who endure with fortitude recitations of La Fontaine and pieces on the piano performed by Napoline, aged four, and Oscar, aged five.[14] The loyalty of the Parisian to the province of his birth brings to Monsieur Lavenaze's house a series of Southerners who interrupt his work, drink his wine, give orders to his servant, and impose on his generosity until he is forced to seek refuge elsewhere.[15] The Pitois family has reached a crisis when the son's appointment to the bar offers to his proud parents a choice between old friends and the simple pleasures and clear-cut moral code of the petty *bourgeoisie*, and the schemes and ambitions of social climbers before whom opens a tempting vista of political and social advancements.[16]

Yes, Monnier knew his Paris, and proved again with what extraordinary sureness of touch he could transcribe the interminable conversations of ordinary people talking as they really do off the stage, outside of literature, even when they are French! No intellectual fireworks, no sparkling repartee, nothing but personalities and banalities which everyone has heard and used a thousand times, until Monnier makes the reader so self-conscious that he is almost afraid to speak lest he talk that way himself.[17]

It is almost a relief to turn to the remaining play, in which Monnier sketched the agelong obstinacy, ignorance, avariciousness, and sharp-tongued shrewdness of the French peasant. In the dialect of the Ile-de-France, familiar to Henry since childhood, he presented types that he must often have seen in his ancestors' village of Parnes, and the reader wonders whether he was mindful of his own grandfather the cooper, when he showed old *Père Pigochet* alternating between sentiment and greed as he tries to get from the doctor a prescription which would end his wife's expensive sufferings.[18]

While Henry Monnier was thus plunging again into literary work, his wife, as they had planned, made her Paris debut, at the Théâtre du Gymnase in 1835. Evidently Paris did not agree with her husband's estimate of her talent, for there is no indication that she ever won a recognized place there. In fact there is a notable absence of any mention at all of Caroline Monnier in the many references to Henry in newspapers and other contemporary writings. Did she share his public appearances or his friends, even in the first years of their marriage?

It would be pleasant to know, for instance, whether Caroline had accompanied her husband to the great ball organized by Alexandre Dumas and given at the Opera, rue Le Peletier, on the fourteenth of January, 1835. This affair was so gay that it outshone all preceding opera balls, whose brilliant tradition went back to the beginning of the century.[19] The artists had spared no pains or expense. The program, for which Célestin Nanteuil had made an etching, announced *tableaux vivants,* directed by Camille Roqueplan and representing Paul Delaroche's *Cromwell* and *Jane Grey*. To Henry Monnier fell the task of organizing various proverbs, comic scenes, and *lazzis* as diversions between the dances. The costumes of the guests were equally elaborate. One of the Déveria brothers must have been very handsome as a Louis XIII cavalier; Mademoiselle Mars, the great actress, though no longer in the prime of youth, dressed as an Italian dancer; a medieval executioner all in red could be seen beside a bald-headed Cupid, fat and insolent, with traditional wings and quiver of arrows and adding to his scanty costume such unconventional touches as bedroom slippers and the red ribbon of the Legion of Honor. Sly old Robert Macaire and his accomplice Bertrand were there, already so popular that no costume ball was complete without them. Monnier chose to appear that evening in the guise of "one who is bored to death," and it is easy to imagine how perfectly he would have conveyed the sleepy stodginess of a respectable shopkeeper or small business man finding himself in a Bohemian gathering whose quips and pranks were beyond his comprehension.

It is quite probable, after all, that Madame Monnier should have preferred not to be there. Respectable women did not attend the opera balls, unless they were bold enough to come for adventure and the liberty of flirtation authorized by the masks. This most famous of the balls set off a wave of renewed enthusiasm. *Tout Paris* began flocking to dance quadrilles to the music of Musard's orchestra, and especially in carnival time, when the gatherings were held once a week, the pursuit of pleasure grew to a frenzy of sensuality. In a few years there appeared a new figure, for whom these lively occasions were a happy hunting ground. This was the *lorette*, the fortune-seeking successor of the less sophisticated and more sentimental *grisette* of Monnier's youth, whose cashmeres and cigarettes and vicissitudes of fortune have been recorded in the drawings of Gavarni and the pages of Nestor Roqueplan. It was the latter who invented the name, because the quarter of Paris behind the church of Notre-Dame-de-Lorette was reserved for those girls called so ironically *filles de joie*, whose life of selling and seeking for pleasure was so short, ending so soon in tuberculosis, insanity, or suicide, or at the best dragging itself out in the trading of secondhand clothing or the degradation of the procuress.*

Although the great ball of 1835 gave Henry Monnier considerable publicity and the *Scènes populaires* were enjoying moderate success, there remained the problem of supporting a wife whom theatrical managers were so reluctant to engage. So Henry and Caroline decided to try the road, in the hope that provincial success would make up for the indifference of Paris. Including in their repertory several of Monnier's familiar roles, they specialized in taking two or three different parts in the same play, thus continuing the tour de force which had made such a hit in *La Famille improvisée*.

They appeared first at Nantes, in December 1835. Henry described to his friend Ferville, an actor at the Gymnase in Paris, the emotions of that evening: "Yesterday we gave our first performance. I had a dreadful fright, which the audience was good enough not to notice, since I was splendidly received . . . My wife ended the program with *La Fille de Dominique;* the poor child didn't receive her drummer boy's costume until she was ready to go on; but finally she did have it." [20] There is a hint in that letter of the material difficulties which were to harass the young couple. They had so little money that they were constantly struggling to provide the necessary costumes. Henry did not hesitate to appeal to his friends, among whom Gavarni was particularly useful, offering much advice and lending to Madame Monnier costumes from his studio. To supple-

* The rue Bréda was particularly notorious at that time. Later it became respectable enough, and the name was changed, to spare the feelings of the residents, to "rue Henry Monnier"! This extends from rue Notre-Dame-de-Lorette and rue La Bruyère to place Pigalle. See C. H. C. Wright, *The Background of Modern French Literature* (Boston, 1926), p. 108, n. 1.

ment their earnings Monnier sold occasional sketches of provincial scenes and types. He did numerous rapidly and cleverly executed portraits, also, which represent the best of his artistic work during that period, but which he usually gave away as the only means of repaying the kindness of actors and artists whom he encountered during his tour. Putting aside for a time the social satire of his Parisian drawings, Monnier gained in vigorous realism, which was probably the most valuable result of the tour.[21]

From Nantes they went on to smaller towns nearby, and arrived at Brest unluckily during Lent. Although Monnier was discouraged by the lack of enthusiasm in that city, he was still optimistic enough to begin planning the organization of a *vaudeville* troupe, with which he hoped to travel as far as Switzerland and Germany. Perhaps because it was the wrong season, however, he found so much difficulty in recruiting actors that he had to give up the project.[22] While he could still speak complacently of Madame Monnier's success, it was not the *succès pyramidal* she had enjoyed at Nantes: "My wife played *la Muette* last Sunday; she made a great impression. She is adored in Brest; she would have played Dugazon's whole repertory if these ladies and gentlemen had not been so lazy." [23]

On the whole the tour was unrewarding, and Monnier's dreams of success as an actor were sadly overshadowed by discouragement as he turned back toward Paris. Having given up his lodgings there, he took Caroline to Parnes, to his father's little property where he had spent so many happy holidays as a boy. From there he wrote again to Ferville, in a curious mood of melancholy mingled with hopes which seem surprisingly ambitious:

> You must have heard from me; I was speaking to you of a project I had had, which I have still, of making my debut at the Français in elderly parts, for I am too old, I feel it strongly, to play in the provinces, and my memory is very lazy . . . What is the situation at the second Théâtre-Français? Would it be easy for me to get what I want there? The answer to that is that I should be nearer Paris; but I do not have lodgings there any longer, and what did I do all the time I spent there? I assure you that sometimes strange ideas pass through my mind, my poor Ferville. But still, let's wait a little longer; however it is pretty sad to live this way! [24]

All his life Monnier clung to his desire to act at the Comédie-Française. How often he must have said to himself that things could so easily have turned out differently for him in 1836! If his friend Perlet had been appointed director of the Odéon that year, Henry's destiny might have been decided, for Perlet really appreciated the peculiar talent of the actor whose naturalistic style was too far ahead of public taste. But regrets were indeed futile when luck appeared to be against him. A note of fatigue and disillusionment sounded for the first time, revealing a new aspect of a nature which had hitherto seemed the incarnation of gaiety and enthusiasm. With facile cleverness Monnier had followed whatever path the fashion of the moment or the suggestions of his friends had opened up to him, but the time had come when the bright successes of his promising youth were dimmed by disappointment and frustrated ambition. There were many years of creative work ahead of him, to be sure, and his real worth had not yet been fully evaluated, but it seemed as though by 1840 he had passed the turning point which led, not upward to the peak of achievement, but down to the lesser level of mediocrity. Perhaps the fault was in his conviction that acting was his regular profession. Art and writing he considered merely incidental means of earning a livelihood, which could be carried on without interfering with his professional career. But for a French actor there can be no real success except in Paris, and Monnier was destined never to reach the summit to which he aspired. The brilliance of his debut was to be equaled, perhaps, in a remarkable period of celebrity after 1849, but his whole life as an actor was marked by unsatisfactory relations with the directors of Paris theaters and repeated attempts to achieve during his road tours the prestige which would assure him more respectful treatment in the capital.[25]

And so in 1837 he and his wife set out again, this time for three weeks in Moulins, then toward the north. In the *Mémorial de l'Allier* for March 7, 1837, there appeared an article on the performances at Moulins, where Monnier offered an elaborate repertory testifying to both Henry's and Caroline's versatility and energy. The writer referred first to the program of March 5:

> That evening the author of "M. Prudhomme" and of "Madame Gibou," the celebrated writer and caricaturist, Henry Monnier, won applause from the Moulinais for *Le Cousin de l'héritière,* one of the most amusing sketches of which he is both author and interpreter, *Vert-Vert* or *Le Perroquet du couvent,*

Le Duel, Le Déjeuner or *Les Comédiens joués.* Monnier, who also made a hit as an actor, gave seven performances in this month of March. His wife, who has not yet left him to run the hazards of the *Roman comique*, his wife and he have both specialized in appearing in the same play in five or six different roles: thus Henry Monnier will play, in a single act, a young greenhorn, an old fop, the oracular Joseph Prudhomme himself, a side-splitting *portière*, a crafty peasant, etc. . . .[26]

The allusion to the *Roman comique* in that passage calls for explanation. The collaboration which had been planned so hopefully was soon to end, for Caroline Monnier had obtained a permanent engagement at the theater of Rouen, and this journey to Belgium and Holland was their last cooperative venture.

The next stop was at Laon, and the effect of their arrival in that sleepy little town has been charmingly recounted by Champfleury, whose lifelong admiration for Monnier dated from his encounter with the actor-artist on this occasion. He was fifteen; it was his first glimpse of a real actor from Paris; he had laughed over the *Scènes populaires* too, and knew that their author was also one of the most famous caricaturists of the day. Now as a member of the orchestra at the theater of Laon, he had the honor of playing the overture which preceded *La Famille improvisée.* Monnier appears to have been well pleased with the full house that day, and even wrote later that people had been turned away, but Champfleury has commented drily that the statement was somewhat exaggerated and that the actors were fortunate if they cleared two hundred francs in a town of six thousand inhabitants "indifferently sensitive to the attraction of intellectual things." [27] It may have been also that the Laonnais were feeling the pressure of hard times, for there was an economic crisis in 1837 and the cost of living was rising for audiences as well as actors.

After a stop at Mons, the Monniers went on to Belgium. There is no record that they played in Brussels, but they must have visited their friends and relatives in that city on their way to Holland. In Amsterdam the theatrical success is again doubtful, but there was profit for the artist. Fascinated by the picturesqueness of the people, Henry did several street scenes which equal in careful observation of types and finished technique his "Marché aux poissons de Billingsgate," in the *Voyage en Angleterre*.[28] On the return trip performances were given at Ypres, Douai, and Arras.

By this time the problem of family responsibilities had to be faced. There were soon three children, two daughters and a son, and Caroline could not continue such a nomad life. According to Champfleury, it was her own decision to separate from her husband and to assume full charge of the children so that Henry might be relieved of a burden which trammeled the free pursuit of his career.[29] Just as there had been in Henry Monnier all his life a rebellious streak which revolted against convention, now he could not give up his independence to settle into the duties of a *père de famille*. It was remarkable that Caroline was able to understand and accept with such tolerance a hard lot which certainly reflects only discredit on her husband. She was evidently a good woman, as she had been a respectable young girl, but the truth would seem to be that if marriage could suit Henry at all, he would have done better to select a wife who could regard with genuine sympathy the vagaries of his nature, instead of assuming an attitude of half-pitying virtue toward her "poor Henry." So for most of their married life they lived apart, until age and infirmity brought the artist to fuller appreciation of Caroline's virtues. Henry took an apartment on rue Ventadour, where he led a bachelor existence, essentially solitary and industrious. There is no indication that any other woman played an important part in his life, or that Madame Monnier ever had reason to question his loyalty.

That for all his independence he was capable of affection his friends knew very well, and now he began to show increasing appreciation of the only family ties which he could not break. While he had had no residence in Paris, he habitually returned after each road tour to the paternal property at Parnes in the Vexin. Here he would rest for a few days with his father, who had retired after a respectable career in government service which had brought him a commission in the National Guard and the red ribbon of the Legion of Honor. A few years later Monnier wrote with deep tenderness that the death of his mother in 1838 caused him violent grief, and that he was constantly concerned over the health of his father:

A few years ago, I lost my mother; I still have my father, very old, and since that loss I am always in mortal anxiety. The loss of my mother is the greatest grief I have experienced; from that moment too I began to feel that I was very old, since I had no mother any longer, and what need I had of one still, when I realized the gap that losing her made me feel. Although my grief has reached a calmer stage, it is for me a wound that will never heal.[30]

It may have been this realization of loss which made Henry more and more assiduous in visiting his father, who displayed the Monnier sturdiness by living some fifteen years longer, to the age of ninety-two.

Grief, frustrated hopes and ambitions, the harassment of a disorganized existence which had neither economic nor spiritual stability, such was the somber tonality of Henry Monnier's personal life at the end of a decade which had opened with the brilliant promise of 1830. The struggle against poverty was to continue all his life. Domestic tranquillity he would enjoy at intervals as he grew older. But whatever melancholy dissatisfaction he must at times have experienced, he remained outwardly the humorist. As a comedian he still entertained his friends; as a practical joker he continued to take part in the ebullient manifestations of the Romanticists; as an artist he joined in the campaign which was gathering momentum against the *bourgeoisie* whose dominance in the monarchy of Louis-Philippe was a bitter consequence of the July Revolution.

X

ARTIST VERSUS BOURGEOIS DURING THE JULY MONARCHY

One of the distinguishing traits of French classicism in the seventeenth century had been an extraordinary absence of the distinction between the artist and the non-artist. This distinction flared into a feud after 1830 with Henry Monnier's generation. The Romantic revolt, with its belief in the fundamental antinomy between society and the individual, its glorification of human passion and the right to happiness, its opposition to social laws and conventions as hindrances to the attainment of that happiness, tended inevitably to condemn the concepts most dear to the middle classes. Insofar as modern civilization is based on respect for law and order, security, tradition, the state and the family, the Romanticists cast responsibility on the Philistine for that civilization, with which they found themselves in conflict. In the July Monarchy and in the King himself they found all those traits they most despised and no redeeming virtues with which to satisfy their own quest for none too clearly defined ideals.

The position of Louis-Philippe was peculiarly equivocal. Although he bore the title of king, his election had been a denial of the doctrine of hereditary kingship by divine right, and the royalists never ceased to look upon him as an illegitimate upstart. The republicans considered him a betrayer of the people, for they realized that the revolution which had brought him to power, giving to France what the aged Lafayette in the first flush of victorious enthusiasm called "the best Republic," had not resulted in the liberty and equality they had wanted. The King's chief support came from the middle class, the bankers and business men who had put him on the throne and who saw in the "upstart" one of themselves, a wealthy property-owner, intelligent and prudent, concerned above all with economic security as the foundation of the family and the state. Clever and diplomatic, Louis-Philippe juggled with the conflicting groups as best he could, but never dared, even had he wished to do so, to refuse to recognize that the *bourgeoisie* was the real ruler of the nation. The phrases "get rich quick" and "the middle of the road" sounded the keynote of that reign, and the financier Laffitte had formulated the business man's philosophy which grew into the dignity of national policy: "I have always considered material good as the least problematic, as the most easily grasped, as the least affected by changes of government . . . a country cannot be given freedom; let it be given the wealth which will soon render it more enlightened, better, and free." [1]

Such a doctrine favored order rather than liberty, prosperity rather than honor. It left no room for sentiments of glory or chivalry, for imaginative flights toward distant utopias. Not that the bourgeois was devoid of yearnings for something which would satisfy his national love of *panache!* This predilection led him, like Monnier's Monsieur Prudhomme, in a curiously paradoxical fashion to combine his support of Louis-Philippe with an increasingly sentimental admiration of Napoleon, the hero whose defeat at Waterloo had been a national humiliation prolonged by the Bourbon Restoration. So he applauded the erection of Napoleon's statue on the Vendôme column in 1833, attended *en masse* the solemn inauguration of the Arc de Triomphe in 1836, and wept appropriately at the return of the Emperor's ashes in 1840. But when it came to demonstrating in his own person the swaggering bravado of a more glorious epoch, the bourgeois was content to serve his country in the National Guard, an organization which to the Romanticists was a base parody of patriotism and chivalry.

What was the place of artists like Monnier in such a society? The utilitarianism which had been the ideal of the enlightened philosophers of the eighteenth century had become a materialism that looked on art as an ornamental but fundamentally useless luxury and the artists as *farceurs* who imposed on society the burden of their irresponsible ways and idealistic dreams. Yearning after greatness and feeling themselves misunderstood by the prudent rationalist, who dreaded whatever threatened the security of his property or of the institutions in which he believed, the young men of the 1830's despised the niggardly pusillanimity of the "shopkeepers" who had chosen as king the incarnation of shopkeeping. The mad young hero of Balzac's *Peau de chagrin* has expressed their dissatisfied restlessness, their longing for experiences and emotions more complex than they could find in contemporary society:

> Since this morning, I have envied only one class of people,—conspirators. I don't know if I shall have the same whim tomorrow, but tonight, the colorless life of our civilization, smooth as the track of a railway, makes my heart leap with disgust. I am passionately enamored of the disasters of the retreat from Moscow, of the emotions of the *Red Corsair,* and the adventurous life of a smuggler. As there are no longer Carthusian convents in France, I would like at least a Botany Bay, a sort of infirmary for the accommodation of little Lord Byrons, who, after crumpling up life as they do a napkin after dinner, have nothing better to do than to set their country on fire, blow out their brains, conspire in aid of a republic, or demand war.[2]

With all that ardent energy, the Romanticists could find no great cause for which to fight after 1830. The heroic struggle against classicism in art and literature had already been won, and the July Revolution confirmed the victory while it scattered the ranks of the victors. The cause of social and political freedom had not yet triumphed completely, to be sure, and the doctrines of Saint-Simon, Pierre Leroux, and Fourier attracted many liberals toward the humanitarian and socialist movements that gained new impetus after the momentary setback following 1830. In Saint-Simon's concept of the industrialist they found further grounds for hatred of the bourgeois, for it was based on the doctrine that the capitalistic middle class, living on unearned income, maintained the worker in the lowest place in society instead of completing the Revolution by elevating him to the high place he deserved as the most important member of society.

While the *bourgeoisie* was entrenching itself as the new ruling class that would dominate the next hundred years, the Romanticists, frustrated along other paths, adopted as their cause the cultivation of personal freedom, the indulgence of passionate individualism, devoting themselves to an almost frenzied pursuit of physical and moral self-expression. As Gautier wrote in the *Histoire du romantisme,*[3] the artist's first rule was to let his thought wander freely where it would, no matter how much he shocked the rules of good taste and propriety. With all his strength he must hate Horace's *profanum vulgus*, which he translated by the scornful epithets of "grocer," "philistine," or "bourgeois." The Romanticism of the 1830's was influenced less by the sufferings of Werther and René than by the cynical Satanism of Don Juan, the Byronic *mystificateur* who delighted in parading his strange perversities for the horrification of lesser men. It was essential that the artist be different from other people.

There seemed to be two ways thus to *épater le bourgeois*. The obvious strategy called for violent repudiation of everything associated even remotely with the *bourgeoisie*, whereas a more subtle technique, adopted by Henry Monnier and some of his friends years before it was defined by Baudelaire, consisted of a coldly disdainful refinement upon middle-class conventions which transformed them into parody.

Many of the younger men, pursuing the cult of their own individuality, set out deliberately to oppose all accepted notions, all conventions in conduct, clothes, and morals. Ironically enough the very cult became such that it tended paradoxically to submerge individuality in the pursuit of passing fads, since the artists were willing to forego complete independence in order better to show the bourgeois that their eccentricities were an organized manifestation against his comfortable smugness. With the common aim of providing amusement for themselves and an outlet for their scorn of the "grocer," they united into various groups or societies, wilder and more elaborate descendants of the *Caveau*, the *Rocher de Cancale*, and other comparatively sedate singing societies which were popular during the Empire and the Restoration, and which Monnier's Joseph Prudhomme had patronized in his youth.[4] Whether they were named *Frileux*, *Bousingots*, *Purs-Sang*, *Infatigables*, *Badouillards*, or *Jeune-France*, these groups were composed chiefly of young painters and writers most of whom never reached as high a place in either literature or painting as in the art of finding ways to *engueuler le pékin*, to use the old term by which the soldiers of the Empire had scornfully designated the civilian.

The *Société des Joyeux*, who called themselves the *Frileux* in the winter, specialized in *banquets lyriques,* at which Charlet, Raffet, Pigault-Lebrun, Béranger, Scribe, and even Hugo and Lamartine observed the fundamental rule that politics were boring and must be excluded. The *Bousingots,* on the contrary, adopted a revolutionary costume, although they devoted their energies, like their successors the *Badouillards,* to the pleasures of eating, drinking, flirting, and playing tricks on the bourgeois. Their sensual escapism was a reaction from the cult of the Middle Ages which was one of the distinguishing marks of the famous group that Théophile Gautier has chronicled in his stories of *Les Jeune-France.* "Daniel Jovard ou la Conversion d'un classique" contains a full-length portrait of these *précieuses ridicules* of Romanticism.[5] The artist was young, handsome, melancholy. He cultivated a noble brow by pushing back his long ringlets, and let his beard grow to give him a medieval appearance and to distinguish him from the clean-shaven bourgeois.[6] As a further means of scandalizing the bourgeois he smoked a pipe, or preferably a cigar, a new fashion so revolutionary that Balzac devoted an article to it in the *Caricature,* the good Dr. Véron prophesied that it would cause a physical, moral, and intellectual transformation of the French, and Madame de Girardin declared still more forcefully that within fifty years the *sexe fort* would be reduced to semisomnolence by tobacco, and that the *sexe faible* would then take control of society.* The *Jeune-France* had definite tastes and occupations. They detested Racine, Boileau, and Voltaire as the literary gods of the *bourgeoisie,* and the National Guard as a symbol of authority founded on wealth, since its members had to be taxpayers. They wrote languorous poetry with a Byronic flavor, to which they signed a British pseudonym. Protesting against the practical, prosaic, and colorless clothes which were becoming more and more the prescribed costume for men, they adopted medieval doub-

* Did these prophets suspect that the habit would spread even into the middle class, until the cigar became symbolic, not of the artist, but of the business man? It has already been suggested that the smoking of the after-dinner cigar, interfering as it did with the traditions of polite society, was partly responsible for the development of the *demi-monde* (p. 62, above, footnote). Balzac, *Oeuvres complètes,* XXXIX, 439–441; Véron, *Mémoires d'un bourgeois,* I, 100–101; Mme. de Girardin, *Le Vicomte de Launay, Lettres Choisies* (Paris, 1913), pp. 292–296.

lets of velvet or satin, designed for themselves jackets and waistcoats of amazing cut and daring color, like the famous *gilet rouge* worn by Gautier at the first performance of *Hernani*, and flaunted those wide-brimmed hats *à la Buridan* which had become almost the *sine qua non* of the artist since the success of Dumas' melodrama, *La Tour de Nesle*.

One of the most notorious headquarters in the war against the bourgeois was an old house, called "La Childeberte," near Saint-Germain-des-Prés, a rendezvous since time immemorial of the artists of the Left Bank. A history of the different generations who lived there forms a record of the changing fads and fashions of Romanticism. The neo-Greeks and Romans of the Empire had given way to chevaliers and troubadours, and they in turn to Orientals; then came a revival of the medieval, when clothes, language, hair, and beards became gothic. After 1830 the artists were *Jeune-France* or *Bousingots*, and their sense of humor seemed to change from the sharp yet delicately intellectual wit of earlier French satire to a blunter buffoonery which they may have learned from the English. While some of their tricks were not unworthy of Monnier or Romieu, their immediate predecessors in the art of practical joking, the latter relied more on a clever understanding of human psychology than on elaborate setting of the stage for their *mystifications*. That Monnier himself sometimes took part in the cruder skirmishing against the bourgeois is attested by Maxime DuCamp, who wrote with his usual rather petty acerbity that Monnier often shared in the nonsense of the younger artists, that he exercised "the resources of a diabolic wit and made himself scarce when the joke took an ugly turn." [7] Perhaps this means that he did not happen to be involved in the encounters with the police which the lodgers of "La Childeberte" had on more than one occasion.*

* The story of the butcher's dog is an example of the grand scale on which "La Childeberte" organized its *mystifications:* One Sunday morning the artists coaxed into the house an enormous mastiff belonging to a neighborhood butcher, and painted stripes on him to make him look like a tiger. Tying a kettle to his tail, they turned him loose just as high mass was ending at Saint-Germain-des-Prés. As the good bourgeois came from church they met the horrifying creature tearing through the square, while at every window of "La Childeberte" appeared a Bedouin, draped in a blanket, wearing a feather duster on his head, and smoking a broomstick.

A decade later Montmartre would begin to attract the artists, and the Brasserie des Martyrs would become the headquarters of the official *Bohême.* Bohemia had not yet been named, however, and Murger, its official chronicler, was too young to realize that it had already begun to exist, scattered here and there about the city. The romantic character of the artist's life, his picturesque disregard of conventional ways of dress or speech, his desire to scandalize the bourgeois, his inability to live peacefully with them, his reputation as a *mauvais farceur,* all these traits which Monnier's generation had revealed with less publicity in the studios of the Left Bank, were crystallized among the *Jeune-France* and the *Bousingots.* Later the groups found somewhat different fashions to follow. The graceful medievalism of the *Jeune-France* evolved into vague melancholy, somber reverie; feeling himself a marked victim of fate, the young poet sought salvation in a mystical neocatholicism, or declined into tuberculosis and an early death. On the other hand the *Badouillards,* with their philosophy of *bon vivant,* became increasingly eccentric in seeking to turn this humdrum life into an orgy of sensuous pleasure. The way was prepared for the bohemianism from which the Realistic movement was to come.

In contrast to this open revolt against bourgeois conventionality, many of the Romanticists expressed their feeling of superiority by the impeccable elegance of their appearance and the coldly phlegmatic indifference with which they masked their antipathy. It seems rather odd that Henry Monnier, with his robust sense of humor on the one hand and on the other the economic restrictions of his hard-working and nomadic life, should have had his part in the *dandysme* of the 1830's. But it must be remembered that as a young *fashionable* of the late Restoration he had cared meticulously for his appearance, and later portraits show the well-groomed head of the actor conscious of a certain nobility of brow and chin, although he never tried to model himself on Beau Brummell as did some of his friends.

A tyrant and purist in matters of dress, Nestor Roqueplan might be named as the *dandy par excellence.* It was he who set the fashion of wearing trousers trimmed with bands of silk braid, and who introduced the latest London cut of tweeds as well as what Gautier called the "complicated equipment of English cleanliness." [8] He is said to have declared that when he had a new coat to be fitted he did not sleep the night before, and that his ambition was to die insolvent and *à la mode*.

Another typical *dandy* was Léon Gozlan, associated with Balzac, Méry, and other journalists of the 1830's. He took pride not only in the exquisite distinction of his dress, but also in the originality of his tastes, genuine or affected. The bourgeois talked of the beauties of nature and dreamed of holidays spent in a suburban villa; Gozlan, like Baudelaire, detested the country and the sentimental praises it received: "Don't speak to me of the execrable lilac, that bluish-purple and pungent flower which grows on the manure heaps of Romainville to adorn the bosoms of the *grisettes* of the faubourg du Temple." [9] He horrified the credulous by affecting to enjoy the taste of human flesh, and when it was rumored that he had been a pirate in his youth and had at one time murdered his captain, he would exaggerate his Marseillais accent in replying: "I killed him, but I ate him, which removed all traces of the crime." [10]

Heinrich Heine, who reached Paris soon after the July Revolution and was to live there until his death in 1856, displayed at that period of his career both the physical and the intellectual traits of the *dandy*. Physically he had, according to Gautier, the blond and robust beauty of a German Apollo, and like Gavarni and Gautier himself, he believed in perfecting the development of his body by vigorous sport. He dressed with care, lived in a comfortable apartment, and took pains to avoid all eccentricities which might mark him as an artist. His participation in the war against the bourgeois was active, but waged chiefly with his pen. The critic Faguet has solemnly deplored the baleful influence of the group surrounding Heine, which turned him into a wit, and even worse, gave him a taste for *mystification:* "Surprising the reader by such an abrupt change of tone, and even of sentiment, and even of idea, that the reader no longer knows where he stands and whether he has before him a serious writer or a mountebank, this is the result of the craze of the time which consisted of 'wanting to astonish the bourgeois.' " And Faguet concluded that Heine had caught from his Parisian contacts the hatred of the middle class which was a "disagreeable malady of the second generation of our Romanticists." [11]

If he had not brought with him the germs of that malady, Heine must have been peculiarly susceptible to it, for as early as 1831 he turned the full force of his cynical wit against the bourgeois in an article on the Salon:

> Has perchance the spirit of the middle classes, of Industrialism, which now pervades the whole social life of France, made itself so powerful in the arts of design, that every picture of our time bears impressed upon it the trade mark of the new supremacy? The Scripture pictures, in which this year's exhibition is so rich, excite in me such a conjecture. There is in the long saloon a picture of "Christ being scourged," whose chief figure, with its grievous face, resembles exactly a director of an unfortunate joint-stock company, who stands before his shareholders and has to give them up his accounts: in truth, the shareholders are also to be seen in the picture in the forms of Pharisees and executioners, who are horribly incensed against the *Ecce Homo,* and appear to have lost much money by their shares . . . There is a William the Conqueror to be seen on whom you have only to put a bearskin cap and he resembles exactly a National Guard who mounts guard with exemplary zeal, pays his bills of exchange regularly, adores his wife, and deserves the cross of the Legion of Honour. Most of the faces have such a pecuniary, selfish, displeased appearance, which I can only explain by the fact that the living original only thought at his sittings of the money which his portrait would cost, while the painter was continually regretting the time which he must spend over his deplorable mercenary service.[12]

In that concluding sentence, Heine expressed the irreconcilable grievance of the creative artist who cannot buy bread unless he sells his products to the man of money. The nineteenth-century Romanticists were goaded to particular rage by that age-old platitude. As the business man attained a position of social stability and prestige, he yielded to the fascination which the arts had always held for him, and became, with considerable condescension, the patron of aspiring young artists whom he commissioned to paint his portrait or, still worse, the portrait of his wife. He thus satisfied his feeling of importance by perpetuating his own likeness or that of his most valuable possession, and had at the same time the rather exciting experience of investing in a luxury which offered no certainty of profitable returns. He was willing to pay what his shrewd business sense considered a fair price, but he expected the artists to deliver satisfactory goods and he felt free to offer comments, criticism, and suggestions, and to insist on alterations to please his own taste, just as though he were buying a suit from a tailor. The painters, on the other hand, believing *a priori* that their patron knew nothing about art and was incapable of understanding it, felt themselves obliged either to risk losing their commission by doing the portrait to suit themselves, or to prostitute their art by pleasing the purchaser.

Such was the situation as it appeared to the writers and artists of the 1830's, and as Monnier, for instance, represented it in the sketch which he incorporated in his *Nouvelles scènes populaires* of 1839, "Le Peintre et les bourgeois." In a series of prints called *Les Artistes,* Gavarni chose to put aside the bitterness of humiliated pride and aesthetic suffering, showing instead the lively humor of the *rapins* and their merry pranks against what they scornfully designate as "a venerable herd of *muffes!*" * [13]

The name of Gavarni evokes almost better than any other the world which the artists created for themselves after 1830, and to which Henry Monnier never ceased to belong, even when his theatrical ventures interrupted his artistic career in Paris. Gavarni's illustrations for Emile de Girardin's *La Mode* had brought him into contact with Balzac, Eugène Sue, Alphonse Karr, Decamps, Raffet, Devéria, Charlet, Grandville, Daumier. Laurent Jan was Gavarni's and Monnier's mutual friend, and Emile Forgues was intimate with Gavarni as early as 1834. With Arsène Houssaye, Roger de Beauvoir, and Albéric Segond, Gavarni formed the elegant group of the *muscadins,* whose *dandysme* showed the usual English influence in impeccability of appearance and politeness of manner, marked by a cold reserve masking a quick imagination and an ardent temperament.†

After Gavarni's talent for designing costumes brought special success to the masked balls, he began to receive his friends on Saturday evenings in his studio, in the rue Blanche between 1835 and 1838, and then for seven years in his famous apartment, rue Fontaine-Saint-Georges. In the room lined with canvases and the neatly stacked tools of the artist, where the skull of Trilby, his pet dog, gave a romantically macabre touch, the guests sometimes exercised

* The untranslatable *muffes,* for *mufles,* suggests the heaviness of oxen or bison, and all that is low-bred and despicable.

† Monnier's comment was: "Ce Gavarni, je ne sais pas comment il fait avec ses maîtresses, il est quelquefois d'un roide, d'un roide! Eh bien, malgré ça, elles l'adorent; oui, elles l'adorent!" Goncourt, *Gavarni,* p. 91.

their wits at parlor games, until Balzac would say with gusty geniality: "Now, if we didn't play any more? if we had some fun?"[14]

Then they would begin a series of charades, *proverbes*, and comic monologues, in which Méry and Ourliac displayed their talents as comedians and mimics, and Henry Monnier topped them all. Never could the guests forget the scene between a painter and the bourgeois who came to have his portrait painted, or the drama of the Jew who had bought an imitation diamond. Balzac was happiest when Monnier brought from his repertory his most side-splitting scenes: a dialogue in broad southern accent between the executioners of Draguignan and Carcassonne; the national guardsman of Brussels who was going to *se prostituer prisonnier;* or Monsieur Prudhomme *dans un mauvais lieu.* Monnier had no longer the slender figure and ardent expression of the young man who had delighted earlier groups in Paris studios, and his personal life offered little but disappointment. And yet he could put aside melancholy thoughts and the problems of a struggling actor, just as he had once been able to forget a lover's quarrel during an evening's fun among his friends, and play the mimic with an art still incomparable.

What seems to have been the special mark of Monnier's humor, whether in improvising pranks to torment the bourgeois or in reciting his monologues, was the imperturbable coldness with which he played, and which was the distinguishing trait of the *dandy*. Baudelaire had not yet formulated the philosophy and code of conduct that gave to his *dandysme* an aristocratic and almost heroic character, but Monnier in his caricature of the bourgeois created a vulgarized version of the *dandy*, even to the details of his physical appearance, which seems almost a predecessor in parody, if that were conceivable, of the *dandy* born of Baudelaire's cult of the ego, which he was to describe later as the pleasure of causing astonishment and the proud satisfaction of never showing it, or of being moved to reveal any other emotion.

It is certainly true that the reaction against the overflowing lyricism of earlier Romanticism was taking the form of a more fastidious restraint. Soon the artists, doomed to lose their battle against the nineteenth-century materialistic spirit, would formulate the aristocratic doctrine of art for art's sake. Under Gautier's leadership they would proclaim that "the visible world exists," [15] but they would be merely elevating into theory what the Romanticists of Monnier's generation had already put into practice, observing the world about them first because they found in it new sources of the picturesque, and then in order better to make fun of it. The Realists would go a step further. Although escape from that external world might be impossible, the artist could escape from himself by fixing his attention solely on it, or still better, could keep intact his own soul by setting the external world as a barrier between himself and an uncomprehending society.

XI

MONNIER'S CONNECTION WITH THE REALISTIC MOVEMENT

As Henry Monnier passed his fortieth year, his life settled into the pattern which it followed for nearly forty years longer. He carried on his three professions, sometimes devoting himself chiefly to acting, at other times working more actively as an artist, and occasionally publishing works which maintained his reputation as a writer. Although professional engagements took him from time to time into the provinces and to Brussels, and once at least as far as Berne and Lausanne, he spent the second half of his life chiefly in Paris and at Parnes. The Revolution of 1848, happening to take place while Monnier was in the country, passed almost unnoticed, with no direct effect on his career such as that of the Revolution of 1830.

Among his old friends, there were inevitably some who disappeared from his life. The comradeship of earlier days with Balzac had cooled, so that Henry saw little of him before his death in 1850. H. de Latouche died in 1851. As the gay friends of the studios settled into the respectable posts of middle age, as government employees or as artists and writers whose works had achieved recognized position, many of them grew away from Monnier. Romieu was not the only one whose official dignity made him reluctant to recall the lively sowing of wild oats which Monnier had shared. Eugène Sue, now champion of social reforms and defender of the lower classes, was no longer at home whenever Monnier chose to knock at the door which had once been so hospitably open to him. The story goes indeed that Monnier was kept waiting more than an hour one day to see his old friend, until he picked up the two silver platters which held calling cards and letters, and set off with them under his arm. That caused cries of "Stop thief!." Monnier was captured and led before Sue, to whom he said calmly: "I knew I'd get to see you!" [1]

Other associates of younger days remained more loyal, although their friendliness sometimes assumed a rather patronizing tone when Monnier sought to profit by their authority or influence, as he was prone to do. After Nestor Roqueplan had become director of Beaux Arts, for instance, Monnier apparently appealed to their mutual friend Cavé to use his influence in obtaining the authorization to present certain plays during his tours of the provinces. Roqueplan's reply shows that Monnier's collaboration in the *Soirées de Neuilly* had not been forgotten: "Cavé knew you in the old days, as you say; but he knows you still, and knowing that I am writing to you, he asks me to give you his friendliest greetings." [2] Mérimée too, a functionary under Louis-Philippe and senator during the Second Empire, was in a position to direct official patronage toward Monnier. It may have been at the time when arrangements were being made to grant Monnier the small pension he ultimately received, that he had the following letter from Mérimée: "My dear friend, our Minister is leaving or is going to leave for Tarbes. He will be back, I think in three or four days. I don't understand too clearly what *bénéfice* you ask of me. If I were Minister of the Church, I would make you abbot of Thélème . . ." [3]

Another old friend was Paul de Kock, one of the most popular novelists of the July Monarchy, whose stories delighted the little *grisettes* and the petty *bourgeoisie* about whom he wrote. In 1845 he built on his property at Romainville, outside of Paris, a small theater where he organized programs during the summer season. According to his *Mémoires*, the list of regular guests was headed for some fifteen years by Henry Monnier. Both men were humorous observers of the same social classes and types, and the work of Paul de Kock not only supplements Monnier's portrayal of contemporary life, but appears at times to imitate it.*

* There are reminiscences of Monnier in *La Grande ville, ou Paris il y a vingt-cinq ans* (Paris, Degorce-Cadot, n.d.): "Une soirée dans la petite propriété" suggests the "Dîner bourgeois"; "Les Dames au marché" and "La Sortie du spectacle" contain dialogue almost as realistic as Monnier's, though less phonetically written. In general Kock describes and explains, not depending, as does Monnier, on the effect of the dialogue. He tends also to give his own sentiments, and sometimes to add a moral lesson. His *Mémoires* (Paris, 1873), pp. 853–857, name among the guests the sculptor Mène, probably Monnier's most intimate friend during the last twenty-five years of his life. Their intimacy may have developed here.

Of the group of caricaturists, Gavarni remained probably the most closely connected with Monnier. There is a picturesque testimonial of their long association as mocking students of the pettiness of mankind, in an illustration in Curmer's famous *Les Français peints par eux-mêmes*.[4] It represents the two artists reclining on a grassy bank, down which come tiny figures who pass one by one through their hands. Gavarni has stopped the progress of one of these helpless puppets and seems to be asking his comrade what fitting treatment they can give him. It is quite likely that the friends did offer each other suggestions and advice. Gavarni may occasionally have borrowed Monnier's ideas for a sketch of manners or a caption, just as Monnier profited by the other's knowledge of costumes. It has even been said that Monnier worked in Gavarni's studio as late as 1861, experimenting with certain technical methods of lithography which Gavarni used. It is certain that their intimacy continued after the increasing popularity of Gavarni's Saturdays forced him to give up keeping open house, for Monnier continued to be welcomed at the house in Auteuil where Gavarni settled after his marriage.

During the theatrical activity of the 1830's Monnier had put aside his artistic work, but after 1839 he resumed it again, producing nearly as much in the next four or five years as he had done between 1827 and 1830. The publishing house of Aubert et Compagnie, which Philipon had turned over to his brother-in-law, was interested now almost exclusively in prints and illustrated periodicals. It produced several new series of lithographs by Monnier: *Récréations* (1839–1840); *Impressions de voyage* (1840), in which the artist turned a satiric eye toward certain provincial types he must have encountered during his tours;* *Les Gens sans façon* (1840), in which the legends vied with the drawings for comic effect;† and *Nos con-*

* For instance, "Les gros bonnets du pays. Le juge de paix, le commandant de place, le conservateur des hypothèques"; also the little scene of manners between a magistrate and the lady for whom he has done a favor: "La sortie de l'audience. 'Vraiment,' dit la grosse dame, 'je vous suis bien obligée, M. Profond, sans votre obligeance mes enfants n'auraient pas eu le plaisir de voir le condamné à mort. Vous dînez avec nous?' "

† Such as the scene in which a small-town neighbor arrives with a long list of errands to be run and many packages to be delivered by his friend who is setting out for Paris: "Voici, mon cher M. Bridault, quelques petites commissions pour Paris . . ." Daumier did a lithograph on the same subject.

temporains (1845–1846), which had previously appeared separately in the *Caricature*.[5]

In addition to these works, which recall the comic and satiric albums of the late Restoration, Monnier made numerous studies and portraits, continuing to sketch country scenes or types during his theatrical tours, or finishing more carefully drawings of heads or stage personages which interested him. As in his earlier work of this kind, there is little caricature, but an accurate observation of facial expression, gesture, costume, a penetrating revelation of character, and in the less frequent landscapes or animal scenes, rendering of homely atmosphere which suggests once more comparison with the work of Flemish artists.[6]

The most interesting part of Monnier's artistic work during this period was, however, in the field of illustration. His decorations for the covers of a group of separately published song sheets, collected under the title *Le Farceur des salons* (1842), may be classed as little more than potboilers, but he made many important contributions to various books which appeared in the early 1840's, studying French, and especially Parisian, manners and customs. Illustrated by wood-engravings—which had temporarily eclipsed the popularity of lithography—essentially though not exclusively humorous in tone, and varying greatly in literary value according to the talents of the contributors, these publications represent the composite effort of different contributors to fulfill a purpose which had been suggested by Balzac even before the July Revolution had added new complications to the transitional bewilderment of French society. In an article in *La Mode* of February 20, 1830, he had complained of the lack of clearly defined mores in a nation which took its fashions in clothes from the French Revolution, in boots from the Empire, in cookery from the Restoration, in carriages from England. He may have borrowed from Montesquieu the idea which he proposed as the goal of a suggested study of contemporary manners: to inquire whether the national character and spirit were in contradiction to the new forms of national government.[7] The innumerable studies which appeared during the July Monarchy corresponded to a similar attempt in the comic and satiric literature of England and Germany to put some order into the chaos of postrevolutionary Europe.

As early as 1834 Ladvocat edited *Paris, ou Le Livre des cent-et-un*, a compilation in fourteen volumes, for which Monnier had made the vignette on the title page. *Babel* appeared in 1840, containing a *scène populaire* by Monnier;[8] in 1841 were published *Le Museum parisien* and *Paris au XIXe siècle*, and *Les Français peints par eux-mêmes* was begun; *Les Industriels* appeared in 1842, *La Grande ville* in 1842–1843, and finally the two volumes of *Le Diable à Paris* in 1845 and 1846. All of these contained drawings by Monnier, and some of them literary sketches also. His illustrations are certainly the best part of *Les Industriels, métiers et professions de France*, whose author, Emile de la Bédollière, seemed overconscientiously aware of his social mission in painting the manners of the working classes for the edification of their social superiors. Monnier's studies of the costumes and tools of each trade, and the imprint of the trade on the face and figure of the workman, offer an excellent example of his characteristic economy in the use of lines and precision of detail.

Les Français peints par eux-mêmes, edited by Curmer, was one of the most successful of these works, treating its encyclopedic subject with comparatively little satire and often with real sympathy even verging on the sentimental. The texts were written by Balzac, Janin, Paul de Kock, Méry, Emile de la Bédollière, Louise Colet, Madame Ancelot, and others forgotten today; and the hundreds of illustrations were furnished by all the illustrators of the period. Monnier did various types in that monumental work, distinguishing himself definitely as a specialist in the study of the lower classes: an old soldier, more moving than Charlet's; the mother of an actress, a commissionaire, a petty bourgeois who poses as the "artists' friend"; the *portière*, for whom he also wrote the text. His figures reveal a sureness of touch marking the mature artist, and a vigor which relies scarcely at all on exaggeration.

The conception of *Les Français peints par eux-mêmes* may have been suggested by the *physiologies* which were so popular at that time, and which represent one of the most curiously romantic-realistic trends of the literature of the July Monarchy. As has often been noted, when the Romanticists did not fly from reality into fantastic realms of the imagination, they sought to represent real men in a real world, with the particular marks which distinguish one individual from another, the picturesque details which differentiate one period from another or one nation from another. The term "local color" came into use to describe this historical sense which was largely visual, tending to translate the analysis of character into terms of external appearance. The Romanticists had not yet reached the pseudoscientific doctrine of the Naturalists, but they already practiced the method of the Realists: the gathering of material, the collecting of information by observation and research. If the data collected concerned past times or distant lands, the result appeared more purely "Romantic"; when they concerned contemporary France, the work would be called "Realistic." *Salammbô* and *Madame Bovary* seem to be at opposite poles, and yet Flaubert's method of documentation was essentially the same in both cases. As a mere boy, he had already used it in the *Leçon d'histoire naturelle*, which is a typical *physiologie*.

The *physiologies* were based on the Balzacian theory that the elements of society can be analyzed according to their milieu, habits, appearance, just as an entomologist classifies the insect world. Perhaps clothes do not make the man, but they show something of his personality and reflect his daily occupation and his economic status. The same is true of all the external details which a careful observer can note as he examines the specimen before him: through them are revealed character and ultimately soul, since the soul, in this materialistic universe, can be only the product of the functions of the body.

Before 1830, the obligatory decorum of social conventions had prevented overfrank liberty in the study of social types. But the method had already been tried, in a series of little books illustrated with lithographs by Monnier, and purporting to present seriously or ironically certain problems of etiquette: *L'Art de mettre sa cravate*, *L'Art de donner à dîner*, *l'Art de se présenter dans le monde*, *L'Art de ne jamais déjeuner chez soi ou de dîner toujours chez les autres*, *L'Art de payer ses dettes et de satisfaire ses créanciers sans débourser un sou.** Balzac was chiefly responsible for the publication

* The English humorist Stephen Potter has recently revived this type of pseudoscientific manual. See his *Theory and Practice of Gamesmanship, or*

of these curious works. He had a hand also in some of the seriocomic *codes* which appeared toward the end of the Restoration with such titles as *Code gourmand*, *Code conjugal*, or *Code civil.* As early as 1825 he had published anonymously a *Code des gens honnêtes* with the impressive subtitle *Prolégomènes: Considérations politiques, littéraires, philosophiques, législatives, religieuses et budgétaires, sur la classe des voleurs*—a typical sample of Romantic interest in the socially disreputable, and of the method of treating with pseudo-scientific seriousness a subject which his contemporaries would consider scandalous.[9] Monnier contributed illustrations to a *Code des amants* and to a *Code du commis voyageur*, a subject with which he showed his familiarity also in the "Voyage en diligence." He illustrated also several *manuels* of the same character: *Manuel de l'amateur de café,—de l'amateur d'huîtres,—du parrain et de la marraine;* and, especially interesting because of resemblances with his more creative artistic and literary work, a *Manuel de l'employé de toutes classes et de tous grades*, and a *Manuel du marié ou Guide à la mairie, à l'église, au festin, au bal, etc.*[10]

The word *physiologie* had been used in 1825 by the clever magistrate Brillat-Savarin, who turned good eating into an art in a book of which Monnier illustrated the third edition in 1829; *Physiologie du goût ou Méditations de gastronomie transcendante.* Balzac adopted the term, announcing in early numbers of *La Silhouette* articles which were begun but apparently never completed: "Physiologie de la toilette," "Physiologie gastronomique"; and publishing in *La Caricature* "Physiologie des positions,"—de l'adjoint,"—du cigare." Other sketches of the same type appeared without the label: "L'Epicier" and "La Grisette," the latter closely suggestive of Monnier's album of *Grisettes* although the lithographs are not mentioned.

In the late 1830's Aubert began publishing the *Physiologies parisiennes*, which appeared as separate fascicules of the *Bibliothèque pour rire*, and then as a series of small illustrated books, each volume

---

The Art of Winning Games Without Actually Cheating (New York, 1948); "Golfmanship, or How to Win Without Actually Cheating" (*Atlantic Monthly*, September 1948); "Lifemanship, or How to Trip the Expert" (*Atlantic Monthly*, May 1949).

usually containing two "specimens." There were dozens of them, by various writers, but it is the fame of the artists which has turned some of them into collectors' items. Here again passes in review the whole gamut of contemporary types: the student, the *grisette* and her successor the *lorette;* the civil servant, presented by Balzac; the *portière*, now described by James Rousseau but twin sister to Monnier's *portière* in *Les Français peints par eux-mêmes.* Monnier did text and illustrations for the bourgeois, of course, but illustrated many others: the bachelor and the old maid, the drinker, the usurer, the *femme honnête*, the journalist, the capitalist, the shopgirl.

The tone of these sketches ranges from frankly comic or satiric to more serious. And again is felt the insistence on picturesque external detail, presented with Romantic irony and yet objectively enough to let the reader make his own deductions about the character. He is reminded, of course, of the seventeenth-century portrait or *caractère*, with the great difference that the nineteenth-century *physiologie* studies social types—what Diderot had called *conditions* —rather than traits of personal character. And yet there can be no doubt that the Romantic satirists and *moralistes* were lineal descendants of La Bruyère and Molière.

While Henry Monnier contributed to these publications which were continuing one of the great traditions of French literature and at the same time practicing the principles of Realism ten or fifteen years before the formation of its doctrines, he was busy also with his own literary work. Another Belgian edition of the *Scènes populaires* was issued between 1835 and 1841, containing all the scenes hitherto published. In 1841 a new volume appeared in Paris, containing seven scenes under the title: *Scènes de la ville et de la campagne.*[12] In 1846 a new edition of the *Scènes populaires* was offered with the title *Œuvres complètes.* His *Physiologie du bourgeois* appeared in 1850. With such indications that Monnier's literary work was being read during that decade, it is understandable that his connection with the Realistic movement should have been literary rather than artistic.

Among the new generation of writers who were beginning to make a name for themselves, there were two who came speedily under Monnier's influence. One was the young journalist, Charles Monselet, fresh from the provinces in 1846, who was introduced to

Monnier by Emile de la Bédollière. At the Divan Lepelletier and wherever the newspaper men gathered, Monselet saw much of the "stout and spectacled man of forty-five," whom he had taken at first for a country gentleman,[13] and with whom he was soon on friendly terms in spite of twenty-five years' difference in their ages. Quickly winning a place as a *feuilletoniste* or, to use the American term, a columnist, Monselet was one of the first to give prestige to this genre so characteristic of modern journalism. Like Paul de Kock, Méry, Gozlan, Champfleury, and Monnier himself, writers whose work never rose above literary mediocrity, Monselet nevertheless added valuable pages to the *petite histoire* which is one of the richest sources of documentation for the social history of Paris.

Gay, witty, gifted with a keen and unsentimental eye for the ridiculous, like Monnier he could produce in a few firmly drawn lines realistic little scenes of manners in which, true lover of Paris, he recognized and preserved the traits which gave the city its characteristic flavor. One virtue these compositions possess which was not learned from Monnier: their brevity. They have a pleasant lucidity of style which recalls the eighteenth-century *moralistes*, somewhat more literary than Monnier's and less realistically stenographic. But the subjects are often similar to Monnier's—such as the "Emotions d'un bourgeois en lisant son journal" [14]—and Monselet showed his admiration by trying to use Monnier's methods of faithful reproduction, and by referring to him repeatedly, comparing him with not very critical enthusiasm now to Carmontelle for his draftsmanship, now to Hoffmann for his skill in composition!

The second writer who devoted to Henry Monnier a lifelong cult, culminating in the affectionate and sympathetic biography which is a precious source of information, was Champfleury. He too came to Paris in the early 1840's, from the provincial town of Laon, where as a boy he had been so thrilled to see Monnier on the stage. The half-satiric, half-realistic form given to Monnier's humorous observation of the lower classes directed Champfleury into the path which was to make him leader of the Realistic movement. Much of his early work contains material borrowed directly from Monnier, including the personage of Monsieur Prudhomme himself, whom Champfleury felt free to use because, he said, Prudhomme was not one individual but many.[15] More significant than such direct borrowing, however, was the influence of tone, technique, and general subject matter.

From Monnier Champfleury learned to look for the grotesque and the ridiculous in the real lives of commonplace people, and thus to exploit the "inexhaustible repertory of middle-class stupidity." [16] He learned to describe with minute accuracy and to record dialogue with stenographic fidelity. In many of his stories, especially those about provincial life, Champfleury followed the method of the *Scènes populaires*, indicating his characters by the briefest description and then letting them talk, giving them individuality by recording their particular jargon and favorite clichés, and achieving a comic effect through the cumulative banality of their conversation. Unfortunately the two writers possessed also a common weakness: Monnier could not teach his disciple selection or composition. While his own scenes, at their best, achieve unity of tone, comic or brutal or simply dull, much of Champfleury's work fails to reach even the humblest place on the ladder of art because of the inability to choose essential details. Such absence of discrimination makes Champfleury, no doubt, a truer realist, since it diminishes the effect of caricature. Fond of humor in art and literature as Champfleury was, he was not fundamentally a humorist himself, and the comic elements of his early stories tend to disappear in the later ones, as Monnier's influence seems to have been replaced by that of Balzac. The latter was, of course, the great god of the Realists, thanks to Champfleury's admiration, and if Henry Monnier enjoys today the prestige of a lesser god, it is because Champfleury first linked his name with Balzac's in that important chapter of French literary history.

When Champfleury came to Paris, he was drawn into the circle of young artists who formed the Bohemia which Henri Murger later chronicled, and which cannot be overlooked in a study of the evolution of Romanticism into Realism. Chintreuil, the Desbrosses brothers, Alexandre Schanne, Murger himself, belonged to a group of penniless but ambitious painters, sculptors, engravers, who called themselves *Buveurs d'eau*, partly in token of their poverty, which prevented them most of the time from indulging in any other drink, and partly because they made of their forced asceticism a symbol of true art. The problems of material existence could not be completely ignored, but the lack of comforts and even of most of the necessities of life was compensated for by a fervent idealism which was the characteristic mark of the Bohemian. Like the artists of the 1830's, these young men vowed undying hatred of the bourgeois: suffering and privation seemed glorious compared with his dull and humbug conception of a wholly materialistic existence.

From the Romanticists they inherited also their notion of the artist as a superior being, gifted with what Victor Hugo had called that *mens divinior* which lifted him into a class apart. The task of the artist in modern life was to raise common man up to his level, a democratic goal which Hugo passed on to Champfleury. He must then concern himself with social and political questions, must study the lives of the people he was called to lead; the world and its ways, objects of his instinctive scorn and hatred, could be considered justifiably to exist as a model for the artist. Everything which furnished material for his art became thereby interesting and bearable, and achieved a reason for being.

A sensitive and idealistic young man, confronted with such a mission on the threshold of his career as painter or poet, might well feel himself torn between the natural impulse to avoid the petty and ugly by taking refuge in his imagination, and the nobler dream of chastizing the petty and destroying the ugly. Champfleury described this conflict in his *Souvenirs et portraits de jeunesse:*

> Two different roads stretched before me at the beginning of my literary life: the one easy, dry, but desolate, the other of more poetic appearance and fragrant with the perfume of plants from beyond the Rhine: I felt myself swept into the quadrille which Henry Monnier made the *bourgeoisie* dance, and at the same time into the rounds of Willis, singing German *lieder*. The almost literal reproduction of the conversations of petty small-town bourgeois pleased me as much as the vague melancholy of the poets of the North.[17]

The final choice was determined by a combination of forces, some of which have already been described. Henry Monnier's talent as a comedian and mimic, improvising scenes for the entertainment of the *Buveurs d'eau*, was a small contributing factor in indicating what kind of "reality" could be interesting, and how it should be studied.[18]

Many contemporary critics of Realism traced its development, not to any literary tradition, but to the materialistic spirit which pervaded all society after the Revolution of 1848. They said that the writers turned to real people and concerned themselves with the external and material aspects of life, just as the philosophers and reformers, whose utopian dreams had been disappointed by the revolution, turned to more realistic projects, to aspirations which could be translated into business terms, to reforms and progress which could be sold as shares and would bring in realizable dividends. There can be no question that every important literary or artistic movement is born of its time, or that the writers and painters of Bohemia, Champfleury, Murger, Théodore de Banville, Baudelaire, Barbara, Courbet, in turning to humble life, the commonplace, the poor, and the outcast, were responding more or less consciously to the growth of the democratic idea, allied with the spread of science. The search for scientific truth encouraged observation of the external world, efforts to measure the importance of environment and the influence of material conditions on the human spirit. But it is equally true that the roots of the Realistic movement reached into the past, and that the Realists remained Romantic at heart. Even when they represented the wretched life and the humble types which were the Paris they knew best, they were invariably attracted to the ugly, the grotesque, the eccentric, or the vicious aspects of reality. Moved at first chiefly by the old Romantic desire to shock the Philistine, they soon found that there was a public ready now to approve of their efforts and take them seriously, and so the doctrine of "sincerity in art" became a watchword of the Realistic movement.

The movement took cognizance of itself in the 1850's, when the definition of Realism was formulated by both its defenders and its critics. A summary of that definition will help to solve one of the major problems in a study of Henry Monnier, by showing to what extent he may accurately be called a realist. The Realist aimed to attain truth by representing the real world, that is by studying contemporary life and manners, through impersonal and scientific observation. Any subject offered proper material, provided that its external aspects were presented through notation of the minutest physical detail; the emphasis was therefore materialistic and sensorial.

Similar objective analysis was applied to the portrayal of character, in which the artist remained completely indifferent to morality. Some critics maintained that he should remain equally passive in the selection of material, imitating nature exactly without any choice or arrangement, simply telling everything he heard and saw, thus achieving a photograph of the external world.[19]

The definitions which had the authority of official pronouncements, however, expressed or implied the need for choice in the selection of material. In Duranty's *Réalisme*, the emphasis on the social mission of the artist showed that although he did not have the right to deform reality in order to falsify its proportions, his duty was to select those aspects which would be comprehensible and significant to the greatest number of people. Champfleury went still further, limiting the study of human nature to the lowest strata, which, he said, supplied the artist with better examples of sincerity in speech and action than did the more sophisticated and refined upper classes. By making an important distinction also between crude reality and literary or artistic realism, he showed that he was conscious of the undesirability of including every detail in a reproduction of life which purported to be a work of art. It is significant to note that both Duranty and Champfleury criticized Henry Monnier as a writer, the former because Monnier saw reality as a series of isolated fragments, which he made no attempt to attach to a picture of society as a whole, the latter because the reproduction of speech in his dialogues was a dangerous example for writers who aimed at an art higher than the comic effects produced in a *vaudeville* at the Palais-Royal or in a novel written to please cooks and concierges.

From the very first, what the critics had praised in Monnier's *Scènes populaires* were his genius for accurate observation of different social classes, especially of the common people, and his talent for the depiction of character. While recognizing his genuine wit and gift for humor and irony, they objected to his choice of boring subjects and his tendency to produce only the shell of reality in photograph or facsimile. Whereas earlier critics appreciated the comic effects produced by his use of exaggeration, the Realists usually deplored this tendency to caricature. On the whole, however, whether to praise as many did or disparage as Flaubert was to do so severely later, there can be no hesitation in fitting the definition of Realism to Monnier's literary work.

He reproduced contemporary life and manners by minute notation of external details and portrayed character in the same way, through tricks and mannerisms of speech. There are many pages which give the impression of a stenographic report, with no setting of the stage, no arrangement of details, no elimination of the insignificant and the digressive. The author rarely betrays his own feelings, although they can sometimes be deduced through the kinds of people he portrays. He does not appear in person to pull the strings, but in his best pages there is a heightening of effect which shows real art. This subtle use of emphasis and exaggeration reveals Monnier's irony, all the more effective because it is suggested obliquely, through dialogue whose apparent naturalness betrays the reader into forgetting that real people's conversation would rarely be so consistently banal, pretentious, heartless, or vicious as it is in the diverse scenes of Monnier's repertory. There is less caricature, however, in his literary work than in his artistic productions; it is as a writer rather than as an artist that he can be called a realist, according to the nineteenth-century definition of that term. It is a remarkable fact that he perfected the genre when Romanticism was at its height, twenty years before it received the definitive sanction of an official appellation.

But Monnier was a precursor of something more than the Realism of the 1850's. He made a contribution also to what the writers of Zola's generation called Naturalism. In 1862 appeared a little group of dialogues called *Les Bas-fonds de la société*, with an interesting introduction showing that the author's goal in this most sordidly unpleasant of his books was the pseudoscientific aim of the Naturalists:

> This book is not written for everyone . . . it is addressed more especially to the bold and vigorous minds which the sight of the whole truth does not frighten, and which by examining, by analyzing that truth, whatever it may be, are sufficiently able and courageous to derive a remedy.
>
> At times we have dramatized what Parent-Duchâtelet [author of a work on prostitution] has described. Our book is as it were a work of social medicine: it

is the physician's speculum. The wound is hideous: a firm eye must resolve to probe it. It is not without sadness that we have decided to turn our pen into a scalpel, and that, after having laughed at the pettiness of this world, we have dared to descend as far as its vices and to look straight in the face the hidden leprosy which devours it.

The philosopher will commend us, the hypocrite will read us in secret, but the depraved, we hope, will shudder upon seeing himself in the mirror which we hold out to him.[20]

This curious preface, the high-flown solemnity of whose style is suggestive of Joseph Prudhomme, fits perfectly into the series of introductions and critical essays which began with Dumas *fils* in the middle of the century to proclaim that the pen must be the instrument of social reform and the regeneration of humanity. Although Monnier had never before expressed a formal conviction of so serious a mission, now he discovered with the most perfect psychological aptness that he had been doing for at least half his life what the disciples of the new sciences were beginning to turn into literature. Whether the idea was his own or his editor's, it led to several editions and reprints of the book, which has rightly been considered one of the chief bases for Monnier's fame.

Three of the scenes had been published much earlier: "L'Exécution" was in the first edition of the *Scènes populaires* (1830); "Un Agonisant" had appeared with the title "La Garde-malade," in the Belgian edition of 1835; "La Consultation" was published as "L'Esprit des campagnes," in the *Nouvelles scènes populaires* (1839). These had been the most somber of the *Scènes populaires,* with little or no comic relief to lighten horrible subjects presented with the utmost cynicism. Monnier retouched them skillfully, shortening the dialogue, omitting irrelevant details, and heightening others calculated to arouse the reader's emotions. It is more effective, for instance, that the patient should die, in "La Garde-malade," instead of continuing to agonize as he does in the original version. In "La Consultation" the cruel avarice and prudent slyness of the old peasant culminate in a defiance of the doctor more violent than their parting words in "L'Esprit des campagnes."

Four other scenes have similar traits of cynicism and brutality, and take their subjects from equally sordid domains. "La Femme du condamné," visiting for the last time the prison cell where her husband is waiting to be executed, is more concerned with carrying away his clothes and watch, which he will not need any longer, than with grief at losing him or remorse over his crime. Her parting advice is that he should see a priest, as a precautionary measure—you never know what may happen—and that he should be brave, as a good example for his little son, who will be coming to see the execution: "Poor child! . . . he doesn't have so much fun as it is! . . ." [21] "L'Eglise française" is a satirical presentation of a new religion, whose priests try to correct by their bonhomie and licentiousness the severity of the "gang of Jesuits" composing the orthodox orders.[22] Although this scene had not previously been published, it is dated 1833, so that it goes back to the period when fantastic sects were springing up in violent reaction to the bigotry of the Church.

The title of "Une Nuit dans un bouge" is self-explanatory. The prostitute has traits which show definite kinship with the Romantic heroines of Hugo's *Marion de Lorme* and Dumas' *La Dame aux camélias:* innocent victim of circumstances, she has not lost her essential purity of soul. There is a touch of melodrama, unusual in Monnier's work, in the mysterious reticence of the client, who confesses at the end that he has probably just murdered another woman's husband. Another dialogue which Monnier must have recited many times, since it is dated 1829, is the short "A la belle étoile," which depends for its effect not only on the two voices, but also on the setting, more fully described than in the other scenes: "Paris, late November, four o'clock in the morning, rue Basse-du-Rempart, opposite the rue de la Paix, and on the boulevard." [23] In this picturesque setting, suggesting the many Romantic melodramas of low life in the great city, Monnier sketched an apache quarrel.

It is a relief to the reader's sensibilities, although the unity of the book is spoiled thereby, that an eighth scene was added to the second edition of *Les Bas-fonds*.[24] "Les Misères cachées," which has no connection with the "lowest depths," is totally different from the other pieces, presenting as it does a grandfather in the exasperating and delightful task of putting to bed his four-year-old grandson. Here there is realism both humorous and charming, without the obvious effort to shock by an accumulation of horror upon ugliness which characterizes the rest of the book. Monnier himself had grandchil-

Portrait of Henry Monnier by Gavarni.

Une Grande Dame.

Promenade à la campagne.

Midi.

Dix heures et demie.

Surnuméraire.

La Famille improvisée.

Monsieur Prudhomme.

Le Pêcheur des côtes.

Vagabond.

Monsieur Prudhomme.

L'Adieu.

La Fuite de l'amour.

Jean Iroux.

Madame Henry Monnier.

Les Voituriers.

L'Huitre et les plaideurs.

La Salle d'attente.

Ecole des orphelins, Amsterdam.

dren by that time, and what a grandfather he must have been! None of the sentimentality of Victor Hugo, but a mock dignity and severe formality which cover the deepest tenderness. Undeniably out of place from the artistic point of view, the scene succeeds paradoxically in demonstrating by contrast with the others the difference between the true representation of real life and that "realism" which was not a reaction to Romanticism, as it has been called, but a prolongation of it.

XII

1849–1877: THEATRICAL VENTURES THE SECOND EMPIRE—OLD AGE

For a few years after 1849, Henry Monnier had considerable success as an actor. His peculiarly natural transposition of life to the stage, which had been enjoyed as a comic novelty twenty years before, was admired now by a public accustomed to greater realism than had been the fashion when Romantic drama was at its height.

He was not the only man who contributed during those years to a slow change in some of the stage conventions so dear to the Conservatory and the Comédie-Française. The famous character actor, Frédéric Lemaître, a specialist in low society, had long shocked classical critics by the realism of his costumes, gestures, and declamation. A few directors had begun to realize the need of giving this kind of acting a more realistic setting than furniture painted on a backdrop, and Monnier's friend, Nestor Roqueplan, had tried the experiment, startling enough in the 1840's, of using real furniture and carpets. Alexandre Dumas had supervised the elaborately accurate costumes and properties of his historical plays. Twenty years later his son went a step further, emphasizing the difference in value between a realistic set, which merely depended, after all, on the mechanical skill of the decorator, and the actor's art, which was essential in creating the illusion of reality.

In the summer of 1849 Monnier appeared at the Théâtre des Variétés, first in a revival of *La Famille improvisée*, wherein a new generation had the opportunity of admiring his skill in taking five different parts, and then in a one-act comedy-*vaudeville*, *Les Compatriotes*, essentially the same scene which had appeared under the title in the *Nouvelles scènes populaires* in 1839. Here again Monnier performed his tour de force of playing a multiple role, rendering with perfect fidelity the amusing accent of the three southerners who came from their home town to harass their old friend in Paris.

Théophile Gautier, who later disparaged severely Monnier's value as a creative artist, accepted as a remarkable feat of "intellectual photography" the ability to give the illusion of complete reality, as Monnier seems to have done in those performances of 1849. In *La Presse* Gautier called the actor the most sincere realist possible, because he succeeded in reproducing with absolute exactness genuine truth. He recognized an element of this realism which the critics of the original production of *La Famille improvisée* had not mentioned—Monnier's careful make-up and choice of costume, apparently remarkable in contrast with the more haphazard practices of other French actors:

> Like the English actors whom he seems to have studied and to whom he is not without some resemblance, Henry Monnier takes the greatest pains with his make-up; and in his case making-up does not mean drawing on your face at random a few lines in burnt Siena or China ink: each touch is thought out, placed where it belongs as if in a picture; the characteristic lines and wrinkles are incredibly right; that red spot near the nostril might have been put there by Balzac; Meissonier alone could find that puce-colored dressing-gown which contains the whole eighteenth century, for the smallest detail has its importance in Monnier's roles: the writer observes, the painter sketches, the actor executes. Hence that perfect harmony, that absolute illusion.[1]

Other journalists gave him equally high praise. *La Silhouette* made an interesting comparison between the characters Monnier created, so natural that they seemed endowed with as much individuality as the people met in real life, and the puppets which passed through the intricacies of the well-made play, losing all character as they were maneuvered on and off the stage in preparation for a cleverly prepared denouement. More than a skillful actor, Monnier had the infinite patience to study human nature and to create an artistic masterpiece in which the critic admired his "melancholy buffoonery . . . comic by dint of its wit, frightening by dint of its truthfulness." [2]

Although his significance as an actor was beginning at last to be appreciated, Monnier's stage career was, as always, a stormy one. Fundamentally good-natured as he seems to have been, his undisciplined individualism revealed itself in misunderstandings and quarrels with stage managers and directors. Perhaps they found his sense of humor as exasperating as it had been to his superiors when he was a young government employee and art student. For anecdotes continue to tell of practical jokes played on fellow actors: A courtier, not realizing that he is wearing his hat over his wig, takes from Monnier a second one just as he steps from the wings to appear respectfully before the king, hat in hand; the monarch's frantic stage whisper of "Take off your hat, you fool!" upsets him so completely that he tries to put on the second one, knocks off the first, and sends it rolling over the footlights.[3] Such a prank would no doubt be detrimental to a conviction that Monnier himself should be taken seriously as an actor, and he never found a director willing to encourage his dream of acting at the Comédie-Française and having a play performed on that august stage. But he never seemed to realize that the fault might lie with him.

When in 1850 the administration of the Théâtre des Variétés was changed, and in spite of Monnier's successful appearances his contract was not renewed, it was with anger and bitterness that he left Paris to play again in the south. In a long and rather pathetic letter to the actor Samson, he poured out his disappointment, and found comfort, as he so often was able to do, in the hope of writing a great masterpiece, producing it with the finest cast he could assemble, and thus avenging himself on the theater which had treated him so unfairly:

> They shall rue it, and it is you whom I entrust, friend, with my revenge. Yes, I am doing a comedy for you, the plan is fixed upon, the first act is roughly drafted, there will be two, in verse, a comedy of character such as the one I had sent you, which I had done alone and which they left on my hands when I asked for a collaborator. There you have the story of my whole life: *facit indignatio versum* . . . Yes, dear friend, never have they known how to make the most of me in the theater, and they have never wanted me to make the most of myself . . .
>
> *Don't speak of my play* before I have read it to you and it has been approved by you. I love your part like one of my children. You will be delightful in it, and if the one I intend for Madame Allan comes as I conceive it, if I can carry it out as well as I want to do, she will be satisfied with it.
>
> Farewell, I am going to rehearse, for I am playing and rehearsing. Remember me to your nice family; we shall do some more charades next winter. I am playing, writing plays, sketching, and doing for the *Siècle* some articles on my journey. Thanks, Monsieur Thibeaudeau, you were a bad actor, you are a stupid director. You will prove it to him. Always your devoted . . .[4]

Monnier's failure to produce a great play for the Comédie-Française or to realize his dream of acting there was certainly not due to indolence on his part. After the busy months in the south he returned to Parnes where he finished the play to which his letter alluded, presumably the unfortunate *Peintres et bourgeois*, his one attempt at a three-act comedy in verse, which was to be given at the Odéon, in 1855. He also prepared for publication in the *Siècle* the *Voyages d'un comédien*, which appeared on March 11, May 22, and July 13, 1851. Correspondence between Monnier and his old friend Louis Desnoyers over these articles shows that their relations continued cordial enough for Monnier to write freely of his plans and hopes:

> I am sending you, my dear Desnoyers, by one of my friends, an article on Nismes to follow those which you have had published already.
>
> I expect to go to see you as soon as I have given the last touch to several things that I have on the stocks, including two plays destined for the Comédie-Française (old style).
>
> In the solitude in which I live I am not in a position to receive much advice, I count on you to know how I stand.
>
> You will see whether your predictions come true, and whether I am as worthy as you have always thought to tackle high comedy, if it doesn't succeed it never will, *car j'ai été dessus tout* . . .[5]

The second play mentioned here must have been *Grandeur et décadence de Monsieur Joseph Prudhomme*, in which Monnier in a sense achieved his revenge on the stupid people who did not appreciate him. Playing the title role at the Odéon in November 1852, at last he gave full stature to the character that had become the most popular in his repertory since its first appearances more than twenty years earlier in monologues, in the *Scènes populaires* and *La Famille improvisée*.[6]

Even the Goncourts, later so unfriendly to Monnier, were enthusiastic over his Prudhomme, calling the play "the second social comedy of the century," the counterpart and complement of Daumier's *Robert Macaire*, since the one represented the promoter and the other the stockholder, and both satirized the bourgeois: "O bourgeois! as if it were not enough that Daumier's pencil had vilified every phase of your existence . . . Here is Monnier, the mocking monographer, the stolid *cabrion*, who puts his arms into the sleeves of your coat, places your spectacles on his nose, assumes your gestures, your brain, your snuffbox, and at the Odéon, before a full house, shows off your disembodied, witless person." Like Gautier, they paid tribute to the naturalness of Monnier's acting in a role which could have become mere farce: "All the more merit in Henry Monnier for having made of it a genuine character when it was so easy to make it into caricature." [7]

How difficult it is a century later to imagine the ephemeral and indescribable quality of an actor's performance! The Prudhomme of Monnier's drawings has the grotesque exaggeration of caricature. While the portraits of Monnier in the role of Prudhomme have a greater flesh-and-blood reality, the impression is still comparable to that made by portraits of Monsieur Jourdain or Mr. Pickwick, comic creations which are also caricatures. There is no doubt, however, that Monnier's bourgeois is less farcical, both in the play of 1852 and in the *Mémoires* of 1857, than in his earlier scenes. The comments of contemporary critics indicate that he must have played with more restraint than formerly, giving to the part a perfection which went beyond mere mimicry or photography and achieved that illusion of reality which is more true than reality itself.

After this success Monnier continued his engagement at the Odéon, but again he began to express dissatisfaction with the parts offered to him, accused the directors of unfairness, and finally presented his resignation, which was apparently accepted with a certain feeling of relief on both sides. Unable to find another engagement in Paris, Monnier was obliged in bitter winter weather to take to the road, where he complained less of physical discomfort than of having to play with fourth-rate provincial companies. Fortunately he found cordial hospitality along the way. At Chartres he was received by relatives of his good friend Noël Parfait, in Brussels by his publisher Hetzel and the artist Madou, and he was able to forget his troubles in gay festivity.

In February 1855 he appeared again in Paris, in a program of two short plays at the Palais-Royal: the "Roman chez la portière," taken from one of the earliest and best-known *scènes populaires*, and adding to the actor's famous character parts the impersonation of Madame Desjardins, the concierge;[8] and "Le Bonheur de vivre aux champs," a new and amusing skit in which Monnier played several rural individuals who contribute to destroy the bourgeois' dream of idyllic country life.[9] The same year another of his plays was produced at the Odéon, although he did not appear in it. This may have been the great masterpiece of which he had written so optimistically to Samson. Written in collaboration with Jules Renoult, *Peintres et bourgeois* tried to turn into a problem play the old enmity which had been amusingly and realistically presented in the *scène populaire*, "Le Peintre et les bourgeois." Since a plot had to be devised, the conflict between the merchant's desire for money and the painter's struggle to express his artistic dreams was resolved for no logical reason by marrying the daughter of the bourgeois to the artist. A few scenes among the *rapins* of a Latin Quarter studio may have contributed to the moderate success of the play.[10] Monnier complained as usual of being badly treated by the management, but found characteristic consolation in the fact that there were not only fifteen performances in Paris, but a comparable number in Lyons, in Marseilles, and in Bordeaux.

In June 1856 Monnier appeared at the Théâtre des Variétés in a new arrangement of *Joseph Prudhomme*, shortened to three acts and "seasoned with couplets," wrote Boutet de Monvel, who remarked that Prudhomme was beginning to take on a somewhat historic character, losing a little of the piquancy of contemporary freshness he had had during the July Monarchy: "Like all political plays, it had become a little dated and already during the Empire required for many people certain annotations." By thus relegating to the past the bourgeois as symbolized in Monsieur Prudhomme, this comment reveals an interesting tendency to repudiate those permanent traits which were to give Monnier's creation its enduring vitality.[11]

Although Monnier's last play gave him another of his multiple roles, it was unsuccessful. It was *Les Métamorphoses de Chamoiseau*, produced at the Variétés in August of that year.[12] Even the author, whose critical sense was seldom keen when applied to his own work, admitted that the play was too hastily thrown together, although, he said, it was good enough for the summer season. The action is based on a series of disguises adopted by Monsieur Chamoiseau in a complicated plot to get rid of his wife by marrying off his daughter, and contains one amusing episode of a mesmerizer which shows that Monnier had not lost his eye for the silliness of passing fads.

With the failure of this play began a particularly trying time. Monnier's father had died the year before, leaving to his son the small family estate of Les Godebins, at Parnes. This property, to which Henry clung as Parisians always cling to whatever bit of land they own in the country, was badly in need of repairs and every expedient was tried that could bring in a little money. The Belgian publisher Hetzel issued a series of reprints of the *Scènes populaires*,[13] but disappointed Monnier by continuing to delay the publication of a new work which had been in his hands, apparently, for ten years or more. This was what Monnier called his *Sacrements*, though it was finally published with the title *Nouvelles scènes populaires—La Religion des imbéciles*.[14] In spite of the startling title, the work was inoffensive enough, as Monnier prudently explained in his preface: "It is well understood that it is not at religious ceremonies that we intend to laugh here; but only at foolish and ignorant people."

The *Mémoires de Monsieur Joseph Prudhomme* were published in 1857,[15] but again Monnier was unlucky, for the publisher was in financial straits and could pay him nothing. The usual expedient of a tour in the provinces brought some relief, at the cost of hardships increasingly fatiguing. Always popular at Lyons, Monnier played there for five weeks, and traveled through the south in his favorite role of the *Malade imaginaire*, the only classical part he is definitely known to have played often and successfully. A little later he was in the north, offering *Joseph Prudhomme* to the inhabitants of Liège, whose cool welcome showed that on the stage Prudhomme's star must have been setting. An attempt to renew his fame in a stupid *vaudeville*, *Joseph Prudhomme chef des brigands*, given at the Variétés in 1860, was a complete failure.[16]

What would years of association with Monsieur Prudhomme suggest to Monnier under such painful circumstances? During the Second Empire the wave of speculation which had begun to flow with the encouragement of Robert Macaire and his prototypes of the July Monarchy had overwhelmed Parisian society in an optimistic rush to acquire overnight fortunes which might be spent the next day on the pleasures of that luxurious era. The sly and unscrupulous promoter whom Daumier represented profiting by the stupid greed of the middle class was replaced by the financial wizard, like Lucien Duplessis in Bulwer-Lytton's *The Parisians,** whose advice was sought even by aristocrats of the bluest blood, not above tripling their income by skillful investments.

For several years Monnier had been enjoying the friendship of a Maecenas in the person of Isidore Salles, himself an amateur poet, friend of writers and artists, whose position as director of the *bureau de la Presse* at the Ministry of the Interior gave him opportunity for official patronage. Salles obtained for Monnier in 1857 a literary indemnity of three hundred francs, tiny, to be sure, but the only recognition he ever received from the government. There were more disinterested services too, as Monnier's letters show, for the actor-artist never hesitated to appeal to his benefactor to use his influence in favor of some young friend in want. And Salles seems to have been the confidant of Monnier's business affairs. Through a letter to him is revealed a curious lawsuit which the artist lost in 1858, concerning some drawings done for the King of Prussia. In another letter Monnier asked for an appointment in order to submit to Salles certain papers explaining a plan for making his fortune. It seems that a friend, entirely respectable and occupying a high position with the railroads, had invited him to lend his name to a project involving a capital of some eight hundred thousand francs, of which Monnier would receive one hundred thousand if his name headed the charter, which had to be obtained through Salles' Ministry. Nothing more is heard of the matter, but it is certain that Monnier never possessed that mirific sum.

A third letter to Salles dealt with theatrical troubles, expressing the familiar grievance against unappreciative directors, who this time had evidently refused a new full-length play in verse which Monnier had submitted to the Odéon and had planned optimistically to offer at last to the Comédie-Française.† Nothing is known of that

* Bulwer-Lytton describes the feverish preoccupation with money and the speculations on the Bourse during the Second Empire.

† In this letter, Monnier was especially angry because the administration of the Odéon excused its refusal on the grounds that it had thought the play written by Marc Monnier. There has been some confusion between Henry Monnier and contemporaries of the same name; see Champfleury, pp. 290–301. These letters to Isidore Salles are published in Marie, pp. 132–133.

play. It may have been referred to in an earlier letter to an unknown collaborator, who was apparently working on a scenario for which Henry was to write the dialogue: "Let us try to be frank: what I must have is a fully outlined plan, scene by scene, on which I can embroider and compose my dialogue, which is child's play for me . . ." [17]

It is interesting that Monnier himself should have realized so clearly his inability to construct a well-organized plan. Whenever a plot was necessary, he had recourse to the help of collaborators. His own talent lay in creating character and writing dialogue rather than in inventing and sustaining action. His great misfortune all his life, which can only be attributed to a lack of critical discernment concerning himself—for he would not have been so clever a caricaturist had he been unable to evaluate other people—lay in the choice of collaborators.* Again and again Joseph Prudhomme or another of Monnier's personages appeared in a *comédie-vaudeville* of no interest. If Balzac, who was fascinated by Prudhomme, had finished any of his projected comedies dealing with that gentleman, a vehicle worthy of Monnier might have given him a more lasting place in the history of the French theater.

On the other hand, would not any play whose plot and action conformed to conventional demands of dramatic construction destroy to some extent the illusion of reality which Monnier created by the very absence of dramatic effects? Perhaps it was his lot to live too soon; Antoine might have found a collaborator able to set Monnier's characters into a "slice of life" which the audience of the Théâtre-Libre would have appreciated as comic relief after the plays of Jean Jullien or Georges Ancey. Or, if Monnier had been Antoine's contemporary, a scene from the *Bas-fonds de la société* might well have appealed to the director who produced such a picture of Parisian low life as Oscar Méténier's *En famille*.

How much Antoine would have admired Monnier's acting is

* What Champfleury called his *rage de collaboration* led Monnier indeed to incredible lengths, even to suggesting that Octave Feuillet, as fellow-author of *proverbes* join him in preparing a play for the Odéon—perhaps the play mentioned above. Feuillet had just made his debut in the *Revue des deux mondes* with polished scenes of the drawing-room type, pleasing to feminine readers. Champfleury, pp. 306–310.

another interesting subject for speculation. Although his natural speech and realistic gestures, make-up, and costumes seem to forecast the so-called reforms which Antoine was to establish in reaction to the stiff conventions of the French stage, Monnier was perhaps too individualistic to fit into Antoine's conception of a theatrical troupe as an ensemble of players "of equal ability, of ordinary talent, of simple personality, who would yield always and in spite of everything to that fundamental law of ensemble." [18]

As is so often the case, Monnier's strength as a monologuist was his weakness as an ensemble actor. He may have been handicapped by a poor memory, since he admitted that he had difficulty in memorizing his lines. In a monologue, such a defect could be concealed by improvisation. An additional handicap to his success on the professional stage, and the fundamental reason why he was so unfortunate in the matter of a vehicle, was the fact that from the very first he was typed. His brilliant performance in *La Famille improvisée* had led to expectations that a similar tour de force would be repeated every time he appeared in a new comedy. He was more and more identified with Prudhomme also, so that it seems as though he never had real opportunity to prove his ability in more varied repertory.

Long before Antoine's time Monnier took part in a curious attempt to create a free theater in Paris in a special genre. Inspired perhaps by the popularity of the marionettes which amused grown-ups as well as children in the Tuileries Gardens, a group of young men decided to set up a marionette theater for adults, where plays would be given to which good Monsieur Prudhomme would never have taken his wife and daughter. Amédée Rolland offered for the Erôtikon Théatron the entrance hall of his small house at 54 rue de la Santé, in the Batignolles quarter. Under the direction of Lemercier de Neuville, a puppet specialist whose *Théâtre des pupazzi* forms an important chapter in the history of modern marionettes, the stage was built, sixteen feet deep and fitted with complicated machinery and elaborate sets. The actor Demarsy, who was something of a sculptor, carved wooden heads for the marionettes, which were dressed by amiable actress friends of the group and worked by Lemercier de Neuville and the playwright Jean Duboys. The lines in each play were to be read by the author himself.

talent, until among the young men who dabbled in literature and the theater during the latter part of the Second Empire scarcely one is widely remembered today. It seems as though repeated frustration of the romantic ideal had caused not only the impairment of physical health and intellectual vigor, but also a renunciation of all effort.

A third revolution had again failed to realize the hopes of the liberals, who saw their republican dreams crushed under the benevolent despotism of Napoleon III. The freedom of the press was limited by rigid censorship and any discussion in which could be detected a strongly political flavor became immediately suspect. In renouncing the responsibilities of personal freedom, the people were reacting against sixty years of restless struggle whose painfully acquired rewards had again and again been offset by disappointment and disillusionment. Now they were told that they had chosen their lot, that they had nothing more to worry about and should give themselves up to a good time. Never had life in Paris been so comfortable, never had there been more money to spend on pleasures and luxuries. Theater lovers were assured of good entertainment by the veterans of the well-made play, Scribe, Augier, and Dumas *fils*. The race track at Auteuil was thronged, and the exclusive Jockey Club became arbiter of masculine manners and morals. For the working class there was more popular entertainment, such as a balloon ascension featuring a man mounted on a pony. This had taken place in 1850, but is a characteristic opening act for two decades of oddities and extravaganzas. The climax came in 1867, when Paris was dedicated as the capital of pleasure in the first international exposition, and all heads were turned by an array of visitors such as had not been seen since the triumphal entry of the allied sovereigns in 1814: the Tsar and the Sultan, the Prince of Wales, William of Prussia and Bismarck, already laying the plans which were to be carried out only three years later.

Contemporary writers complained bitterly of the decadent materialism of the period. Everywhere cheap substitutes, they said, were replacing the solid values of the old days: cotton had taken the place of good wool and linen, imitation jewelry was all the rage, palates dulled by beer drinking no longer appreciated fine wines.

Just as charity had become organized philanthropy, so pleasure had become debauchery, and good taste had vanished with individual liberty.* An attitude of sterile negation replaced the more constructive optimism of the generation of 1830. The Romanticists too had seen the evils of contemporary life, but they had dreamed of remedying them and they had expressed their hopes in the language of noble sentiments and poetic aspirations. In spite of their mockery of middle-class ideals, or perhaps by that very mockery, they had kept their respect for a few sacred tenets.

To pessimistic critics it seemed as though the generation of the 1860's respected nothing, not even its own deepest feelings. It had learned from the Realists to beware of excessive lyricism. Fearing to sound insincere if it voiced high-flown sentiments, it adopted a pose of indifference which tended inevitably to become genuine inability to feel deeply. As the word "virtue," having become the property of political orators and professional moralists, could no longer be pronounced without mockery, there was hesitancy in admitting the existence of the thing itself. The spirit of mockery, which is so essentially French, assumed a special form to which was given the name *la blague*. The *blagueur* was different from the *mystificateur* of earlier days. His sense of humor was less frankly Rabelaisian, more blasé; he was less likely to play jokes on your person than to make fun of your ideas and your convictions. One of the characters in Augier's *La Contagion* attributed this attitude of derision to the low moral and intellectual level of a generation which with feigned or genuine indifference labeled as pedantic whatever it could not understand. A later and more tolerant study of the mid-nineteenth century by Paul Valéry defined *la blague* as a kind of shame, concealing a deeply rooted unwillingness to expose sacred things to the devastating positivism of modern science.[21]

The group of young men whom Monnier encountered at the Théâtre Erotique represented some of the most deplorable traits of

* Such criticism is comparable to the complaints of certain middle-aged Frenchmen in the 1920's and 1930's: Mechanized production, imported from America along with high-pressure advertising, has destroyed the national genius, which reached its highest expression in the painstaking handwork of the past; in the speed and standardization of modern life the essential character of Paris has been lost.

that generation. Drinking their beer at the Brasserie des Martyrs, they dabbled in a republicanism composed of unenlightened admiration for the French Revolution, adored Rabelais without reading him, and, realizing that they could never hope to enter the temple of art and letters, called themselves rebels and indulged in scornful criticism of other more industrious and wholehearted worshipers. They were indeed far from fulfilling Balzac's or Hugo's glorious conception of the artist!

The artistic productions of Henry Monnier's old age are of more value than his last dramatic work. Here he continued to fill his role as observer and castigator of the weaknesses and follies of mankind, presenting with an enlivening point of satire numerous scenes of manners which form the largest part of his production after 1860. These scenes were done in ink or pencil, or more often in water color with a strengthening of outlines and shadows by the addition of pen work. In both medium and composition they suggest Daumier more closely than did any of Monnier's earlier work. In such pictures as the "Lecture d'un testament," with its group of legatees whose faces show all degrees of expectation, greed, and disappointed hope, or "Un rasoir," who crushes his glassy-eyed victim under the weight of his aggressive stupidity, or "L'Huître et les plaideurs," in which the fable is illustrated by a fat and periwigged magistrate who offers in each hand an oyster to his discomfited clients, vigorously drawn figures dominate a simple setting, in contrast to Monnier's earlier habit of placing small people against a minutely detailed background. That he could achieve charm as well as truth in the portrayal of character is shown by the little scene, "Dans un salon," which represents a fresh and graceful young girl seated beside her elderly mother, listening presumably to a parlor performer who is not visible. In this case the scene is completed by an unobtrusive suggestion of elegance in the background.[22]

Monnier continued to do portraits, especially of actors in costume, but his favorite subject was still Monsieur Prudhomme, occupying his pedestal of pompous self-righteousness. As Henry was his own model for Prudhomme, it is interesting to note that with the invention of photography he found a new technique. Champfleury tells how he used to pose before the camera, in various positions expressing particular emotions, later working from the photographs. Being what would today be called extremely photogenic, he was able in this way to preserve facial expressions and gestures, which he studied and copied not only in his drawings but also in his acting. When the ordinary daguerreotypes and stiffly unnatural photographs of the period are compared with sketches made from Monnier's photographs, the vivacity and expressiveness of the latter suggest that he would have made a fine moving-picture actor!

During the last years of the Second Empire and after the Franco-Prussian War, Monnier frequented the studio of the sculptor Jules-Pierre Mène, at 19 rue de l'Entrepôt. As long ago as 1833 Monnier had begun to inscribe the name of Mène on sketches and water colors, and their friendship seems to have grown with passing years until Mène became the most congenial companion of Monnier's old age. Just before the war broke out in 1870 they took a trip together to Contrexéville, in the Vosges, where Monnier may have tried the waters to allay the increasing severity of his gout, and each of them made as a souvenir of this excursion a portrait of "M. Prudhomme à Contrexéville." Besides innumerable scenes of manners and portraits of Prudhomme in various characteristic situations, Monnier illustrated for Mène a volume of the *Bas-fonds*. But all these indications of the close sympathy between the two men are less revealing, perhaps, than Henry's habit of dashing off a sketch instead of a letter to his friend, such as the picture of "M. Prudhomme portant des dossiers" bearing the inscription: "My dear Mène, M. Prudhomme will tell you that today I am dull. Are you like me?"—or a portrait of Monnier-Prudhomme, seen from the rear, his fat body buttoned tightly in Prudhomme's long coat, as he waddles on gouty feet toward the studio of Mène, with the caption: "M. Prudhomme devouring the distance from the rue Ventadour to the rue de l'Entrepôt." [23]

In Mène's studio might be encountered, until his death in 1870, that other comrade of youthful days, Alexandre Dumas, still a great talker, who held the center of the stage until Monnier was heard climbing the stairs. Then everyone would wait expectantly to see what character the old actor would adopt for his entrance and what new *mystification* he would devise. After the war the group was augmented by occasional appearances of Charles Gounod and by the frequent presence of another of the younger men who were Monnier's good friends, the engraver and print collector Hector Giacomelli.*

It is pleasant to think that the man who had given so generously of his talent for the entertainment of his comrades should still be welcomed among the artists whose appreciation must have meant much to him. Until he was too ill to enjoy such social pleasures, Monnier continued his lifelong habit of dining out. In the homes where in earlier days he had been the center of the party, he was given his place beside the fire after dinner and left undisturbed to enjoy his pipe and his nap, during which it was his custom to shade his eyes by pulling down his wig. When the wig was put back into place it was a signal that the others need no longer talk in whispers and that Henry Monnier was ready to join the conversation. He was still gay, still quick to flare up at a suspected affront, such as the indignity of having to wait for his dinner. Some people accused him of avarice, because he never refused a free meal; they would have been astounded to realize the genuine poverty concealed by a pride which kept him always immaculately dressed and ostensibly free from the pecuniary worries confided only to a few intimates. Even when a sale of his works was organized by his friends the profits were scanty, because it was so hard to believe that a man was in great need who dined with such lively appetite and told his clever stories with a sparkling vigor almost as dramatic as the pantomimed monologues of younger days.[24]

The apartment on the rue Ventadour continued to be Monnier's Paris headquarters. He must have been there during the war, for after the Théâtre des Variétés was transformed into a hospital, Monnier came to entertain the wounded soldiers. Dignified and clean shaven like the heavy father of comedy, wearing gold-rimmed spectacles on his Roman nose and a capable and self-satisfied air, the old actor would tell his comic or indelicate stories as he solemnly took snuff from his snuffbox and looked about him with the serene imperturbability of Monsieur Prudhomme.[25]

* Giacomelli's painstaking and delicate illustrations of birds make him a successor of Audubon.

In the good season Monnier spent much time at Parnes, leading the peaceful life of a country gentleman in the simple but comfortable old house at Les Godebins. His son and daughters were all married, and it seems that the faithful Caroline was appreciated at last, for Henry wrote to his old friend Madou, still living in Brussels, that his wife was, as she had always been, the best of wives and mothers.[26] Monnier was no great hand at gardening, as was rather caustically observed by a good peasant neighbor who used to help Madame Monnier with the housework, but he liked to wander about with a pruning knife in his hand, inspecting his orchard and strolling in what he called pretentiously the "path of sighs." In a letter to Mène he described his rustic existence, typically that of the Parisian who, like the bourgeois whom Monnier himself had so often made fun of, has retired to the country to end his days among his own radishes and apple-trees:

Parnes, July, 1874.

It is Sunday, and pouring rain, so my family will not go to mass. I resign myself to that all the more readily because it gives me an excuse for not accepting an invitation in the neighborhood where we would have to drink and eat as they drink and eat in the country.

I have here an exceptional location, half-way up a hill; I command the whole region, no one overlooks me. I have contrived not to be seen: trees conceal my house, whose windows looked out on a bare plain, and they cut me off from it. I am quite isolated, and at the end of my garden is an orchard which leads to the village. To get there I cross the Cudron, a charming little shady brook with ducks and cows, which I fully expect some day to show to the whole Mène family, and even to the Barbediennes.

My cider has turned out very well, and I offer myself what my father called *lampées* of it with a fine rich *galette* which they are making for me today; I'm going to have a treat! And to think that if it weren't for this fine Republic, I should be so happy in my little manor house, six months of the year, then the others, in retouching and mounting . . .

You would be very surprised to see me here with a spade in my hand, and my wife slipping beautiful roses.

I have taken up again the volume at which I have been working part of this summer, then I intend to do some cows and landscape . . .[27]

A true Parisian could not be content for long in that rural setting, and Monnier was still busy with restless and hopeful projects. A letter to Giacomelli told that he was working hard on a text illustrated with wood engravings:

You cannot imagine the work I have had to do since we saw each other. I have written approximately one volume, that is to say that with my corrections and the trouble it has caused me I have done at least two. When I write I tire, especially because ideas come thick and fast and I have the greatest difficulty in putting them together, the whole thing accompanied by drawings on paper and on wood.

After that interesting sidelight on his method of working, the letter continues rather pathetically:

Then topping everything, worries of which you know a part. I will admit to you that I should have had a more peaceful old age. When people see me they think me the luckiest of mortals. The contrary is more nearly true. Fortunately the happiness of my friends does not make me jealous, and your last letter set me to rights, especially coming one day when I was, as the English say, full of *blue devils.*

That Monnier was capable of deep affection toward his friends is shown by the more cheerful conclusion of the letter:

Indeed what to complain of when one has friends like those I possess, who appreciate me enough to tell me about their windfalls, like this last one you have just sent me. Madou, my old friend Madou, has written to me; his letter is so good and friendly that I shall have to give up my trip to Vienne [?] in order to go to Brussels to take over the apartment which he has had arranged *à mon fait exprès,* as they say around here. I have a few *sous,* he tells me in closing his letter.

Doncques à bientôt, cher ami, mes hommages et amitiés.
Toto corde
Henry Monnier.

My love to the people at Chesnay. Tell them that I think of them, and of the happiness I shall have in seeing them soon again.[28]

Monnier did in fact go to Brussels that year and had the pleasure of seeing again the Belgian artists Madou and Verboeckhoven. To the former he revealed an ambition which only Prudhomme could have conceived, the desire to be decorated! It seems that he had once been dining in company with several Academicians, who expressed surprise that such a prominent actor had never received that honor. The idea had stayed in Monnier's mind, and he decided now to ask Madou to start a movement in Brussels in the hope that the impetus might reach Paris. This ambition, like the wish to act at the Comédie-Française, was never fulfilled, and Monnier died still unreconciled to the failure of his career as an actor.

In addition to the gout which made it more and more difficult for him to get about, he suffered from asthma and had to sleep sitting in an armchair. For two years he was confined almost entirely to his apartment, where he died, true Parisian to the end. After his death in January 1877, among the many articles about him in newspapers and periodicals there appeared an account of one of the last visits he had received. It was New Year's Eve and the artist was busy preparing the traditional calling cards for the next day, writing in his most florid hand a witty word for each of his special friends, even sketching here and there the profile of Monsieur Prudhomme. On the table beneath the lamp lay a water color portrait of himself in the costume of Prudhomme, which he had been copying from a photograph by Carjat. Greeting his caller with hospitable warmth, the old man got up to show how well he was able to walk without a cane and boasted proudly that he had not had a cold all winter. "Furthermore, unparalleled attentions!" he added in Joseph Prudhomme's stentorian voice, for the benefit of his wife and children in the next room. He was not eager to venture out of doors, however, for he had decided that walking was a waste of time and that he preferred to stay peacefully in his armchair. How did he pass the time? By reviewing his classics. And he began to recite the scene between Orgon and Cléante, in *Tartuffe:*

> Les bons et vrais dévots, qu'on doit suivre à la trace,
> Ne sont pas ceux aussi qui font tant de grimace,
> Eh quoi! vous ne ferez nulle distinction
> Entre l'hypocrisie et la dévotion? [29]

He stopped to light his pipe, and when it was drawing well, he began the scene again, this time giving it as it was played when he was young by Saint-Aulaire and Baptiste *cadet*. "Yes, they spoke through their noses like that, and everyone thought it was charming. There were also people in those days who wrote tragedies called *Parthénopenon* or perhaps *Artaxercès*. They used to call that 'gathering laurels in the sacred wood where dwells the Muse.' " Then Monnier began to speak of the friends he had outlived and of the changes in Paris, especially in his quarter where they were tearing down the old windmills. His quiet apartment was the same, however, with his father's portrait in water colors, Henry's portrait by Gavarni, the study of a horse's head by Géricault, a page of manuscript music signed by Rossini. As his guest rose to leave, Monnier promised to read to him soon a play he had nearly finished, which he intended to offer to the Palais-Royal.[30]

This play may have been one which Champfleury had suggested, much to his succeeding embarrassment. He had said casually a year or two before that he considered Monnier's "Partie de campagne" one of his most theatrical scenes. From that moment on, Monnier gave him no peace, insisting that they collaborate in what he was sure would be a first-rate comedy. He would furnish the incidents from his own childhood experiences and family memories and Champfleury would supply the action. Only a week or two before his death, when Champfleury went to see him he was greeted by the opening lines of *their* play: "The curtain rises. The doorbell rings. Offstage a woman's voice: 'Wait a moment, I am in my nightgown.' 'What difference does that make? Open anyhow.'" After this the asthmatic old actor wheezed out fragments of a *vaudeville* he had heard as a child, "La Leçon de botanique," of which he recited in Prudhomme's pompous manner a father's moral lesson to his daughter: "Remember, *especially in the future*, that it is better to place one's secrets in the bosom of a father than in that of a flower." [31]

And so at the end he relived the dearest part of his life, which had been the theater.

Henry Monnier's funeral was held at the parish church of Saint-Roch and his body was escorted by a procession of the painters, sculptors, musicians, actors, and writers who had known and respected the originality of his talents and the charm of his personality. He was to be buried at Parnes. At the Gare Saint-Lazare, after the formal speeches were ended, the casket was lifted on to the train. As the porters were struggling awkwardly with their burden, one of them was heard to pronounce a "caption" which Monnier himself could not have surpassed: "Just pull the parcel a little to the right." [32]

XIII

MONNIER, BALZAC, AND FLAUBERT

Of the great writers of the nineteenth century the two whose work shows the closest affinity to Henry Monnier's are Balzac and Flaubert. The former is more directly connected, so closely in fact that Monnier can be given the honor of having furnished him with certain elements in his great study of French society. In Flaubert's case there is no indication of direct borrowing, but a comparison of the two writers, who had before their eyes the same objects and reached similar conclusions about them, serves as a double check on the veracity of their observations.

A few days after Monnier's death there appeared in *L'Illustration* a brief article which started a prolonged and sometimes bitter discussion of the relations between Monnier and Balzac, and the latter's indebtedness to Monnier. Reporting a conversation with Balzac many years before, the artist Bertall quoted him as saying:

> Henry Monnier is a very curious person, very strange and very witty. But with him everything is superficial, he represents better than anyone our unbelieving, mocking era, sceptical and unaware of its own significance. Without guidance, without criterion, and without a goal, when he makes fun of Monsieur Prudhomme, he does not even know he is making fun of himself.

After this comment Balzac added the words which proved to be so inflammatory:

> You will see how precious he has been to me in giving to my work the aspect of the times. You will find him everywhere mingled with the action, and you will hear his mocking laugh sounding at every moment through the anthem of passions, sentiments, and dreams. My Bixiou is Henry Monnier; I have emphasized certain of his traits; I have enlarged him a little, but it is he himself.[1]

When Champfleury published his biography of Monnier two years later, he took up the matter again, reproaching Balzac for having painted such a disagreeable and unjust portrait but not attempting to deny the likeness. Immediately he received a letter from Monnier's widow, protesting against the comparison with Bixiou:

But how does it happen that you, who appreciate him better than anyone, who seem to love him sincerely, you should have recalled that infamous article of M. de Balzac's, if indeed it is done as a portrait of Henry Monnier? Because of a few points of resemblance, it is to my mind a malice which does more harm to its author than to the one against whom it is directed. And the *Figaro*, which I thought a friend of yours, published: "*the most perfect, the most finished, the most striking portrait, as well as the most unpleasant, is the one which bears Balzac's signature.*" And first of all, for a portrait to be *perfect*, it must be a likeness, and M. Balzac's filthy personage, who *insulted especially what he did not understand*, has never, thank God, borne the slightest likeness to Henry Monnier. Forgive me, dear sir, but I can not tell you how that article offended and grieved me . . . I was so happy with those memories which you retrace so clearly before my eyes and which, even while they moved me, made me feel a certain comfort at seeing him alive again! And here is this tiresome article which comes to spoil all those good memories . . .[2]

It is easy enough to understand Madame Monnier's protest, for there is little to like in the caricaturist and practical joker whose unprincipled existence, as it is shown in *Les Employés*, *La Rabouilleuse*, *Splendeurs et misères des courtisanes*, *La Muse du département*, and other novels, is distinguished by the exercise of a malicious tongue and a talent for pitiless mimicry. Bixiou is at times so devilishly clever, however, that he arouses admiration in spite of the disapproval Balzac nearly always conveyed in presenting him. Perhaps that tone of disapprobation expressed the bourgeois side of Balzac's genius, while the artist delighted in Monnier's similar talents. That he did have Monnier in mind may be accepted conclusively from a frank suggestion made in 1843, when Monnier was preparing to contribute to an illustrated edition of the *Comédie humaine:* "See if you can do yourself as Bixiou, whom I recommend to you." [3]

There are certainly closer resemblances than Madame Monnier was willing to admit between Bixiou and the life and character of Henry Monnier. The similarities are indeed so great that it is hard to decide when they cease to be valid and when it becomes fallacious to consider Bixiou as a true and complete portrait. His physical description might be Monnier in his twenties: "Short but well-formed, with delicate features, remarkable for a vague resemblance to Napoleon, thin lips, a straight, flat chin . . . blond, with thrilling voice and sparkling eye . . ." He too is always elegantly dressed, with the easy manners of a man of the world. Like Monnier he has studied painting, and has taken up caricature, supplementing his salary in a government office by doing illustrations and vignettes. Clever and impertinent, he teases his fellow employees and is frequently in hot water with his superiors, who evaluate him severely as possessing much ability but little steadiness and sense of deportment. And as had happened in Monnier's case, his conduct prevents advancement and leads finally to dismissal. For he spends his time in mercilessly ferreting out the vulnerable points of his associates and in devising and carrying out practical jokes, in the manner of the skilled *mystificateur*:

Famous for his jokes, he varied them with so much skill that he always obtained a victim. His great secret in this kind of work was to find out what each one wished; he knew the road to all the castles in Spain, to the dreams about which a man may be mystified because he is inclined to believe in them himself, and he would hoodwink one for hours at a time. Thus this profound observer, who possessed the greatest tact in playing a joke, had not the faculty of using this power to induce men to further his fortune or to advance his promotion.[4]

He is an excellent mimic also, and his comic impersonations suggest Monnier's. One of his famous tricks at the Ministry, for instance, is to imitate the great Dr. Gall delivering a lecture on phrenology. In *La Peau de chagrin* there is a lively example of his talent as an after-dinner entertainer:

"Come, Bixiou, let's have a classic farce! Give it to 'em!"
"Do you want me to give you the nineteenth century?"
"Listen!"
"Silence!"
"Put a mute on your muzzle!"
"Will you hold your tongue, you Chinaman!"
"Give him some wine and keep him quiet, the child!"
"Now, Bixiou!"

The artist buttoned his black coat to the neck, put on his yellow gloves, and made himself up with a horrible squint to mimic the *Revue des deux mondes;* but the uproar drowned his voice, and it was impossible to hear a single word of his raillery. If he did not represent the century, he did at all events represent the *Revue*, for he did not understand himself.*

* The squint refers to the editor Buloz, whose defective vision won him the nickname of the *Polyphème de la rue Saint-Benoît*. Balzac's pun in the last sentence is unfortunately lost in translation: "car il ne s'entendit pas lui-même." *La Peau de chagrin,* p. 81.

Although Bixiou's personality is on the whole much more disagreeable than Henry Monnier's, there are so many points of similarity that this comparison offers an excellent illustration of Balzac's method of basing a portrait on a living model, sharpening the focus in the manner of the skilled caricaturist, to detect and develop latent traits or tendencies. However exaggerated the result may appear to be, the features of the original can still be recognized. At first it is almost purely Monnier:

> A tireless hunter after *grisettes*, a smoker, a jester, a man who dined out and attended many supper parties, always tuned to the highest pitch, as brilliant in the green-room as in the balls given by the *grisettes* in the Allée des Veuves, he was as witty at table as on a pleasure party, as gay at midnight in the streets as in the morning when he first jumped out of bed; but gloomy and sad at heart, as is the case with most comedians.

Then the lines deepen and the effect begins to change:

> Moreover this artist, really profound, but only by flashes, swung to and fro in life like a swing, without thinking of the time when the cord would break. His lively wit, his profusion of ideas, caused him to be courted by all who were accustomed to appreciate brilliancy of intellect; but not one of his friends liked him. Incapable of withholding a witty saying, he would compromise his two neighbors at table before the first course was served.

This malice, which in Bixiou's case reaches a height of genuine vindictiveness in the *mystification* by which he foils Philippe Bridau's ambitious schemes, revealed itself in Monnier under sufficient provocation, but it was counteracted by an essential good humor and by a real capacity for affection, traits which Bixiou lacks. To a certain extent the rest of Balzac's description might be applied to Monnier: "Notwithstanding his outward gaiety, the spirit of dissatisfaction with his social position would pierce his sayings; he aspired higher, while the fatal demon hidden in his soul prevented him from possessing the gravity which imposes so much on fools." In Henry's case the discontent that he sometimes showed was not so much with his social position as with his failure to rise to the heights of theatrical success, of which he never ceased to dream. In the manifold promise of his early career, and in his own inability ever to understand clearly his own limitations, he may well have inspired the words with which Bixiou's portrait ends: "No sorcerer could foretell the future of a young man in whom every talent was incomplete." [5]

Such appears to be the extent to which Balzac exploited his friend as a model. Further study of their relationship throws light not only on various aspects of Balzac's technique, and the probable source of some of his material, but also on the character and temperament of both men. For they were in many ways alike. Exactly the same age, they had even a slight physical resemblance, although Monnier was far handsomer. When they began the close association during which Monnier illustrated many books published in Balzac's printing shop, and later when they worked together on *La Silhouette* and *La Caricature*, natural congeniality made them friends. They had the same love of life and laughter, the same Rabelaisian sense of humor, the same keen eye for the oddities of appearance and manner which are often the distinguishing marks of character. No one enjoyed more wholeheartedly than Balzac the scenes acted by Monnier in the studios, and Balzac's praise of his lithographs definitely established Monnier's reputation as a comic artist.

It was Monnier's faithful reproduction of social types which delighted Balzac, who recognized both the artist's originality and the subtly intellectual quality which marked his satire at its best. In an article in *La Mode* for October 2, 1830, he paid Monnier the tribute of comparing him with Charlet, Hogarth, and Callot, saying that, like these artists, he had preserved living types which would otherwise have been forgotten. More original than Charlet, Monnier appealed to the handful of thinkers capable of appreciating his art, and Balzac called him "the most satiric, the wittiest, of our cartoonists," whose genius would be recognized as equal to Hogarth's when his work was more fully known to the public.[6]

In another article, published in *La Caricature*, May 31, 1832, Balzac analyzed more fully his friend's art, explaining the qualities which made it intellectual rather than popular:

Henry Monnier has all the disadvantages of a superior person, and he must accept them because he has also all the merits. No cartoonist knows better than he how to seize upon an absurdity and express it, but he formulates it always in a profoundly ironical manner. Monnier is the personification of irony, English irony, well calculated, cold, but piercing like the steel of a dagger. He can put a whole political life into a periwig, a whole satire worthy of Juvenal into the back view of a fat man. He finds unsuspected relevancies in two attitudes, and contrasts a plump dowager armed with spectacles, and a slender young girl, in such a way that you make fun of your closest kin.—His eye is always bitter, and his drawing, quite Voltairian, has something diabolical about it.—He dislikes old men, he dislikes quill-drivers, he detests the *épicier;* he makes you laugh at everything, even women, and he offers you no consolation.

He addresses himself to all men strong enough and mighty enough to see further than the others, to scorn others, never to be bourgeois, in short to all those who find in themselves something left after disillusionment, for he disillusions. Now such men are rare, and the higher Monnier rises, the less popular he is.[7]

This article contains probably the most famous criticism of Monnier's work, cited by later admirers of Monnier not only because they have found it penetratingly accurate, but also because it has flattered the astuteness of their own judgment.

The qualities which Balzac admired are certainly found in his own work: irony whose underlying bitterness disenchants without consoling, the power to evoke a character through notation of external physical details. In the work of both men there are other technical similarities, some of which have been considered rather defects than merits of their style. Delacroix objected, for instance, to the method, perfected by Monnier and often used by Balzac, of seeking a realistic and comic effect through the almost phonetic notation of speech.[8] Other contemporary critics disliked the use of reappearing characters, a device employed by Monnier in his earliest repertory of improvised scenes and in the 1830 edition of the *Scènes populaires*, and by Balzac in *Le Père Goriot* in 1834. Monnier's readers took for granted that the types he had first created in the studios should reappear in the *Scènes populaires*, but it was not until much later that the value of the method was appreciated in the *Comédie humaine*.

Both writers were criticized also for the lack of conventional form in their work, Balzac's early novels being as independent of artistic rules as Monnier's plays. A comment on the impression produced by Balzac in 1836 might equally well be applied to Monnier: ". . . the resolve to express exactly what you observe . . . means being sure of giving to the work thus produced all the interest of reality; but it means also accepting the verbiage, the incoherence, the diffusion of real life."[9] It would be interesting to know whether Balzac had begun by deliberately experimenting with Monnier's technique, which he consciously modified later, or whether the more careful construction of the later novels was due to the gradual development of a skill that Monnier never possessed. As the Realists of the middle of the century realized, the formlessness which so often gives to Monnier's work the boring dullness of ordinary life makes him the greater realist, although Balzac is incontestably the greater artist.

In the cases where the two men handled the same subject, it is possible by a comparison of dates to determine what material Balzac may have borrowed from Monnier. Some of the clearest examples of probable borrowing are found in the studies of life in the civil service, where both could draw to a certain extent on their personal experiences as clerks, but where Monnier had the advantage of more extensive firsthand knowledge. His album of lithographs entitled *Mœurs administratives*, which appeared in 1828, set the stage for the later literary works and presented the typical *dramatis personae*. *La Caricature* of November 25, 1830, contained a sketch by Balzac called "Le Garçon de bureau," a dialogue between two elderly clerks who complain of their new chiefs because the latter do not understand the traditional protocol of the ministry, where things were better in the old days.[10] In the 1835 edition of the *Scènes populaires* Monnier published his "Scènes de la vie bureaucratique," which are little more than a commentary in dialogue form on the earlier lithographs. Balzac's novel *Les Employés* appeared in 1836, containing the various types already sketched by Monnier, with analysis and amplification of the traits which the latter had illustrated more briefly and objectively: the laziness, disrespect, self-seeking, and humbug of the typical functionary. It is interesting to note that Balzac still inserted occasional passages in dialogue form, as though he could not get away from Monnier's scenes.

It has been said that many of Balzac's sketches published in periodicals of the early 1830's could have taken their place in the *Scènes populaires*. They were brief bits of photographic realism, sometimes in descriptive form, such as the scene of departure in "La Cour des Messageries royales," sometimes in dialogue, like the "Départ d'une diligence." [11] The evident resemblance in subject matter, form, and tone, between this little scene and Monnier's "Voyage en diligence" suggests that Balzac took the idea from his friend. Although Henry did not publish his famous sketch until 1842, he had been acting it for years, and it was one of Balzac's favorites.

The way in which Balzac turned Monnier's album of *Grisettes* into a *physiologie* has already been mentioned.[12] Another and more serious accusation of borrowing has been made by Champfleury and others, who have affirmed that Balzac took from Monnier the life of Napoleon told in a gathering of peasants by an old soldier, in *Le Médecin de campagne*.[13] Monnier's "Précis historique de la Révolution, de l'Empire et de la Restauration" had been published in the *Scènes populaires* in 1831, and may have suggested the comic method used by Balzac, but could scarcely have supplied much material for his longer and more complete life of Napoleon. Even if Monnier had another monologue, unpublished and closer in content to Balzac's masterpiece, it is difficult to see how the accusation of plagiarism could be substantiated.[14] In another case, however, Balzac's use of material taken from Monnier seems to be incontrovertible. The story of Ravenouillet, in *Les Comédiens sans le savoir*, must have been suggested by "Les Compatriotes." In fact Balzac not only summarized the subject of Monnier's play before adding as it were a final comic touch, but had the story told by Bixiou, as though in indirect acknowledgment of its source.[15]

Thus far it has seemed that Balzac could have borrowed certain subjects and situations from Monnier's published or unpublished work. It might be expected that he would put into the *Comédie humaine* the most complete of Monnier's characters, Monsieur Prudhomme, but such is not the case. The honest clerk Phellion, of *Les Employés* and *Les Petits bourgeois*, is a humble Prudhomme, possessing the latter's middle-class virtues but never rising to his economic or social importance. To supplement his scanty salary he teaches history, literature, and elementary morals in a girls' school. He lives in a small house decorated in the solemn bad taste of the petty *bourgeoisie*, likes to receive old friends with whom he discusses politics and the arts, is an officer of the National Guard and a member of the "reading committee" at the Odéon. Like Prudhomme he is both pompous and dull, destined to be a foil for the wit of his associates

There is nothing in the tone of this letter to indicate that Henry Monnier had received from Balzac the blow which, according to Champfleury, he never forgave. In the case both of Bixiou and of Prudhomme, Balzac's very frankness showed that he intended no disloyalty, no surreptitious betrayal of friendship. It was Monnier's role to serve the creative artist by supplying him with some of the raw materials from which Balzac constructed his great picture of French nineteenth-century society. Monnier also demonstrated the value of a method of documentation which Balzac used, and which was to develop into the realistic technique adopted by Flaubert.

There is a spiritual kinship between Monnier and Flaubert clearly recognizable without any proof that the one directly influenced the other, or that they were personally acquainted. They both possessed a trait which reached its fullest development, perhaps, in the second generation of French Romanticists, the obsession with contemporary reality, not because they loved it, or saw in it as the Classicists did a symbol of universal humanity, but because they found in the study of their contemporaries a weapon for avenging themselves on human stupidity. It was this need to demonstrate his superiority over his fellow men which led Flaubert, when he was little more than a child, to begin collecting information on the nature, manners, and habits of the bourgeois, data which he used in *Madame Bovary*, in *Bouvard et Pécuchet*, and in the *Dictionnaire des idées reçues*. It was a feeling of rebellion against his own middle-class environment which developed in him the spirit of mockery, expressed by the *farces* which he and his boyhood friends in Rouen composed when they were not acting tragedies *à la* Victor Hugo in his father's billiard room. The *garçon*, a strange invention whose stupid laugh punctuated the boys' conversation and interrupted their games, was a grotesque creature comparable to the types created by Traviès, Daumier, Monnier, and the other satiric artists of the July Monarchy. As Flaubert grew older, his dislike of the times he lived in and the society to which he belonged took the form either of escape into past centuries and exotic lands, or of a kind of self-torture which compelled him to a study of his contemporaries. Here his only relief was in that Romantic laughter which is supremely ironic.

Flaubert was not yet seventeen when he published an essay which showed, if not the direct influence of Henry Monnier, at least a resemblance striking enough to herald the debut of Monnier's great successor as historian of the nineteenth century's middle classes. This was "Une Leçon d'histoire naturelle: genre commis," appearing in *Le Colibri* of March 30, 1837. It is a *physiologie* of the Clerk, his appearance, habits, tricks of speech, and all the details noted by the young writer can be checked against the portrait of the species in Monnier's *Scènes de la vie bureaucratique*. The same enormous *redingote* forms the distinctive carapace, its capacious pockets containing a cold lunch. When the clerk has shed its protective bulk, he piles wood in the stove and hugs its glowing heat, for he is a cold-blooded creature. His amusements are innocent ones such as a game of dominoes at a neighborhood café after he leaves the office, but he takes them seriously, and on their success depends the degree of affection shown when he reaches home and the wife whom he calls in moments of expansion *mon épouse*.[18]

It must have been soon after this early realization of the humor and satire to be found in the observation of reality that Flaubert began collecting material for the *Dictionnaire des idées reçues*, which was found after his death in the dossier of notes pertaining to the unfinished novel *Bouvard et Pécuchet*. According to Maxime Du Camp, the dictionary was to have been a methodical grouping of the hackneyed phrases and platitudes, the *prudhommismes* which both amused and exasperated Flaubert as he noted their frequent use in everyday speech. Flaubert said himself that the book would appear to be the "historical glorification of everything people approve of," presented in such a way that the reader would not know whether the author were serious or not, but that after he had read it, he would not dare open his mouth lest he find himself using one of its truisms.* In that way Flaubert would be avenged on the Philistines whose love of conventionality, order, and tradition makes so difficult the artist's effort to express the originality of his genius.[19]

This work, which was to be Flaubert's supreme condemnation of the bourgeois, was often in his thoughts as he was writing *Madame*

* Flaubert would have enjoyed Frank Sullivan's cliché expert, Mr. Arbuthnot, who appears occasionally in the *New Yorker*, for example, "The Cliché Expert Testifies on Baseball," *New Yorker*, August 27, 1949, pp. 22–25.

Bovary. Homais represents a preliminary incarnation, so to speak, of the ultimate victim. With his belief in progress and his worship of that pseudoscience which has the undisciplined character of magic; his anticlerical ideas; his recognition of the newspaper as the strongest weapon of a society which is governed by propaganda rather than by enlightenment; his professed scorn of the government, tempered by his ambition to wear the red ribbon of the Legion of Honor; with his complacent pride in his wife and children, and the self-assurance which blinds him to his own ignorance, Homais is first cousin to Joseph Prudhomme.*

The resemblance is so evident, in fact, that it suggested to Henry Monnier the idea of turning the novel into a play, in which he would of course take the part of the apothecary. The letter which he wrote to Flaubert on this subject may help to explain why the latter refused persistently and with increasing acerbity to allow the dramatization of *Madame Bovary:*

30 December, 1857.

Monsieur,

I have indicated to many of our friends all my admiration for *Madame Bovary:* many authors, the majority, have seen in me the apothecary, so they had me write the play, and after it was written I offered it to a director who accepted it and I am rehearsing it, all this without your permission. In two hours I am leaving for Reims where I am going to give several performances. Please be good enough, Sir, to let me know whether your intention is to have *Madame Bovary* played, and whether you consider me capable of taking the part of the apothecary . . .[20]

* A comparison of their professions of faith serves to confirm this relationship: *Madame Bovary* (Paris, 1930), p. 106: "I believe in the supreme Being, in a Creator, whoever he may be, it matters little to me, who has placed us here below to fulfill our duties as citizen and *père de famille,* but I do not need to go, in a church, to kiss silver platters, and to fatten from my pocket a lot of jokers who are better fed than we! For one can honor Him as well in a wood, in a field, or even while contemplating the ethereal vault, like the ancients. *My* God is the God of Socrates, of Franklin, Voltaire, and Béranger! I am for the *Profession de foi du vicaire savoyard* and the immortal principles of 89!" *Mémoires de Monsieur Joseph Prudhomme,* I, 195: "Certainly I am not the enemy of Catholicism, I have always thought and I still think that a religion is indispensable to the masses; but the enlightened man finds sufficient nourishment in the sublime philosophy of Socrates, Jean-Jacques Rousseau, Plato, and Monsieur de Voltaire. It is in the presence of nature that I like to address my prayers to the sovereign Architect of the universe."

The condescending tone of this letter, and the liberty which Monnier was prepared to take, may seem astonishing as the relative importance of the two men is viewed with the perspective of nearly a century, but it must be remembered that Flaubert was an unknown writer whose first novel was creating quite a scandal, and that from Monnier's point of view the young man might well have felt honored if a celebrated author-artist-actor, twenty years older than he, wished to create the role of Homais.

It is impossible to prove that Monnier, who knew everyone, ever met Flaubert. In a letter to Baudelaire in 1860, Flaubert mentioned Monnier, but in an ambiguous way which could be an allusion to the *Scènes populaires* rather than to the actor himself: "*Le Théo* gives no sign of life, *la Présidente* is charming as usual, and every Sunday at her house I rival in stupidity Henri Monnier." [21] The only other letter in which Monnier is named was written to Maupassant in 1876: "How can one have a taste for words as meaningless as this one: 'Naturalism?' Why has that good Champfleury been left with 'Realism,' which is nonsense of the same stamp, or rather the same nonsense? Henry Monnier is no truer than Racine." [22]

Whether Flaubert knew Monnier personally or not, these references show casual familiarity with his work, and there is further evidence that he was intimately acquainted with Monsieur Prudhomme. Not only did he scatter in his letters frequent *prudhommismes* such as this: "Are you condemned to Villenauxe for life? 'Is not Paris enough to be pitied, *belle dame?*' as M. Prudhomme would say." [23] He also used the name of Prudhomme to represent the bourgeois: "Are you studying Prudhomme these days? He is gigantic. He admires Musset's *Rhin* and asks if Musset has done anything else." [24] It is interesting to note that Prudhomme appeared most frequently in the letters after 1870, as though Flaubert thought of him often during his last years, when he was working on *Bouvard et Pécuchet* and the *Dictionnaire des idées reçues*. One letter he wrote from beginning to end in the most florid style, signing it: "Prud'-homme." [25] Did he perhaps remember that he had once, *mirabile dictu*, been called a second Prudhomme? That had been after the publication of his second *Education sentimentale*, in the provincial newspaper *La Gironde*, whose critic no doubt intended by that seemingly incongruous epithet to recognize in Flaubert Monnier's gift of depicting human nature with a semirealistic, semi-ironic touch.

With *Bouvard et Pécuchet* Flaubert went beyond ironic realism into a realm of caricature where he is more comparable to Daumier than to Monnier. In the two heroes of this book the stupidity of mediocrity is brought to its ultimate crucifixion. Their efforts to absorb universal knowledge become an immense parody of the modern scientific spirit, with its faith in the printed word, the demonstrated proof, the prescribed formula. Reducing infinity to their own limited terms, they think they can do anything, but they never realize that the thing they can not do is to fathom their own crassitude. Monsieur Prudhomme is capable of affection and enthusiasm; Bouvard and Pécuchet have no likings or admirations. They are the automata of Flaubert's vengeance.

The *Dictionnaire des idées reçues*, which Flaubert undoubtedly intended to incorporate in some way in the novel, might almost have been composed of notes taken from Monnier's works. For it is possible to find parallels for item after item of the *Dictionnaire*, not only in the *Mémoires de Monsieur Joseph Prudhomme* but in Monnier's other studies of the bourgeois, such as the *Scènes de la vie bureaucratique*, the *Physiologie du bourgeois*, and *Les Bourgeois de Paris*. A few examples chosen at random show the closeness not only of thought, but often of phraseology:

The *Dictionnaire* gives: "DIVORCE. If Napoleon had not divorced, he would still be on the throne," an opinion which Prudhomme had expressed: "From the day when Napoleon committed the irreparable mistake of divorcing Josephine, I foresaw the fall of the Empire," [26] and Madame Bergerat, in "La Garde-malade," had already blamed all of Napoleon's troubles on the same cause. The life of an *émigré* is summed up in the *Dictionnaire:* "EMIGRES. Earned their living by giving guitar lessons and making salad," or as Prudhomme had written in the *Mémoires:* "Valère is in exile, Dorante is giving lessons in the minuet to the Russians, Damis is teaching the English the art of seasoning salad . . . A sad life, anyhow, the life of the *émigré*." [27] Prudhomme's flowery phrase: "luxury, that cankerworm of empires," [28] appears tersely in the *Dictionnaire:* "LUXURY. Ruins nations." When Prudhomme follows the bourgeois tradition of taking his wife to Italy on their honeymoon, he might have been prepared for Madame Prudhomme's disappointment, for the *Dictionnaire* says: "ITALY. Gives many disappointments, is not so beautiful as they say." And Prudhomme's jealousy of the young traveling salesman whom they meet during their trip is justified by the statement in the *Dictionnaire* that a singer of *romances* always pleases the ladies.

In this work Flaubert reached many of Monnier's conclusions concerning the bourgeois' ideas about literature and the other arts: He would rather be able to say that he knows an author or actor personally than read his books or see him play, but his effort to win the friendship of such a celebrity is inspired either by the hope of an invitation to dinner or of complimentary tickets, or by envy which finds spiteful satisfaction in discovering that the intimate habits of important personages make them mere mortals like the rest of us. All actresses are a potential menace to the bourgeois' sons, as Monsieur Prudhomme has learned to his sorrow; all artists are *farceurs*. But the professional critic inspires tremendous respect because he occupies a position of authority. For the fundamental tenet of the bourgeois' creed is still, of course, that society is based on respect for authority.

Flaubert's bourgeois agrees with Monnier's that good penmanship is the first essential of success. They are both fond of dogs, whose loyalty is a lesson to mankind. They are both afraid of drafts. They both read the newspapers assiduously, although they disagree violently with most of them. The one unfailing topic of conversation is the weather, about which they always complain. And they both feel that being out after midnight is immoral. The *Dictionnaire des idées reçues* has been accepted as a document of reliable information concerning the average opinions of the French middle class between 1850 and 1870. The comparison with Monnier shows that those opinions were essentially the same between 1830 and 1850, and that two listeners peculiarly sensitive to clichés might reach identical conclusions about both generations. It must be admitted that their conclusions remain remarkably valid even today.

Flaubert the perfectionist never brought to complete maturity his conception of the bourgeois as the incarnation of a single type of the nineteenth century. Monnier's bourgeois had been born fully developed, needing only the accumulation of details to achieve perfection. The correspondence in which Flaubert revealed himself much more fully than in his novels has left no doubt of his intention in his lifelong pursuit of human folly. He wanted to avenge himself, but on what? Fundamentally, like all romanticists, on the inescapable fact that he too was human, was mediocre, had his limitations and his follies. He could not escape from himself, but in knowing himself, like Montaigne, he could reap the satisfaction of complete disillusionment. Henry Monnier, who left no volumes of self-revelatory letters and rarely expressed his intentions and aims, did once record his attitude toward Joseph Prudhomme, and he used words almost identical with those of Flaubert: "Prudhomme was a vengeance." [29]

XIV

THE TRIUMPH OF MONSIEUR PRUDHOMME

Monsieur Joseph Prudhomme has had to be mentioned repeatedly during this study as he appeared in the course of Monnier's theatrical, literary, and artistic career. In order to understand his importance, it is necessary to examine his background, to know something of his history and of his place in French literature, and to trace the progress of his growth from a comic character identified with its creator, Henry Monnier, to a symbolic type which exists quite independent of Monnier, just as John Bull and Uncle Sam are personages whose inventors have long been forgotten. Prudhomme does not have such universal renown as these two figures, to be sure, but his social and political significance is great enough to warrant the conviction that he represents modern France fully as legitimately as does the more dramatic and alluring Marianne who has become more or less accepted as the national symbol. It is certainly true that a study of Prudhomme is invaluable in a comprehension of the great middle class which dominated French life between 1789 and 1940.

Monnier once said that he had conceived Joseph Prudhomme in 1829, at the Café des Cruches, where he had used General Beauvais as his model. According to Champfleury, the type had been suggested to him even earlier by a Monsieur Petit who had been his superior at the Ministry of Justice.[1] Whatever traits this worthy functionary may unwittingly have contributed to the personage take on added significance from the fact that he did not disappear entirely from Monnier's life, as Champfleury implied by making no further mention of him after Monnier left the Ministry. At some time during the late 1840's, when Monnier was already busy expanding his scenes and sketches into the full-length play which was to present Prudhomme in his full dimensions, Monsieur Petit reappeared, evidently interested now in journalism, appealing to his former subordinate for an introduction to the editor-in-chief of the *Siècle*, Monnier's old friend Louis Desnoyers. It is a temptation to read a double meaning into the letter that Monnier obligingly wrote for him:

> My dear Desnoyers, I am sending you one of my good and former *camarades de bureau* of whom I have spoken to you. He would intend to give you something for the *Siècle*. He will bring it with him.
>
> You will be grateful to me for having given you the opportunity to know M. Petit.[2]

Those who delight in pursuing sources may wish to believe that Prudhomme's name and profession were suggested by an old treatise on penmanship, by one Preud'homme of Paris, but there is no evidence that Monnier had seen this work.[3] It is less coincidental that there should have been in Paris during Monnier's youth a school of penmanship directed by the Saintomer brothers, and that Joseph Prudhomme called himself *professeur d'écriture, élève de Brard et Saint-Omer*. Whatever may have been the original sources of inspiration, Monsieur Prudhomme quickly became a synthesis of many elements for which it would be supererogatory to seek a single living model. The traits and attributes which Monnier gave him must be assembled from the sketches, lithographs, and water colors which reproduced his portrait between 1830 and the artist's death, and the literary works in which he appeared during that period. Since Monnier made portraits of himself as Prudhomme in the various plays in which he took the part, it is possible also to form some idea, however scanty, of the stage Prudhomme.

Physically he is short and stout, with a round bald head adorned with a single tuft of hair on top and a fringe behind, prolonged in side whiskers which extend well over his cheeks. His full double chin is clean shaven. The curve of his mouth with its protruding lower lip indicates complacency as well as stubbornness, and belies the benevolent effect of the round spectacles behind whose rims the eyes have an expression of perpetual and naïve surprise. His massive head rises from the folds of an enormous white cravat which nearly covers the ears in a stiff framework contributing greatly to his air of unbending dignity. In dress, Monsieur Prudhomme prefers substantial quality to the latest fads of fashion. His well-cut tail coat has wide lapels which open to disclose a snowy waistcoat buttoned over his portly front. Below hangs a watch fob, and the trousers descend to trim white gaiters over well-polished boots. His manner is calm and polite, with more than a touch of old-fashioned elegance in its formality. His voice is strong and resonant, and he speaks with a precision of diction which matches the preciousness of his language. His pompous style has an opulence of form which only too often masks the poverty of its thought.

Such is the individual who appears in several of the *Scènes populaires* and in *La Famille improvisée*, is the hero of the five-act play *Grandeur et décadence de Monsieur Joseph Prudhomme*, and of the *Mémoires de Monsieur Joseph Prudhomme*. The first glimpse of him, in "Le Roman chez la portière," reveals his restrained and deprecating manner, and that love of sententious phrases which causes him to say, in asking the concierge for a light: "Everything is finally extinguished . . . The taper is the image of life." When he is called as a witness at the trial of Jean Iroux, in "La Cour d'assises," he gives his testimony with an air of pompous condescension toward the court as well as the prisoner, and takes occasion to make his first profession of political faith.[4] At the "Dîner bourgeois" his politeness becomes an attitude of restrained gallantry toward the ladies, and his hitherto solemn manner yields to the frivolity of an after-dinner song and the relating of anecdotes. An unfortunate Englishman who is present, and whose knowledge of French is limited to the word *bonjour*, is treated with charitable superiority and advised to apply himself to studying the language, since, as Prudhomme says, "by working nothing resists man," and "all men are made to esteem each other." He hates the English, however, as he declares frankly in "Un Voyage en diligence." Perhaps this feeling is sharpened by the innumerable irritations of the journey, although Monsieur Prudhomme bears them with the philosophic words: "One must take the rough with the smooth." Even the unsatisfactory food and poor service of the inn where they stop to lunch merely cause him to remark: "It would be so agreeable to travel if the inns could reconcile their interests and those of the travelers," and he devotes himself to making polite conversation with his fellow passengers. His curiosity leads him to ask indiscreet questions, but he does not wait for the answers, preferring to talk about himself and his vast experience. For he remembers the *Ancien Régime* and the Revolution, and all the subsequent changes in France, and that is why he can say tranquilly: "Nothing that is done in our time surprises me." He does allow himself to express indignation, however, at the beggars who surround the coach when it halts, saying that the authorities should not permit such annoyance, but should force the wretches to earn their living by honest work, as other people have to do. And he becomes really agitated at anything which shocks his sense of the propriety due to the presence of ladies, as inevitably happens in the course of the journey. In "Scènes de mélomanie bourgeoise" Monsieur Prudhomme is solemn and dull, declares that he never travels, dislikes negroes, enjoys the guitar, and would willingly recite a poem or two. He unbends enough to join with dignity in the game of *les propos interrompus*, comments on each musical rendition that it is "full of interest," and sums up thus his feeling toward that great art: "Music is a very fine thing . . . It charms our moments of leisure and poeticizes our existence."

La Famille improvisée presents the writing master in a much lighter vein, ready to kiss the servant and indulge in gay badinage, so long as proper respect is shown those things which he considers serious: "I am of a light and facetious nature, I love to laugh, but I never joke about public matters, I am entirely devoted to the established order . . . Long live the established order . . . Long live all which contributes to our happiness! Long live the constituted authorities, may the municipal guard and its august family live forever!" *

In the comedy *Grandeur et décadence de Monsieur Joseph Prudhomme* there is a tremendous expansion of Prudhomme's activities and importance. It is the beginning of 1848. During the July Monarchy his financial speculations have prospered, his position as an officer in the National Guard has brought him prestige and influence in his quarter, he is invited to a royal ball, about to go into politics,

* Flaubert, *Dictionnaire des idées reçues:* "BASES. Of society, are (*id est*) property, the family, religion, respect for the authorities.—Speak with anger of them if they are attacked."

and hopes to be decorated, when the February Revolution overthrows all his dreams and sends him temporarily into retirement in the country. There he tries to console himself by introducing agricultural innovations among the peasants, but his political ambition has been aroused, and when his former associates in the National Guard present him with a testimonial sword—"This sword is the best day of my life!"—he cannot resist the temptation to run as a candidate for the National Assembly. As a businessman he is at the height of his career, with a finger in everything: the development of the dirigible balloon, a mining project at Montmartre, the management of a newspaper, jury service, the presidency of a philanthropic society. If he could marry his daughter to a title, he would desire nothing more except the red ribbon of the Legion of Honor. But the silly girl remains faithful to a lover who represents to her father all that is useless, irresponsible, undesirable, for he is a writer! In 1852, with the Second Empire well established and the power of the middle class diminished, Monsieur Prudhomme loses the election, finds himself too old for the National Guard, and is forced to accept a son-in-law whose play has been received with such success at the Comédie-Française that it is he, and not Prudhomme, who is finally decorated. The times have changed indeed since Prudhomme began his career.

The *Mémoires de Monsieur Joseph Prudhomme* fill in the details of his life, and show most completely his role in French society during the first fifty years of the nineteenth century. As a youth he is apprenticed to his uncle, a bonnet-maker, but he yearns for higher things than a modest career in business. He thinks of becoming an actor, and when this ambition is discouraged, he decides first to write a great tragedy in verse, then to try his hand at painting. He joins one of the singing societies so popular during the Empire, falls in love with a *grisette*, becomes a *rapin* in a studio, works for a short time as a supernumerary in a government office, and falls victim to a *mystificateur*, all in the best tradition of the period. With the Restoration he hopes to come at last into the post he would have inherited from his father, who was writing master to the royal stable boys, but when Louis XVIII disregards his request, he turns away from the Bourbons, practices his profession in private, and accepts the July

Revolution calmly with the hope that since the new regime cannot be worse, it may be better than its predecessor.

Prudhomme's first wife having died, he marries a second time, for his honeymoon taking his one long trip, the traditional journey to Italy. He had two children by the first Madame Prudhomme, a daughter Lydie, a modern young lady with Republican leanings and practical ideas, who refuses the penniless count her father chooses for her, and—unlike the daughter in the play—marries a businessman with prospects at court; and a son Anatole, who is a great disappointment because of his idleness. Since Anatole shows no interest in work of any kind, his father finally hopes to make an artist of him, and persuades him to take up photography. It is Madame Prudhomme's ambition which directs the course of her husband's life during the monarchy of Louis-Philippe. Seeing the increasing social importance of the financier, she urges Prudhomme to invest the inheritance which has given him independent means in a seat on the Exchange. There for a time he witnesses the mania for speculation which is sweeping France, but his efforts to satisfy all the relatives who bring him their savings, and the feeling of constant insecurity which accompanies the operations of high finance, make Prudhomme so unhappy that when an opportunity comes to sell his seat at a profit, he seizes upon it with relief. His next venture is in theatrical administration. Madame Prudhomme is pleased to be able to offer complimentary tickets, but the problems of dealing with the artistic temperament of actors and playwrights are complicated for her husband by his efforts to keep up with the latest ideas in stage setting. The expense of going from extreme realism to complete fantasy nearly ruins him. Anatole falls in love with the leading lady and is challenged by her brother because his father will not consent to his marrying an actress. Monsieur Prudhomme, whose conception of honor, like Monsieur Poirier's, is more practical than aristocratic, prevents the duel by promising that the marriage shall take place after Mademoiselle Rosa has completed her three years' engagement with his company, a delay which he confidently hopes will arrange the matter to his satisfaction. He is obliged also to aid his son-in-law, who still gives promise of great business acumen but is in need of capital.

By this time Prudhomme's fortune is seriously diminished, and his wife has not yet achieved the social position she wants. The golden opportunity for both of them comes when Monsieur Prudhomme is offered the directorship of a newspaper, with a salary which assures them of a comfortable living, and a prestige which surrounds him with flattery and gives him a delightful feeling of importance, while in reality he has nothing to do. The policies of the paper are determined by the stockholders, and Madame Prudhomme takes charge of its less serious features, such as art, literature, and drama. Her Thursdays are attended by men of letters, she organizes lotteries for charity, patronizes young musicians, and attends the first night of every play. It seems as though at last, in his old age, Monsieur Prudhomme has reached perfect security and happiness, as he exclaims: "I bless Providence every day, and I declare that for a good bourgeois without ambition and desirous of finishing his career peacefully, there is no post today more pleasant, more enviable, than that of the director of a newspaper." [5]

But there is a *Postscriptum* to the *Mémoires:* a brief note saying that suddenly Monsieur Prudhomme finds himself completely ruined, loses his position because his name no longer has any value, loses his son who marries the actress and goes off on a tour of the provinces, has the sorrow of knowing that his daughter is forced to support herself by teaching in a boarding school, and sees his wife inconsolable over the reversal of their fortunes. So ends the career of Monsieur Prudhomme, for whom money, that most unstable of possessions, had been the basis of existence.

Lest there be any doubt that Joseph Prudhomme was intended to represent the bourgeois, the *Mémoires* declare explicitly that in recording the complete history of a personage who had up to that time been an object of mirth and caricature, the author intended to bestow upon his hero the honor he deserved as the personification of his century, the era of the middle class. Since he was the typical bourgeois, no one had a better right than he to address himself to his contemporaries. "You may do and say what you please," he said, "everything is bourgeois today. The aristocracy exists no longer, the democracy does not yet exist, there is only the middle class. You have only transitional ideas, opinions, manners, literature, arts, instincts; hail then Joseph Prudhomme, the man of the transition, that is to say of the middle class!" [6]

So the Prudhommes of the nineteenth century tried everything, from the arts to high finance. They reached the climax of their importance during the reign of Louis-Philippe, when the government favored their efforts to enrich the state by enriching themselves and rewarded them with political power and social prestige. They promoted the new inventions springing up like mushrooms as the industrial age gained momentum: the development of photography and chromolithography, the manufacture of shoes and buttons by machinery, the chemical composition of matches, the first steps toward the perfection of the sewing machine. Means of communication and transport were being improved as rapidly as public prejudice would allow. The old canal systems were repaired and completed, but when the question of railroads arose, there proved to be several stumbling blocks. The Prudhommes are always slow to adopt novelties which threaten the established order of things, and the building of railroads was a menace, not only to the rights of private property but, even worse, to the tranquillity of the country districts where agriculture and animal husbandry would be ruined by the ravages of the steam horse. When the first line was being projected, between Paris and Saint-Germain, Thiers called it a "plaything" for Paris and prophesied that it would never carry a passenger or a package, and when a few years later many lives were lost in an accident, the Prudhommes saw a divine warning in this catastrophe.* [7] It was not until 1842 that the great financial houses, the Rothschilds and their competitors, were willing to accept a national railroad program which threatened to cut their private profits. At about the same time transatlantic steamboat service began to be organized, and in 1845 money was provided for the first electric telegraph line, between Paris and Rouen. Although poets would have scorned to commemorate the great battle between colonial sugar and the beetroot industry, and no artists painted the dramatic scenes at the Bourse or the Chamber of Deputies, it was a time of epic business ventures in France, as in many other parts of the world.

* George Eliot's *Middlemarch* presents amusingly the arguments against the construction of railroads in England at this same period.

Such commercial and industrial activity was accompanied by the fever of speculation which was responsible for the rise and fall of the Prudhomme fortunes. Money was the root of happiness, for it meant security and material well-being, and the middle class drew all its power from the possession of wealth. The privileges which it guarded most jealously were based on economic status: the right to vote and hold office, the right to serve as a juryman, and as a member of the National Guard. In order to understand Joseph Prudhomme's emotion on the day when his fellow guardsmen presented him with a sword, it must be realized that the National Guard had both political and social significance. Its position as protector of the State gave it considerable power in the administration of public affairs, as well as enormous private and individual prestige. The reorganization of this body, which had been suspended by Charles X, had been one of the first acts of the July Monarchy and was a masterly means of assuring the devoted support of the *bourgeoisie*.

For all his apparent naïveté, Monsieur Prudhomme was not without acumen and proved to be justified in his ultimate choice of journalism as the great profession of the middle class. The modern newspaper was conceived and launched during the July Monarchy, a product of the spirit of business enterprise whose invasion of realms hitherto reserved for intellectuals and artists contributed to the Romanticists' animosity toward the bourgeois. Realizing that its newly acquired power could best be consolidated through control over ideas, the *bourgeoisie* hastened to monopolize the press. Until the last years of the Restoration, there had existed two kinds of journals in France: on the one hand the official press devoted to the expression of political doctrine, or combining politics and literature, as did *Le Globe;* on the other hand small, violently independent publications like *Le Corsaire* or *Le Figaro. La Revue des deux mondes*, founded on liberal principles in 1829, soon became a pillar of middle-class conservatism, as did *Le Journal des débats*.

The great innovations in journalism were the work of Emile de Girardin, whose most important single achievement was the establishment of *La Presse*, the first daily newspaper with no political affiliations and a policy of enlightening the public by an impartial presentation of facts. In order to reach the whole population, for the first time cheap daily copies were sold instead of limiting the sale to expensive annual subscriptions, so that to Emile de Girardin must be given credit for making newspapers the universal habit they have become. He introduced also the innovation of financing the paper through paid advertisements, thus inaugurating what in some ways has proved to be one of the curses of modern journalism, the need to satisfy the advertisers. Girardin also introduced the daily serial story, giving to journalism the added luster of such a union with literature.*

The first number of *La Presse* appeared on July 1, 1836, and its editor struck at once the popular note of a social problem to be solved: how to achieve the most happiness for the largest number. This was the keynote of the July Monarchy, and Emile de Girardin represents much of the best and some of the worst in that era. Well-meaning as he was undoubtedly, he nevertheless followed the current of his time in making of journalism a delicately balanced combination of idealism and commercialism. Its mercantile character was sure to dominate as soon as a newspaper became the organ, not of a group of men concerned with the promulgation of ideas or doctrines, but of a group of stockholders interested in increasing the value of their property. After that, as Joseph Prudhomme discovered, it was not necessary to have ideas so long as one's name was respected on the market place.

Had Monsieur Prudhomme been younger or more ambitious, he

* It might perhaps be noted that Monnier had coöperated with Girardin in his first journalistic venture, *Le Voleur*, which had appeared in 1828 with the avowed policy of reprinting articles stolen from other publications, since its young editors had no means of paying for new material. In 1829 Girardin started *La Mode*. These little papers prospered, but the Revolution interrupted their success. Girardin then founded the short-lived *Silhouette*, which set a model for the satiric journals succeeding it. He showed his genius for seizing upon a popular idea and encouraging it to develop into a national institution when he established *La Garde nationale*. This paper, appearing in September 1830, announced a program of bringing into communication with each other all the national guardsmen of France, in order to strengthen their unity and to work for the preservation of civil rights and public order. The enthusiastic reception it received made its owner's name a household word. Girardin's bold and fertile mind continued to launch new and important ideas, which his energy and perseverance crystallized into success. He conceived the project of establishing savings banks in small towns and rural regions, and he published a *Journal des connaissances utiles* as the organ of this movement.

might have made his position as director of a newspaper a stepping-stone toward political power. For that other great bourgeois, Adolphe Thiers, had been a journalist when he helped to bring Louis-Philippe to the throne and to establish the constitutional monarchy in which he played such an important role. There was undeniably something *prudhommesque* about Thiers, even in the dignity of his short body, the resonance of his voice, the immaculate whiteness of his neckcloth, the regularity of his features, which bore some resemblance to those of Henry Monnier in the latter's old age. And his characteristics were essentially bourgeois: an industriousness which set him at work early in the morning, a love of order which molded his life into a regular program, interrupted occasionally, like Prudhomme's, by the indulgence of a whim or fancy such as the collecting of hummingbirds or tropical plants. He dabbled in art to the extent of frequenting print sales, but he spent his money prudently on copies rather than in the ruinous extravagance of originals. He knew what he liked, however, and made categorical pronouncements concerning the merits of an artist or a dancer, loved the theater, and could be aroused to ardent enthusiasm over a new idea. He would throw himself wholeheartedly into the study of it, think and talk of nothing else, until, like Bouvard and Pécuchet, he dropped it to take up something else. In politics and statesmanship Thiers relied on facts and figures, based his decisions on practical sense, on logic and expediency rather than on abstract justice, and defended the simple, solid virtues of family loyalty, modesty, reasonableness, which were embodied in the king he had chosen to serve, and which he hoped to see glorified in the republic for which he planned.[8]

Thiers appeared thus to two of his contemporaries, the aristocratic and royalist D'Althon Shée, whose point of view was that of a cultured politician, and the man of letters and student of human nature, Dr. Véron. The latter must inevitably enter into a discussion of Joseph Prudhomme, for his *Mémoires d'un bourgeois de Paris*, which appeared within a year of the *Mémoires de Monsieur Joseph Prudhomme*, is an important document in a study of the ideals and spiritual values of that middle class to which he and Prudhomme were both so proud of belonging. How well Véron expressed the bourgeois ideal when he ended an analysis of contemporary society with the words: ". . . in spite of all the political upheavals, our society is regaining its taste for reason, calm, justice, the love of family and the passion for work." [9] But his admiration for the *esprit gaulois* which gave to the *bourgeoisie* its clear-sighted realism, its intolerance of the follies and mistakes of its superiors, did not prevent Véron from diagnosing with blunt sincerity its great weakness, its self-satisfaction. Ready to laugh at others, the bourgeois was too often blind to his own childish vanity, the instability of his opinions and interests, his unreasoned prejudices, his secret vices. For his character had not improved since La Fontaine had described it in *Le Rat et l'éléphant:*

> Se croire un personnage est fort commun en France:
> On y fait l'homme d'importance,
> Et l'on n'est souvent qu'un bourgeois.
> C'est proprement le mal françois:
> La sotte vanité nous est particulière . . .

In seeking other sources for Monsieur Prudhomme than the observation of French society during the July Monarchy, it is possible to say that Henry Monnier had one literary model for the *Mémoires.* This was *Jérôme Paturot à la recherche d'une position sociale*, by Louis Reybaud, published in 1842.[10] The hero, a candid young man inclined to plunge enthusiastically into new experiences without foreseeing where they will lead, spurns the honest career of bonnet-maker which is opened to him, as to Prudhomme, by an uncle lamentably ignorant of culture. He passes through a series of adventures like those of Monnier's hero: after being the one hundred ninety-eighth poet of the Romantic School and a member of the lowest, or vegetarian, *carré* of Saint-Simonists, where he soon finds that he has nothing to eat at all, Paturot becomes involved in fraudulent speculation in Moroccan bitumen, then in the publication of a newspaper which lures its readers by the ultramodern method of offering premiums for new subscriptions. When this system proves ruinous, Jérôme is fortunate enough to obtain a position on a more prosperous paper, subsidized by the government. This is his moment of triumph, but his fall is as rapid as Prudhomme's. After an attempt at suicide, in good Romantic tradition, he realizes that a prosaic commercialism is after all the surest guarantee of his daily bread, takes over his uncle's business, becomes a patron of art, and goes into politics, until he becomes bankrupt and is obliged to retire to the country. There like Candide he turns to gardening, and ends his life grafting fruit trees and improving the stock of Brussels sprouts. This book had a moment of great success, which no doubt encouraged Monnier to attempt a similar episodic biography, based on a satiric study of the same social sphere.*

Such were the contemporaries of Monsieur Joseph Prudhomme, but his ancestors go far back into French literature. Among the burghers of the medieval farces and *fabliaux*, whose hope in life was a well-filled purse and the skill to outwit those who threatened it, rises the self-seeking Maître Pathelin, whose shrewdness is outdone by his vanity. The aristocratic ideals of honor and chivalry had little appeal for those natures whose physical timidity was greater than any exaltation of the soul which might urge the sacrifice of self to a higher spiritual cause. Deeply rooted in the practical realism of an established position and material possessions, Prudhomme's family tree represents a static force holding firm against the attacks of dynamic idealism, but like the oak in La Fontaine's fable, it is vulnerable whenever self-confidence exceeds good judgment.

By the time Jean-Baptiste Poquelin revolted against his father's wish to establish him in his own comfortable business, choosing instead the discomfort and uncertainty of an artist's life, the heredi-

* There was another figure, half real, half legendary, that may have contributed to the formation of Joseph Prudhomme. A certain person named Calinot or Calino was employed in an antique shop and frequented a restaurant popular with the Bohemians. One day he appeared carrying a seventeenth-century cane with a handsome knob which gave it great value. Complaining that the cane was too long, Calino had the knob cut off, and when his protesting friends asked why he had not shortened it from the bottom, he replied, "It was the top that bothered me!" From that day on, poor Calino's name became proverbial, he had the dubious honor of being put into a *vaudeville*, and his remarks, genuine or apocryphal, were finally collected by the Goncourt brothers, who claimed to be his official biographers. According to them it was he who first said of Napoleon: "If he had remained a captain of artillery and Josephine's husband, he would still be ruling France," one of those popular dicta which keep reappearing mysteriously with no discoverable source or origin. See Goncourt, *Quelques créatures de ce temps* (Paris, 1878), pp. 81–91; Xavier Aubryet, *Les Jugements nouveaux* (Paris, 1860), p. 59, quoted in Georges Doutrepont, *Les Types populaires de la littérature française* (Bruxelles, 1926), pp. 494–495; D'Alméras, *La Vie parisienne*, pp. 77–78.

tary traits of the bourgeois were clearly defined. He was a man of property, devoted to his possessions, of which his family was an important unit; hardheaded and conservative in business and politics; individualistic by temperament, but finding in a government post the security and prestige he desired. Being socially inexperienced, he was often ridiculously naïve in his social climbing, and it was this trait which made him such a perfect subject for comedy. Molière turned into farce Monsieur Jourdain's efforts to learn manners and polite accomplishments, but the works on etiquette which appeared in great numbers during the seventeenth century had already been parodied in a little book called *Le Bourgeois poli*, published in 1631.[11] Here in a series of realistic dialogues were presented the bourgeois and his wife as they went about their daily life, interviewing the butcher and the draper, being treated by the apothecary and the doctor, and receiving their guests with the endless formalities reflected two centuries later in the pompous manners of Monsieur Prudhomme.

On the whole the seventeenth-century bourgeois had a fairly honorable place in literature. If his pretentious vulgarity was absurd, there was not yet any great harm in it, and the honest common sense of Gorgibus and Chrysale was allowed to triumph over the *esprits oisifs* who spent their time at poetry and music. Monsieur Jourdain was ridiculous because he indulged for a brief moment in the folly of a dream, but Madame Jourdain, with her solid grasp of realities, had the middle-class qualities which Molière admired.

On the threshold of the eighteenth century stands Turcaret, the financier, a more menacing figure than the essentially humble and well-meaning Monsieur Jourdain, because his moral sense is twisted into pride over the very unscrupulousness with which he has amassed his fortune and his power. This glimpse of danger, however, even strengthened by the bursting of Law's Mississippi Bubble, which foreshadowed the disasters accompanying the development of speculation during the reign of Louis-Philippe, was soon forgotten in the growing tide of sentimental admiration enveloping the bourgeois after the middle of the century. For the utilitarianism of the Enlightenment found in the middle-class businessman a symbol of the good citizen, and the humanitarian belief in man's innate goodness made him an object, not of ridicule or scorn, but of respect and tenderness.

Everything about him became interesting, and it sufficed to present him with his homely virtues displayed in his daily family life, in order to arouse sympathy and admiration. In Diderot's *Père de famille*, in Sedaine's *Philosophe sans le savoir*, Monsieur Prudhomme's ancestors attained a degree of perfection which many of their less meritorious descendants have complacently continued to accept as the birthright of the *bourgeoisie*, without stopping to weigh the qualities of family affection, personal integrity, community loyalty, against the defects born of prudence, narrow-mindedness, and possessiveness brought to the fore after the French Revolution.

During the long "century of transition" when, as Monnier said, France was no longer ruled by the nobility and was not yet a democracy, Monsieur Prudhomme's family tree spread its branches wide. As usual, his successors can be most easily recognized in the theater, both on the stage and in the audience, for this has always been Prudhomme's special domain. The enlargement and simplification of emotions and ideas through the focus of the stage satisfy his taste for the observation of his fellow beings, while the social atmosphere of the entertainment gives him the additional pleasure of showing off his wife, his daughter, and the comfortable state of his pocketbook. Ponsard's *école du bon sens* and the dramas of Dumas *fils* flattered the bourgeois by treating with serious respect his ideas of morality and his social problems. On the other hand, by that quirk of human nature which makes us laugh at our contemporaries and neighbors without being made uneasy by the suspicion that their foibles and follies may be our own, Monsieur Prudhomme applauded the comedies of Augier and Labiche, many of whose personages were his near relations.

Monsieur Perrichon, writing in the hotel registry at Chamonix: "How small man is when one contemplates him from the height of the *mère de Glace!*" and consenting complacently to pose for posterity in a painting: "Myself and Mont Blanc . . . tranquil and majestic!" is first cousin to Monnier's philosopher who enlightens his daughter with the aphorism: "Take man from society, you isolate him."[12] Monsieur Poirier is speaking for the businessmen of the family when he says: "I tell you that commerce is the true school for statesmen. Who will put his hand to the helm, if not those who have proved that they knew how to steer their own bark!" And he shares the family prejudice: "Let the arts be protected, very well! but the artists, no! . . . they are all loafers and profligates. Things are told of them which make your flesh creep, and which I wouldn't let myself repeat before my daughter." [13]

Louis Veuillot, a disillusioned critic of the materialism of the mid-century, who condemned the *bourgeoisie* for its "democratic" lack of good manners and absence of respect for spiritual values, realized nevertheless that its importance was increasing as its members took possession of domains where Prudhomme had scarcely dreamed of entering. In his creation Coquelet, Veuillot incarnated a new and powerful branch of the family: "Coquelet is not Prudhomme; he occupies a higher rank, he has received a more careful upbringing. It is Coquelet who is *par excellence* the child of higher education . . . Prudhomme admires Coquelet, and Coquelet disdains him. Prudhomme does business in a small way; Coquelet is a man of letters, poet, artist, lawyer, an employee of high rank, a politician. In the National Guard, Prudhomme never rises above the rank of captain; Coquelet became a colonel."

This disdainful attitude with its rather unfair derogation of Prudhomme's abilities and accomplishments, does not prevent a recognition of the many ties which unite the two. For more than one Prudhomme daughter brings in marriage to a Coquelet son the substantial dowry her father has accumulated in the grocery or drug business, and the Prudhommes, who are susceptible to sentiment, have been known to marry for love, and the hope of social advancement, a Coquelette with no dowry at all. Thus the tribe has increased, until it has reached all the positions of importance: "They have a seat in the Assemblies, in the tribunals, many of them are fifth-class Academicians, they edit almost exclusively the *Revue des deux mondes*. There are some very pious ones, and they are almost the only Catholics to whom secular offices are not closed." And finally Coquelet, Prudhomme, and Company become the most powerful bank in the world, and thus rule over everything, including arts and letters: "They place orders everywhere, all Parnassus works for them. They choose the artists whose renown marks them out. Reputation is enough. And they pay according to the reputation. Only they impose their own taste." And their taste is for art which shows that although life is earnest its severest trials can be forgotten if we look always on the sunny side, which is the side of love, "that rascally little Cupid." [14]

If Coquelet represents the financial and political interests of the upper middle class during the Second Empire, another aspect of bourgeois egoism was typified by Villiers de l'Isle-Adam in the grotesque personage Tribulat Bonhomet. While Homais might be called an apostle of modern science, Tribulat Bonhomet is its high priest, for he is an atheistic physician, the pretentiousness of whose scientific experiments is equaled only by their stupidity. Villiers de l'Isle-Adam seems to have made of this figure a constant companion, like Flaubert's *garçon*, and attributed to him a series of aphorisms which he collected, like the comic and foolish phrases which Monnier put into the mouths of his characters and Flaubert gathered for his *Dictionnaire des idées reçues*. When he sought, as Vigny had done in *Chatterton*,* a symbol of the poet's destruction by the bourgeois, he found it in Tribulat Bonhomet's most memorable experiment, the killing of swans in order to hear their dying song.[15]

It is a relief to turn from this sinister figure to the more frankly comic social reformer and freethinker Monsieur Cardinal, whose family fortunes were told by Halévy in the early years of the Third Republic. As candidate for the position of inspector general of the minds of the rural population, he combines Prudhomme's faith in the sanctity of appearances with the Voltairianism of Homais, bores one to death with Utopian schemes evolved by a genius which society has not yet learned to appreciate, is the personal enemy of the Jesuits, and is supported in dignity by the love affairs of his daughters. In Monsieur Cardinal solemn humbug and ambition are combined with an amoral quality which is his distinguishing trait.[16]

* Lord Beckford represents perfectly the Romanticist's notion of the Philistine (see Act III, sc. vi). If Vigny based his personage on the real William Beckford, who was Lord Mayor of London the year before Chatterton's death, it would be interesting to know whether he realized that the fortune augmented by this shrewd merchant enabled his son William to devote himself to the arts, and to express his taste for the ultraromantic not only in personal eccentricities but especially in the fantastic novel *Vathek*, which is the younger Beckford's chief claim to fame.

The decadence of Monsieur Prudhomme, which Monnier had announced at the beginning of the Second Empire, was marked at the end of the century by a Symbolist reincarnation and caricature beneath the grotesque mask of *le père Ubu.* Jarry's *Ubu roi* shows "stupidity triumphant, crushing with the sledge-hammer which it uses as an argument everything which might be art, intelligence, delicacy, intelligent initiative. It is the inefficient functionary, the poor leader, the stupid general. It is the State itself and its administration, when it blindly enforces regulations without considering the consequences. Ubu represents authority turned imbecile." [17]

Gluttonous, greedy, brutal, cowardly, this baroque symbol of human stupidity seems far removed from Joseph Prudhomme, and yet at the end of his extraordinary adventures, after escaping from the Russians and Poles with whom his ambition and self-confidence have brought about the most ridiculous of wars, Ubu takes on the very tone and manner of Prudhomme as he declaims: "Ferocious and inhospitable sea which bathes the land called Germany, so named because the inhabitants of that country are all cousin-germans." And as Mother Ubu answers admiringly, "That's what I call erudition; they say that country is very beautiful," he replies: "Ah! gentlemen! beautiful as it may be, it is not so fine as Poland! If there had been no Poland, there would be no Polish!" [18]

The reign of Joseph Prudhomme continued for forty years longer, in a prolongation marked by moments of surprising youthfulness and vigor. In Moroccan speculation where Jérôme Paturot had found only ruin, Topaze makes a fortune; Knock has a cynically expert knowledge of human nature which makes Homais, by comparison, both naïve and innocent. Jules Romains' *Hommes de bonne volonté* give to their expanding enterprises an international importance such as the nineteenth-century Prudhommes would not have dreamed of.

Prudhomme's history as an independent literary figure began a century ago, when Champfleury wrote the worthy gentleman's impressions of the Salon of 1846. In the next few years articles appeared over Prudhomme's signature, and he was given credit for editing two collections of humor. In the repertory of Lemercier de Neuville's marionette theater Prudhomme figured in a dozen plays where his comic possibilities were exploited in various roles. In 1920 Prudhomme made a speech at the unveiling of his own statue at Sceaux, and a few years later a story came out that he had received the visit of his English cousin Samuel Pickwick. This visit is rather dramatic, for Pickwick falls in love with Prudhomme's young wife. In seeking proofs of this betrayal, Prudhomme discovers that Pickwick's diary is quite illegible, so everything is settled amicably when he offers lessons in penmanship.[19]

Monsieur Prudhomme has rarely inspired poets, but once, at least, he has been the subject of a sonnet. Could it have been the potent influence he exerts which led Verlaine to open with a pun and trace his portrait with such delicate irony?

Il est grave: il est maire et père de famille.
Son faux col engloutit son oreille.–Ses yeux
Dans un rêve sans fin flottent insoucieux
Et le printemps en fleurs sur ses pantoufles brille.

Que lui fait l'astre d'or, que lui fait la charmille
Où l'oiseau chante à l'ombre, et que lui font les cieux
Et les prés verts et les gazons silencieux?
Monsieur Prudhomme songe à marier sa fille

Avec monsieur Machin, un jeune homme cossu.
Il est juste milieu, botaniste et pansu.
Quant aux faiseurs de vers, ces vauriens, ces maroufles,

Ces fainéants barbus, mal peignés, il les a
Plus en horreur que son éternel coryza,
Et le printemps en fleurs brille sur ses pantoufles.[20]

Although the bourgeois has always had a place in French literature, it is evident that his literary role owed its growth in importance and complexity in the nineteenth century to factors which were chiefly political and economic. That Henry Monnier's conception of Monsieur Prudhomme should have achieved greater and more lasting fame than any of the other presentations of the type was due partly to the fact that he was triply impressed on public imagination, through Monnier's three media of creation. He thus became with unusual rapidity a very familiar figure and entered into the public domain long before Monnier had completed his own studies of Prudhomme. Comic artists wishing to caricature the average Frenchman found themselves using him as their model. For years he was one of the favorite subjects, for instance, of Cham, who published in *Le Charivari* a whole history of Prudhomme's share in the events of the Second Empire: his zeal as a national guardsman, his part in the Crimean War and the war against Italy, his departure on an expedition to China, his chauvinistic views of the Prussian question. Later cartoonists, Guillaume and Forain, specializing in the bourgeois, gave their newly rich businessmen the portly figure, bald head, and gold-rimmed spectacles of Monsieur Prudhomme, recognizing in him the representative, no longer of a social class, which had become far too complex to be cast into a single mold, but rather of a certain type of mentality, of a certain stage in man's intellectual and spiritual development.

It is this conception of Prudhomme which makes him the natural butt of youth's mockery, as he was represented on a magazine cover a short time before the war of 1914–1918. Under the caption "Papotages de Fantasio" appeared Prudhomme, accompanied by a modern girl teasing and tormenting him.[21] And this universal Prudhomme who continues to reappear in each generation inspired in 1921 a poster of the Comité Français de Propagande Aéronautique, showing the ghost of Joseph Prudhomme, dated 1842, perched on the shoulder of a modern bourgeois and looking at an airplane, as he says: "*I* did not believe in the railroad." *

If further proof of Prudhomme's vitality were needed, it could be found in the way he has been attacked and defended ever since Monnier created him. Those who attributed his early popularity to the fact that he appeared as an antidote to the feverish passions and languorous melancholy of Antony and the other Romantic heroes saw in him the personification of good sense, reassuring banality, a solid mediocrity which reinforced those two pillars of the modern

* Prudhomme's definitive acceptance as a type has come with the dictionaries' inclusion of his name as a simple noun, with its derivatives. Larousse defines *la prudhommerie* as "character, language analogous to those of Monsieur Prudhomme"; *prudhommesque* as "sententiously banal." A *prudhommade* is a "sententious saying in the manner of Joseph Prudhomme," and there has even been coined the verb *Josephprudhommiser* (in Benjamin Crémieux, "Les Lettres françaises–Questions de grammaire," *Les Nouvelles littéraires,* May 17, 1924, p. 4, col. 6). See Doutrepont, *Les Types populaires,* p. 291.

state, the family and the social order. His sententious pedantry, his silly prejudices, the flowery inappropriateness of his empty rhetoric have been condemned as manifestations of his stupidity and ignorance, but the immense power of his egoism, his dignity, the fundamental sincerity of his materialism have made him representative of that *juste milieu* which has been called the foundation of modern France.

When the twentieth century has tried to relegate Joseph Prudhomme's old-fashioned ways to a bygone era, proclaiming in his stead the birth of a new and modern *bourgeoisie,* it has found that the average Frenchman still reveals many of the traits which Monnier defined so shrewdly.[22] More sophisticated in taste than he used to be, he has become quite bold in his willingness to accept the unusual and the incomprehensible. But he still enjoys the familiar more than the strange, and would rather be flattered by having his own notions confirmed than suffer the wounded vanity of seeing them refuted. His love of order leads him still to classify and codify his ideas into formulas to which he clings with an instinctive realization that on them is built the whole fabric of his self-assurance. When his essential respect for virtue leads him periodically to examinations of his soul, he renews his profession of faith in the value of daily work and the sanctity of the family.

A glance at Monsieur Prudhomme's literary forbears and descendants has shown that he is far from being an isolated phenomenon peculiar to the nineteenth century. An analysis of his mental processes and the concepts by which he lives has revealed him as the symbol not of a social class but of a permanent human type, which happened to achieve special significance in France during the nineteenth century. That Henry Monnier's second-rate talents should have perfected him is one of those tricks of circumstance by which the master *Mystificateur* brings together at the climactic moment an artist and a fully ripened idea.

NOTES

NOTES

Chapter I—Childhood

1. *Nouvelle galerie des artistes dramatiques vivants* (Paris, 1855), I, xiii.

2. Sara Woodruff, "Henry Monnier" (unpublished dissertation, Middlebury College, 1938), p. 11. For other references to this data, see Larousse, *Grand dictionnaire universel du XIXe siècle;* "Henry Monnier," in *Temple Bar,* LII (London, 1878), 355; Aristide Marie, *Henry Monnier* (Paris, 1931), p. 7. Incorrect dates given by Champfleury, *Henry Monnier* (Paris, 1879), p. 1; Henri Beraldi, *Les Graveurs du XIXe siècle* (Paris, 1890), IX–X, 76; Eugène de Mirecourt, "Henry Monnier," in *Les Contemporains* (Paris, 1857), LXXVI, 5; Webster's *New International Dictionary* (1935). The works by Marie and Champfleury will hereafter be cited by author's name only.

3. See Spoelberch de Lovenjoul, "Henri Monnier et ses épaves" *Lundis d'un chercheur* (Paris, 1894), chap. ix, nos. 20, 21, 33.

4. Charles Simond, *Paris de 1800 à 1900* (Paris, 1900), 279–280.

5. Labretonnière, *Macédoine; Souvenirs du quartier latin dédiés à la jeunesse des écoles; Paris à la chute de l'empire et pendant les cent jours* (Paris, 1863), p. 98.

6. *Ibid.*, pp. 208–209, 218.

Chapter II—Government Service

1. Scribe et Dupin, "L'Intérieur de l'étude, ou Le Procureur et l'avoué," in *Fin du répertoire du Théâtre Français* (Paris, 1824), XXXVI, 132.

2. Balzac, *Les Employés* (transl. by M. W. Artois, Philadelphia, 1896), p. 186.

3. *Ibid.*, p. 188.

4. *Ibid.*, p. 90.

5. *Ibid.*, p. 93.

6. Prudhomme's signature became an inseparable part of the personage. See Flaubert, *Correspondence* (Paris, 1930), VI, 419: letter signed "Prudhomme," with the note: "N.B.–*Un parafe impossible.*"

7. Dumas, *Mes mémoires* (Paris, 1899), ser. 3, p. 126.

8. *Fin du répertoire du Théâtre-Français,* XXXVIII, 248.

9. *Ibid.*, p. 266.

10. Champfleury, p. 13.

11. Compare Champfleury, p. 339.

12. "Scènes de la vie bureaucratique," in *Scènes populaires* (Brussels, 1835); "Scènes de la France administrative," in *La France administrative* (Paris, 1840–1842).

13. See Champfleury, p. 13, n. 1.

Chapter III—Art Student

1. See Audebrand, "Henry Monnier," *Illustration*, LXIX (January 13, 1877), 19.

2. I, 139–184: "Les Ateliers."

3. *Ibid.*, p. 162. Compare Flaubert, *Dictionnaire des idées reçues*, in *Bouvard et Pécuchet* (Paris, 1923), p. 416: "ARTISTES. *Tous farceurs.*"

4. Madame Ancelot, *Les Salons de Paris* (Paris, 1858), p. 59; compare Véron, *Mémoires d'un bourgeois de Paris* (Paris, 1856), I, 262.

5. Champfleury, p. 16, quotes N. Roqueplan, in *Le Constitutionnel* (August 3, 1863): "Je voudrais bien que monsieur *Gros eille* la bonté de regarder ma figure" (that is, the sketch he was working on); or "Ah! monsieur *Gros ayez* la bonté de regarder ma figure!"

6. See Mespoulet, *Images et romans* (Paris, 1939), p. 15: song sung in 1819 at the Variétés, in *Les Bolivars et les Morillos.*

7. *Contes philosophiques*, I, in *Oeuvres complètes*, XXVII (Paris, 1925), 15.

Chapter IV—England

1. Letter mentioned but not quoted, in P.-A. Lemoisne, *Eugène Lami* (Paris, 1912), p. 20.

2. Marie, p. 30: letter to Guittard, from London, June 20, 1828.

3. *Ibid.*, describes series published or offered for sale in London, the most important being: p. 240, *Modes et ridicules* (1825); p. 246, *Récréations du cœur et de l'esprit* (1826); pp. 249–250, *Rencontres parisiennes;* p. 252, *Voyage en Angleterre* (1829).

4. Champfleury, pp. 358–363. Compare Balzac, *Œuvres diverses,* II, in *Œuvres complètes,* XXXIX (Paris, 1938), 144–145.

5. A. Jal, *Esquisses, croquis, pochades . . . sur le Salon de 1827* (Paris, 1828), p. 395.

6. See Marie, pp. 27–28: this description corresponds closely to that of Bixiou in Balzac's *Les Employés.*

7. Quoted in Blanchard Jerrold, *Life of Cruikshank* (London, 1882), II, 45; see also p. 48 (note), p. 55.

8. See Marie, p. 256.

9. *The Tour of Dr. Syntax in Search of the Picturesque; Dr. Syntax in Search of Consolation; Dr. Syntax in Search of a Wife.* Published in Ackermann's *Poetical Magazine* beginning in 1809, then in book form.

10. *Paris France* (New York, 1940), p. 24. For a somewhat different approach to the same conclusion, see anonymous editorial quoted by T. S. Eliot, in "The Function of Criticism," *Selected Essays 1917–1932* (New York, n.d.), p. 16: "The English character . . . 'obstinately humorous and nonconformist.'" As early as 1837–1838 the English fashion of hiding feelings under a mask of boredom and cynicism had reached Russia; for example, the Byronic Pechorin in Lermontov's *A Hero of Our Times.*

Chapter V—Development of Illustration

1. For a catalogue of Monnier's work during this period, see Champfleury, pp. 328–345; Marie, pp. 241–254. Marie includes the following series, although

some of them are undated: *Boutiques de Paris; Esquisses parisiennes; Les Grisettes; Jadis et aujourd'hui; Mœurs parisiennes; Paris vivant; Passetemps; Les Petites félicités humaines; Les Petites misères humaines; Rencontres parisiennes; Six quartiers de Paris; Le Temps, sa brièveté, sa longueur, sa fuite; Vues de Paris;* etc.

2. See *Mémoires de Monsieur Joseph Prudhomme,* I, 283–286: a lyrical evocation of the *grisettes* of his youth.

3. See Jal, "La Gaîté et les comiques de Paris," *Nouveau tableau de Paris au XIXe siècle* (Paris, 1834), II, 263 ff.

4. *Le Charivari* (Paris, September 15, 23, 1868).

5. *Ibid.*, September 15.

6. Marie (p. 38) describes this sketch and suggests the above interpretation.

7. Gautier, *Portraits contemporains* (Paris, 1874), p. 226.

8. *Histoire du romantisme* (Paris, 1877), p. 53.

9. Ferdinand Langlé, *Les Contes du gay sçavoir* (Paris, 1828). Monnier designed the vignettes at the head of the following tales: "Le Prisonnier du Mont Saint-Michel," p. xxxvii; "La Dame Lige de la fausse monarchie du diable," p. cxi; "Le Clocheteur des trépassés," p. cxliii.

10. See Champfleury, *Henry Monnier,* pp. 376, 390, 393; *Vignettes romantiques* (Paris, 1883), pp. 385, 386; Charles Asselineau, *Bibliographie romantique* (Paris, 1874), p. 258.

11. *Chansons de Béranger:* see Marie, pp. 245, 265; Champfleury, p. 376. *La Morale en action des Fables de La Fontaine:* see Marie, p. 267; Champfleury, pp. 385–386.

12. *La Coupe et les lèvres,* "Dédicace."

Chapter VI—Monnier and His Friends

1. II, 111–112. This allusion is the only indication I have found that Monnier knew Nodier or may have gone to the Arsenal.

2. *Biographie pittoresque des députés, portraits, moeurs et costumes* (Paris, 1820).

3. For further details of this elaborate hoax, and material on Latouche, see the definitive study by Ségu, *H. de Latouche.*

4. II, 103–108.

5. See Nodier's preface to *Trilby* (*Nouvelles,* Paris, 1871, p. 104), acknowledging his debt to Latouche and expressing his admiration of him; Emile Deschamps' presentation of him to Hugo as his mentor; the prestige Latouche acquired by editing the poetry of André Chénier in 1819 (Léon Séché, *Le Cénacle de Joseph Delorme,* Paris, 1912, I, 212 ff.; Ségu, *H. de Latouche,* pp. 87 ff.).

6. Letter undated, quoted by Champfleury, p. 125.

7. II, 111.

8. See Albert Cim, *Mystifications littéraires et théâtrales* (Paris, 1913), pp. 129–134. Virginie was supposed to have given birth to a son before leaving the island, this being the reason, in fact, for her being sent away.

9. Letter to Stendhal, quoted by Pierre Trahard, *La Jeunesse de Prosper Mérimée* (Paris, 1925), I, 234–235.

10. Ancelot, *Les Salons de Paris,* pp. 66–68.

11. Henri d'Alméras, *La Vie parisienne sous le règne de Louis-Philippe* (Paris: Michel, n.d.), pp. 52–53.

12. Dumas, *Mes mémoires*, (1898), X, 256. See J. R. Boulenger, *Sous Louis-Philippe: Les Dandys* (*nouvelle édition augmentée*, Paris, n.d.), p. 286.

13. Mirecourt, "Henry Monnier," p. 27.

14. Dumas, *Mes mémoires* (1899), IV, 218.

15. Dumas, *ibid*., pp. 215–216; Champfleury, p. 70.

16. Champfleury, p. 71.

17. Quoted by Champfleury, p. 223.

18. Théodore de Banville, *L'Ame de Paris* (Paris, 1890), pp. 104–105.

19. Jal, *La Gaîté et les comiques de Paris*, pp. 317–318.

20. Quoted by Champfleury, pp. 78–79.

21. See Berthet, "Silhouettes et anecdotes littéraires," *Revue de France*, III (May 1, 1877), 320–322. The "Voyage en diligence" of which Berthet gives some details, and which he says was never published, seems different, indeed, from the published scene bearing that title, which has no Englishman asking to descend *pour ioun tout petit chose*, and does not end with the accident from which the postilion emerges to remark: *En voilà de la propre ouvrage! . . . quelle omelette!* I have combined details given by Berthet with some taken from the published scene. See *Scènes populaires* (Paris, Dentu, 1864), pp. 237–337.

22. *Lorgnette littéraire* (Paris, 1857), p. 149.

23. *Pensées* (Paris, L. de Bure, 1823), II, 70–71.

24. Cim, *Mystifications littéraires*, p. 4, note. For the history of famous *mystifications* in France see also Larousse, "Mystification," *Grand dictionnaire universel du XIX*[e] *siècle* (Paris, 1874); Augustin Thierry, *Les Grandes Mystifications littéraires* (Paris, 1911); Roger Picard, *Artifices et mystifications littéraires* (Montreal, 1945).

25. *Mémoires de Saint-Simon* (Paris, Hachette, 1890), VII, 57–60.

26. Voltaire, *Œuvres complètes* (Paris, 1882), XLVIII, 119.

27. I, 260–261.

Chapter VII—Caricature

1. See Baudelaire, "De l'essence du rire et généralement du comique dans les arts plastiques," *Curiosités esthétiques* (Paris, 1868), pp. 359–387; also Giraudoux, "Sur la caricature," introduction to *Arts et métiers graphiques*, XXXI (Sept. 15, 1932), p. 3: ". . . vengence at its highest degree, which one can wreak on oneself, man on man, in the loathing or hilarity which the fact of belonging to the human race inspires in him . . . The great and the middle class have a horror of caricature because it avenges, at the expense of existing mankind, a humanity which does not exist." See Paul Gaultier, *Le Rire et la caricature* (3rd ed., Paris, 1911), pp. 3–6; 35–36; Arsène Alexandre, "L'Esprit français; Les Caricaturistes," *Pages d'histoire 1914–1916*, ser. 8 (Paris-Nancy, 1916).

2. Hogarth's influence on the moralizing tendency of French literature in the eighteenth century can be traced through Diderot. His contribution to the growth of realistic literature is found in Rétif de la Bretonne's *Paysanne pervertie*, suggested by the *Harlot's Progress*, and the *Paysan perverti*, whose subject was taken from Hogarth's *Rake's Progress*. See M. W. Burger, *Histoire des*

peintres de toutes les écoles: école anglaise (Paris, 1867), p. 14: refers to Philarète Chasles, *Hogarth: influence en France.*

3. *La Silhouette, Journal des caricatures, beaux-arts, dessins, mœurs, théâtres,* etc., I (Paris, 1830).

4. Vol. III (New York, 1932), bk. IV, p. 81.

5. Benjamin Antier, Armand Lacoste, Alexandre Chapponier, under pseudonymes of Benjamin, Saint-Amand, Paulyanthe, *L'Auberge des Adrets,* presented at the Ambigu-Comique, July 2, 1823.

6. *Works of William Makepeace Thackeray* (London, 1911), XXII, 183.

7. I, 187.

8. Raymond Escholier, *Daumier peintre et lithographe* (Paris, 1923), pp. 124–128.

9. See Champfleury, pp. 353–354.

10. *Mémoires,* II, 3.

11. Champfleury, p. 386: "Une des planches interdites par la censure fut celle du *Lion devenu vieux.* Voulant montrer à quel degré d'humiliation peut arriver l'homme que la fortune a abandonné, il avait assis sur le rocher de Sainte-Hélène Napoléon, décrépit, triste et recevant un coup de pied d'un officier anglais. Dans une autre, interdite également, il avait fait un égoiste d'un chanoine et pris parmi les gens d'Eglise le *Rat qui s'est retiré du monde.*" Eugène Desmares, *Les Métamorphoses du jour ou La Fontaine en 1831* (Paris, 1831): the titles of the *Fables* parodied and given political significance. See Marie, p. 267.

12. John Grand-Carteret, *Les Mœurs et la caricature en France* (Paris, 1888), p. 222: caption of an anti-Romantic drawing of the early 1830's.

Chapter VIII—*Scènes populaires*

1. *Nouvelle galerie des artistes dramatiques vivants.*

2. Paris, Levavasseur & Urbain Canel, 1830.

3. pp. xii–xiii.

4. p. x.

5. p. 38.

6. See Morienval, *De Pathelin à Ubu, bilan des types littéraires* (Paris, n.d.), p. 153.

7. p. 54.

8. p. xiii.

9. Scribe, "La Loge du portier," *Fin du répertoire du Théâtre-Français,* XXXVIII, 185–241. The *portier* was frequently presented in the *physiologies* and sketches of manners abounding between 1830 and 1848. For example, "Les Portiers," and "Les Voisines du faubourg Saint-Germain," in *La Silhouette,* I, 89–91, 97–99; James Rousseau, "Physiologie de la portière," *Les Physiologies parisiennes* (Paris, n.d.). Balzac sounds a humanitarian note in describing the miseries of the *portier's* life in *Les Comédiens sans le savoir, Œuvres complètes,* XIX, 328–329.

10. Monnier & Gabriel, *Le Roman chez la portière, folie-vaudeville en un acte,* Théâtre du Palais-Royal, February 10, 1855 (Paris, Galerie Théâtrale, Magasin Central de Pièces de Théâtre, 1855, 1857, 1860, 1869). Isabelle Fusier, *L'Exécution, deux tableaux tirés des Scènes populaires,* Nouveau Théâtre, Oc-

tober 10, 1921; see Woodruff, "Henry Monnier," p. 79: this play presented Titi, Lolo, Prudhomme, and other characters from the *Scènes populaires,* and was very successful.

11. *Proverbes dramatiques* (Berlin & Paris, 1781), p. 15.

12. See p. 93, above. *Proverbes dramatiques* (Paris, 1835); *Œuvres complètes* (Paris, 1851).

13. Vitet, *Scènes de la Ligue* (Paris, 1883), I, "Introduction." Quoted by Marthe Trotain, *Les Scènes historiques. Etude du théâtre livresque à la veille du drame romantique* (Paris, 1923), p. 48.

14. Mérimée tried the historical genre in *La Jacquerie, scènes féodales* (Paris, 1828). See Delécluze, *Souvenirs de soixante années* (Paris, 1862): From 1819 to 1830 these men attended the regular Sunday gatherings. Delécluze describes Cavé and Dittmer as "enlevés par le tourbillon romantique . . . ayant mis la main à l'oeuvre pour réaliser les théories proposées et réformer l'art dramatique" (pp. 228–229). The theories would be Stendhal's in *Racine et Shakespeare* (Paris, 1822): use of prose in serious plays, subjects taken from national history, etc. I have found no proof that Monnier himself belonged to Delécluze's group.

15. *Scènes populaires* (2nd ed., Paris, 1831).

16. *Scènes contemporaines,* I (Paris, 1828); II (Paris, 1830).

17. See L.-J. Arrigon, *Les Années romantiques de Balzac* (Paris, 1927), pp. 6–8.

18. See *Œuvres complètes,* I (1912): "La Maison du Chat-qui-pelote," first published with the title "Gloire et malheur," and "Le Bal de Sceaux."

19. *France in 1829–30* (London, 1830), I, 268. See also II, 371: "Whoever has not read '*Les Soirées de Neuilly,*' has still to read one of the pleasantest productions of the modern school of French literature; light, yet philosophical—humorously, not sarcastically illustrative of living manners."

20. See "Les Marrons du feu," in his *Contes d'Espagne et d'Italie.*

21. In *Le Tiroir du Diable: Paris et les Parisiens* (Paris, 1850), pp. 1–53.

Chapter IX—Monnier as an Actor

1. *Nouvelle galerie des artistes dramatiques vivants.*

2. Duvert, *Théâtre choisi* (Paris, 1879), I.

3. Dumas, *Mes Mémoires,* VIII (1898), 173–174; see Ségu, *H. de Latouche,* p. 283.

4. July 1, 1832.

5. Champfleury, p. 194.

6. *Scènes populaires dessinées à la plume* "par Henry Monnier, ornées du portrait de M. Prudhomme, du facsimile de sa signature, et de 6 gravures à l'eau forte par E. Verboekhoven" (Paris, Levavasseur, Bruxelles et Londres, Librairie Romantique, 1830) Champfleury says (p. 317) that in spite of the title page the book appeared only in Brussels, and contained 7 etchings by Verboekhoven. This book is listed as very rare. See Asselineau, *Bibliographie romantique,* p. 308.

7. *Scènes populaires,* "dessinées par Henry Monnier, 2e édition, augmentée de 2 scènes et de 2 vignettes" (Paris, Levavasseur, Urbain Canel, 1831). See page 88, above.

8. Bruxelles, Deprez-Parent.

9. Balzac, *Œuvres complètes*, XXXIX, 300–303: "La Cour des Messageries Royales," *La Caricature* (February 17, 1831); 477-478: "Départ d'une diligence," *La Caricature* (February 9, 1832).

10. *Scènes populaires* (Paris, Dentu, 1864), p. 265. Another, abridged version of the "Voyage" appeared in *Les Annales politiques et littéraires* (Paris, April 4, 1926), pp. 379–380.

11. *Scènes populaires* (ed. Dentu), p. 346.

12. *Scènes populaires dessinées à la plume* (4th ed., Paris, Dumont, 1836–1839; 4 *tomes*, 2 vols.).

13. "Le Peintre et les bourgeois."

14. "Les Petits prodiges."

15. "Les Compatriotes."

16. "Les Trompettes."

17. Compare Flaubert's aim in writing the *Dictionnaire des idées reçues: Correspondance*, III (Paris, 1927), 66–67.

18. "L'Esprit des campagnes."

19. For a description of such a ball, see Balzac, *Splendeurs et misères des courtisanes*, opening pages.

20 Champfleury, p. 102: letter of December 30, 1835.

21. See Marie, pp. 212–213: "Le Vieil acteur," 1835; "Portrait d'homme en redingote verte," Douai, 1837; "Portraits de l'acteur Lambert," Lyon, October 1843, April 1844; etc.; p. 265: "Les Aniers de Moulins," *L'Art en province* (Moulins, 1839).

22. There is no confirmation of Monnier's statement in the *Nouvelle galerie des artistes dramatiques vivants* that he became director of a company which performed for 18 months in Belgium, Germany, Prussia, and France.

23. Champfleury, p. 107: letter to Ferville.

24. Champfleury, pp. 107–108: December 16, 1836. Marie, who quotes part of this letter (pp. 99–100) interprets it oddly enough to show that Monnier had regained hope while he rested at Parnes.

25. A letter to Louis Desnoyers, dated *21 février 1841*, written while Monnier was acting at Troyes, says: ". . . J'ai quitté Paris depuis un mois environ et me trouve fort bien jusqu'à présent de mon émigration si la capitale ne veut plus de moi ou du moins MM. les directeurs la province en veut bien et nous le prouve. Nous restons encore à Troyes une quinzaine puis nous allons à Auxerre Joigny. . . . Si vous avez quelques amis dans ces parages indiquez-les moi je les irai visiter . . ." (from the Gentili di Giuseppe Collection deposited in the Houghton Library of Harvard University).

26. Marie, p. 100.

27. Marie, p. 112.

28. See Marie, p. 212: "Un matelot hollandais," "Scène de rue à Amsterdam," both dated 1837; p. 229: "Marchands de poissons à Amsterdam," not dated.

29. Marie, p. 198.

30. Marie, p. 162: letter from Nice, February 19, 1844.

Chapter X—Artist versus Bourgeois

1. Quoted by Jules Guex, *Le Théâtre et la société française de 1815 à 1848* (Vevey, 1900), p. 139.

2. Transl. by G. Burnham Ives, *The Magic Skin* (Philadelphia, 1899), p. 61.

3. p. 64.

4. *Mémoires de Monsieur Joseph Prudhomme*, I, 264 ff.

5. *Les Jeune-France* (Paris, 1885), pp. 71–95.

6. In the *Histoire du romantisme* (p. 21), Gautier says that when he joined Hugo's *cénacle* there were only two full beards in France, which gave great prestige to their wearers, Eugène Devéria and Pétrus Borel. See footnote, page 61, above.

7. *Souvenirs littéraires* (Paris, 1892), I, 75.

8. *Histoire du romantisme*, p. 176.

9. Paul Desfeuilles, *La Vie littéraire sous le second empire: Charles Monselet et la critique anecdotique* (Paris, 1927), p. 254.

10. Gautier, *Portraits contemporains*, p. 147. For Gozlan's friendship with Monnier see page 56, above.

11. *Propos littéraires* (Paris, 1902), pp. 159–161.

12. Transl. by William Stigand, *The Life . . . of Heinrich Heine* (London, 1875), II, 27.

13. Goncourt, *Gavarni l'homme et l'œuvre* (Paris, 1912), p. 183.

14. Goncourt, *Gavarni*, p. 169.

15. Quoted in *The Goncourt Journals*, translated by Lewis Galantière (New York, 1937), p. 46: May 1, 1857.

Chapter XI—The Realistic Movement

1. Mirecourt, "Henry Monnier," p. 68.

2. Quoted by Champfleury, p. 69.

3. *Ibid.*, p. 70.

4. p. 72. See discussion of the work later in this chapter.

5. "Vieux lions," "Demoiselle à pourvoir," "Le Jour de la blanchisseuse," and many others, including a complacent bourgeoise who pronounces a sentence sometimes attributed to Prudhomme: "Je n'aime pas les épinards, et j'en suis bien aise, si je les aimais, j'en mangerais, et je ne puis pas les souffrir." According to the *Intermédiaire des chercheurs et curieux*, V, 479 (August 25, 1869), Monnier did not invent this legend, which appeared in Dugast de Bois Saint-Just, *Paris, Versailles et les provinces au XVIII*e siècle (1809), II, 331. For a complete description of the series listed above, see Marie, pp. 257–258.

6. As, "Intérieur de cuisine avec un chat," "Etude du village de Tain," "Paysan assis," "Cour de ferme avec animaux," etc. See Marie, pp. 213–215.

7. Balzac's complaint recalls Stendhal's gloomy prophecy; see p. 32 above.

8. *Les Mécontens*, II, 156–176.

9. *Œuvres complètes*, XXXVIII, 66–71; 452, note.

10. For bibliography see Champfleury, pp. 363–369.

11. *Œuvres complètes*, XXXIX, 11, 47, 62, 277, 400, 411, 439.

12. 1841 is probably the correct date for the publication also of *L'Ami du château*, or *Le Chevalier de Clermont*, republished sometimes under the one title, sometimes under the other. This was a historical novel by Elie Berthet and Monnier, an unfortunate collaboration which adds nothing to Monnier's reputation, although it is further evidence of his versatility. It recalls his youthful plunge into the *genre troubadour* with his illustrations for *Les Contes du*

gay sçavoir, and his sometimes overconfident willingness to try his hand at any venture.

13. Desfeuilles, *La Vie littéraire,* p. 213.

14. *Théâtre du Figaro* (Paris, 1861), pp. 207–219.

15. For a list of borrowings from Monnier and a discussion of his influence, see Emile Bouvier, *La Bataille réaliste* (Paris, n.d.), pp. 65–69.

16. *Ibid.*, p. 69.

17. (Paris, 1872), p. 127.

18. See Schanne, *Souvenirs d'un buveur d'eau,* speaking of Monnier's monologues: "La seule indication de ces histoires donnera, j'en suis sûr, un revenez-y de rire à ceux qui ont eu la bonne chance de voir le grand humoriste mettre en scène et faire parler tout le monde bizarre qu'il avait créé." Quoted by Bouvier, *La Bataille Réaliste,* p. 64.

19. For this summary, and discussion of the theories of realism, see Weinberg, *French Realism: The Critical Reaction 1830–1870* (Chicago, 1936), esp. chap. iv and pp. 194–195.

20. I quote from the edition of 1866 (Amsterdam).

21. p. 78.

22. p. 64.

23. p. 81.

24. Paris, n.d.

Chapter XII—Theatrical Ventures

1. *La Presse* (July 8, 1849). A letter to Louis Desnoyers, postmarked *15 août 1849,* shows that several weeks after Monnier opened in these plays he was still working on his costume. This letter reveals also some of the strain which he felt at reappearing on the Paris stage more than twenty years after his early successes: "Mon cher Desnoyers vous sentez que vous n'êtes pas de ces gens qu'on oublie. Mais j'étais si peu certain du succès de ma dernière machine que j'ai mis de la coquetterie à ne pas me montrer dans le cas où j'étais alors. Ce n'est que d'hier justement que j'ai commencé à m'asseoir la pièce étant donnée j'apporte à mes costumes certains changements, certaines améliorations, qui ne seront faits que la semaine prochaine alors je vous invite avec l'aimable Madame Louis Desnoyers mademoiselle et charmante Christine Louise Desnoyers et M. Petit, si je peux me le procurer. A bientôt, Henry Monnier." From the Gentili di Giuseppe Collection deposited in the Houghton Library of Harvard University. For M. Petit, see chapter XIV, pp. 186–187.

2. *La Silhouette* (September 23, 1849).

3. Mirecourt, "Henry Monnier," p. 61.

4. Quoted by Marie, pp. 120–121: letter from Montpellier, June 27, 1850.

5. Parnes, *11 juillet 1851;* from the Gentili di Giuseppe Collection deposited in the Houghton Library of Harvard University. In a letter dated Rouen, *4 mai,* Monnier had expressed some dissatisfaction because his travel articles were cut too much: "Mon cher Desnoyers Voilà la suite de mon voyage dans le midi je vous enverrai Nismes, Avignon, Marseilles, etc.: je trouve que vous m'avez terriblement écourté mon Aigues-Mortes je ne m'en plains pas–il y avait passablement de longueur mais pour Montpellier si vous pouviez me donner deux feuilletons je vous en serais bien obligé . . . Votre tout dévoué . . . J'ai

lu ma pièce à Samson qui (*sic*) j'ai trouvé ici elle est de son goût. Nous verrons ça cet hiver" (same collection).

6. Monnier et Gustave Vaez, *Grandeur et décadence de M. Joseph Prudhomme* in *Théâtre contemporain 1790 à 1853* (Paris, 1853). An undated letter to Desnoyers seems to belong to this period of dramatic triumph. In it Monnier signs himself "Lafon de la Comédie Française," as if to indicate his hope of realizing his ambition at last. His use of Prudhomme's flowery style is to be expected at a time when he was absorbed by the role, but the mention of his son is surprising, for allusions to his family are very rare: "Je ne sais mon cher Desnoyers si la visite de Mon. mon fils est oui ou non inopportune. Il se prétend engagé par votre aimable demoiselle. Dans tous les cas ne vous gênez pas avec lui je l'enverrai prendre si cela vous convient entre 3 et 4[h] de relevée. Je saisis l'occasion qui se présente pour vous témoigner toute ma reconnaissance de l'aimable accueil que vous et votre aimable dame (aux pieds de laquelle je dispose le tribut de mes hommages) m'avez offert d'une manière gracieuse." From the Gentili di Giuseppe Collection.

7. *Mystères des théâtres*, 1852 (Paris, 1853), pp. 480–483.

8. Monnier and Jules Gabriel (Paris, 1855; several later reprints).

9. Published Paris, 1855; republished with the title "Les Voisins de campagne," in *Scènes populaires* (1879), II, pp. 231–280.

10. Published Paris, 1856.

11. *Les Variétés 1850–1870* (Paris, 1905), pp. 16–17.

12. Published Paris, 1856.

13. *Les Petites gens, Scènes parisiennes* (1857); *Galerie d'originaux, Croquis à la plume, Comédies bourgeoises, Les Bourgeois aux champs* (1858).

14. Champfleury, p. 321: This is the same as the *Petit tableau de Paris* which precedes it in Champfleury's bibliography. See Marie, pp. 60, 203: Paris edition published by Dentu (1861 ?).

15. Paris, Librairie Nouvelle, 1857.

16. Clairville, Gabriel, and Monnier (ms. lost, never published; see Marie, p. 134).

17. Marie, p. 140 (September 9, 1856).

18. S. M. Waxman, *Antoine and the Théâtre-Libre* (Cambridge, Mass., 1926), p. 132: refers to a brochure by Antoine (May 1890).

19. For accounts of the *Théâtre Erotique* see Alfred Delvau, *Le Théâtre érotique sous le bas-empire français* (Paris, n.d.); Lemercier de Neuville, *Histoire anecdotique des marionnettes modernes* (Paris, 1892), *Souvenirs d'un montreur de marionnettes* (Paris, 1911).

20. *L'Enfer de Joseph Prudhomme*, "dialogues agrémentés d'une figure infâme et d'un autographe accablant; Paris, à la sixième chambre" (Bruxelles, 1866 ?).

21. See Emile Augier, *La Contagion, Théâtre complet*, vol. V (Paris, 1890), Act I, sc. 3, p. 298. Valéry, "*Rapport sur les prix de vertu, lu dans la séance publique de l'Académie Française, 20 décembre, 1934*," *Variété IV* (Paris, 1938), 169.

22. For further descriptions, and reproductions of Monnier's late work, see Marie, pp. 163, 175–176, 178, 179, 180.

23. See Marie, pp. 211–228: many works autographed for Mène between 1869 and 1874.

24. *Catalogue des tableaux, aquarelles, dessins, bronzes, etc. offerts par divers artistes à Henry Monnier, dont la vente publique aura lieu, Hôtel Drouot, salle no. 5, le jeudi 20 mai 1875, à deux heures et demie.* Works by Bellangé, Corot, Daubigny, Isabey, Millet, etc., as well as by Monnier's more intimate friends, Lami, Madou, Mène. A preface by Champfleury indicates that Monnier's ill health had revealed his poverty.

25. See Boutet de Monvel, *Les Variétés*, pp. 154–155.

26. For earlier mention of Monnier's son see note 6 above. One daughter married Emile Gaudy, an actor at the Théâtre des Arts in Rouen and later a *pensionnaire* of the Comédie-Française; the other married the Marseillais actor Portalès, also on the stage in Rouen and Paris. The son of one of these daughters became an artist and was present as a young man at a ball given in 1904 for the benefit of the comic artists. See Woodruff, "Henry Monnier," pp. 4–5. There was also a grandson, Charles-Henry Monnier; see *Catalogue des aquarelles, dessins et croquis, par Henry Monnier, provenant de la collection de M. Gustave Cohen* (Paris, 1929).

27. Marie, p. 184. Monnier was particularly fond of the tranquil cows of Normandy.

28. Ms. dated March 15, 1873, in my possession, generously given to me by Professor Charles Livingston, of Bowdoin College.

29. Act I, sc. 5.

30. Albert Delasalle, "Ma dernière visite à Henry Monnier," *Les Nouvelles de Paris* (January 11, 1877); quoted in Champfleury, pp. 177–183, but dated incorrectly 1876. See Marie, p. 192.

31. Champfleury, pp. 171–172.

32. Philippe Burty, "Henry Monnier," *L'Art*, IX (May 1877), 177–184. This anecdote may be apocryphal, but Monnier would have enjoyed it.

Chapter XIII—Monnier, Balzac, and Flaubert

1. Bertall, "Henri Monnier," *L'Illustration* (January 13, 1877), p. 27.

2. Marie, pp. 81–82: letter dated June 17, 1879, attached to Champfleury's personal copy of his *Henry Monnier*.

3. Marie, "Balzac et Monnier," *Les Nouvelles littéraires* (March 7, 1931), p. 8. In *La Maison Nucingen* one of Bixiou's most brilliant *tours de force* is called by Balzac "une de ces terribles improvisations qui valent à cet artiste sa réputation auprès de quelques esprits blasés" (*Œuvres complètes*, XIV, 348). I have mentioned the resemblance between Monnier and Bixiou in chapter II.

4. *Les Employés*, pp. 136–139.

5. *Les Employés*, pp. 139–140. The final sentence is my own translation. For the foiling of Philippe Bridau, see *La Rabouilleuse*, pp. 577–578. The elaborate mystifying of Gazonal in *Les Comédiens sans le savoir* is an example of the impersonal way in which Bixiou sometimes uses his talents.

6. *Œuvres diverses*, II, 144–145, in *Œuvres complètes*, XXXIX.

7. *Ibid.*, p. 538. Monnier said almost the same thing of Balzac's tendency to disillusion his readers, which kept him from having the popular appeal of writers who expressed a more idealistic conception of human nature. See Marie, pp. 80–81, letter to Noël Parfait, August 21, 1857: "Balzac, malgré son immense nature, a le grand tort de nous jeter la mort dans l'ame; il est navrant, il ne

croit à rien, il ne croyait à rien non plus; c'est le seul homme auquel je n'ai pas connu d'âme ni même le désir d'en avoir."

8. *Journal d'Eugène Delacroix*, III, 408, July 22, 1860: "Malgré l'opinion surfaite du mérite de Balzac, je persiste à trouver son genre faux d'abord et faux ensuite ses caractères. Il dépeint les personnages, comme Henry Monnier, par des dictons de profession, par les dehors, en un mot; il sait les mots de portière, l'argot de chaque type. Mais quoi de plus faux que les caractères arrangés et tout d'une pièce?"

9. Eugène d'Izalguier, "La Vieille fille," *Phalange* (November 20, 1836), vol. I, cols. 434–435; quoted in Weinberg, *French Realism*, p. 53; see also, pp. 54, 72.

10. *Œuvres diverses*, II, 208–209.

11. *Ibid.*, pp. 300–303, 477–478.

12. See page 137, above.

13. *Œuvres complètes*, XXIV, 170–189. See Champfleury, p. 96, n. 1.

14. It is far more likely that Monnier's Napoleon was the source of another *Vie de Napoléon racontée dans une fête de village*, a comedy by Alcide Tousez, given at the Théâtre du Palais-Royal in 1834. The monologue forming the central part of this little play is much funnier than Balzac's text, and contains many phrases and turns of wit close enough to Monnier's manner to suggest the possibility that it was inspired by Monnier's unpublished scene. See the following passages. p. 5: "V'là donc mon homme qui est né, très bien! . . . ses parents que dans une parfaite débine, le mettent à l'école militaire, rempli de dispositions, avec un petit chapeau à trois cornes, les mains sur le dos, imitant déjà son portrait . . ." The Directoire: "le gouvernement de cette époque, qui était composé de cinq particuliers ornés de plumes." p. 6: In Egypt are found *cocodrilles:* "Je n'ai jamais cru aux *cocodrilles;* je les considère comme des animaux fabuleux, mais, dont la morsure est très dangereuse, au dire des botanistes." The Pyramids: "ainsi nommées, vu leur forme pyramidale." Austerlitz: "Ils parlent tous allemand! je ne sais pas comment ils font pour se comprendre!" Seeking a second wife, Napoleon says to the Emperor of Austria: "'A la demande générale du public, j'aurais besoin de votre fille, dont je suis très épris, n'importe laquelle' . . . L'empereur d'Autriche, voyant un homme très bien, et qui avait une bonne place, lui donne sa fille complètement." Published Paris, 1834.

15. *Œuvres complètes*, XIX, 327–328. The dates of publication confirm this conclusion: "Les Compatriotes," 1839; *Les Comédiens sans le savoir*, 1846.

16. *Lettres à l'étrangère* (5th ed., Paris, n.d.), I, 431: to Mme. Hanska, October 10–12, 1837.

17. Coll. Lovenjoul, A. 283: letter from Balzac, August 23, 1848; A. 308, fol. 574: Monnier's reply.

18. See Flaubert, *Œuvres de jeunesse inédites*, I (Paris, 1910), 198–203; Monnier, *Scènes populaires* (1835).

19. See *Correspondance*, II, 237–238; III, 66–67, 337. For other early allusions to the *Dictionnaire*, see III, 105, 139, 175, 295. See DuCamp, *Souvenirs littéraires*, I, 169.

20. *Madame Bovary*, *Notes*, p. 524. See *Correspondance*, IV, 245–246: Flaubert's decision not to commercialize his art by consenting to the dramatization.

21. *Ibid.*, IV, 366.

22. *Ibid.*, VII, 377. See the criticisms of Monnier's realism in the 1850's, pages 143–144, above.

23. *Ibid.*, VI, 288: to Mme. Roger des Genettes, October 6, 1871.

24. *Ibid.*, VI, p. 138: to George Sand, August 3, 1870. Other references to Prudhomme in letters to G. Sand: VI, 117, 353; VII, 11.

25. *Ibid.*, VI, 417–419: to Baroness Lepic, September 24, 1872.

26. *Mémoires*, I, 272.

27. *Ibid.*, p. 238.

28. *Ibid.*, p. 279.

29. Woodruff, "Henry Monnier," p. 85: letter, March 4, 1863.

Chapter XIV—M. Prudhomme

1. See Chapter V, page 46; Chapter II, page 20.

2. Letter dated only 7 *mai*, from the Gentili di Giuseppe Collection deposited in the Houghton Library of Harvard University. This could be May 1849, as in another letter from the same collection, dated *15 août 1849*, Monnier mentions Petit again. (For text, see chapter XII, note 1.) Inserted in this letter is a fragment containing the sentence: "M. Petit trouve heureuse l'idée que j'ai eue de devenir M. Proudhon il constamment dit Proudhon." In spite of the carelessness of Monnier's style, here is a glimpse of a man obviously made to be a foil for his wit and a model for his study of human stupidity.

3. *Essai instructif de l'art de l'Escriture, où par une nouvelle méthode le mystère de l'Escrivain est clairement découvert et expliqué par le nombre ternaire et autres enseignemens; Avec une ample digression sur les vérifications et comparaisons des escritures et signatures; Outre les maximes importantes de l'Art; par R. Preud'homme, Maistre Escrivain-Juré à Paris. A Paris, chez l'auteur, à ses frais; Chez Samuel Petit, dans la cour du Palais, à la Bible d'or; et chez Hernier Clousier, au Palais, sur les degrez de la Sainte-Chapelle; M.D.C. XXXIX.* See *L'Intermédiaire des chercheurs et curieux*, I, 160 (August 10, 1864); G. d'Heylli, *Gazette anecdotique, littéraire, artistique et bibliographique*, lère année, II, 186 (Paris, September 30, 1876).

4. See above, Chapter VIII, p. 90.

5. II, 267.

6. I, 2.

7. See J. B. Wolf, *France, 1815 to the Present* (New York, 1940), p. 96; A.-J. de Marnay, *Mémoires secrets et témoignages authentiques* (Paris, 1875), p. 187.

8. This composite portrait is taken from Edmond D'Althon Shée, *Mes mémoires* (Paris, 1869), I, 256–258; and Véron, *Mémoires d'un bourgeois*, II, 286, 317–318; III, 285–287.

9. III, 37.

10. Paris; vols. II and III appeared in 1843 with the title: *Jérôme Paturot à la recherche d'une position sociale et politique. Jérôme Paturot à la recherche de la meilleure des républiques* (1848) is less interesting to compare with Monnier.

11. *Le Bourgeois poli, où se voit l'abrégé de divers complimens selon les diverses qualités des personnes, oeuvre très-utile pour la conversation; A Chartres chez Claude Peigné, imprimeur, 1631. Réimprimé à Chartres, Garnier, 1847;*

Par François Pedoüe, chanoine de Chartres. In Edouard Fournier, *Variétés historiques et littéraires* (Paris, 1859), IX, 145–213.

12. Labiche & Martin, *Le Voyage de M. Perrichon,* Act II, sc. vii; Act III, sc. viii. See Marie, p. 219, water color dated 1861: Prudhomme with his daughter; the sentence was one of his favorite sayings.

13. Augier, *Le Gendre de Monsieur Poirier,* Act I, sc. iv, vi.

14. Louis Veuillot, *Les Odeurs de Paris,* 3rd. ed. (Paris, 1867), pp. 407–442.

15. Auguste Villiers de l'Isle-Adam, *Tribulat Bonhomet* (Paris, 1896). See Lucien Refort, *La Caricature littéraire* (Paris, 1932), pp. 29–32; Morienval, *De Pathelin à Ubu,* pp. 248–249.

16. *Monsieur et Madame Cardinal* (1873), *Les Petites Cardinal* (1881); published together as *La Famille Cardinal* (1883). See Morienval, *De Pathelin à Ubu,* pp. 222–225.

17. *Ibid.,* pp. 269–270. See Gertrude Jasper, *Adventures in the Theatre: Lugné-Poe and the Théâtre de l'Œuvre to 1899* (New Brunswick: Rutgers University Press, 1947), pp. 222–236.

18. Alfred Jarry, *Ubu roi ou les Polonais* (Paris, n.d.), pp. 180–181.

19. Champfleury, "M. Prudhomme au Salon," *La Silhouette* (March 22, 1846), republished in *Contes vieux et nouveaux* (Paris, 1852), pp. 202–223. *Le Passe-temps comique* (Bruxelles, 1850); *L'Encyclopédie pittoresque de calembours* (Paris, n.d.): both "mises en désordre par Joseph Prudhomme." L. de Neuville, *Paris pantin* (Paris, 1863); *Nouveau théâtre des pupazzi* (Paris, 1882). "L'Apothéose de Joseph Prudhomme, par le Bonhomme Chrysale," *Annales politiques et littéraires* (July 18, 1920), pp. 43–44. Léon Deutch, "Samuel Pickwick chez Joseph Prudhomme," *Revue française* (March 16, 1924). See Woodruff, "Henry Monnier," pp. 73–75.

20. "Monsieur Prudhomme," *Poèmes saturniens* (1866), in *Œuvres complètes,* I (Paris, 1923), 53. Prudhomme has even made a brief and curious appearance on the stage since the curtain fell on Monnier's final performance of the role. In 1931 Sacha Guitry produced a two-act sketch based on an imaginary episode in Monnier's life, in which the artist is shown in the role of Prudhomme, the evening of his public debut. It must have been an amusing tour de force. Guitry's bill at the Théâtre de la Madeleine included *M. Prudhomme a-t-il vécu?* and Monnier's *La Femme du condamné,* produced for the first time. See Jacques Deval, "A travers les théâtres," *Revue des deux mondes* (December 15, 1931), pp. 942–943; "Les Théâtres," signed "R. de B.," *L'Illustration* (November 14, 1931), p. 355.

21. See Woodruff, "Henry Monnier," p. 71: *Fantasio* (Paris, August 1, 1912–July 15, 1913).

22. See Emmanuel Berl, *Mort de la pensée bourgeoise* (Paris, 1929); *Frère bourgeois mourez-vous? ding! ding! dong!* (Paris, 1938); René Dumesnil, "Le Bourgeois à l'ombre d'Hernani," *Formes et couleurs* (Paris, 1945), Vols. III-IV.

SELECTED BIBLIOGRAPHIES

SELECTED BIBLIOGRAPHIES

A. MONNIER'S LITERARY AND ARTISTIC WORK

It seems unnecessary to reprint here information which is already available in works listed in section B of this bibliography. In the notes full references have been given to all editions of Monnier's work which have been discussed. In the Index of Monnier's Works are listed all artistic and literary works mentioned; this list forms a fairly complete bibliography.

B. STUDIES OF MONNIER

Aubryet, Xavier, "Synthèse de la sottise–Monsieur Prudhomme," *Les Jugements nouveaux, philosophie de quelques oeuvres* (Paris, 1860).

Audebrand, Philibert, "Courrier de Paris," *L'Illustration* (January 13, 1877).

Babou, Hippolyte, "Henry Monnier aux enfers–scènes de l'autre monde," *La République des lettres* (January 21, 1877).

Banville, Théodore de, "Le Témoin," *L'Ame de Paris, nouveaux souvenirs* (Paris, 1890).

Bertall (Charles-Albert d'Arnoux), "Henri Monnier," *L'Illustration* (January 13, 1877). Famous article naming Monnier as Balzac's model for Bixiou.

Burty, Philippe, "Henry Monnier," *L'Art* (May 20, 1877). Interesting study of M. as actor, and enemy of the bourgeois.

Bury, R. de, "Les Débuts d'Henry Monnier, humoriste," *Mercure de France* (February 1, 1927).

——— "Les Théâtres," *L'Illustration* (November 14, 1931).

Catalogue des aquarelles, dessins et croquis, par Henry Monnier, provenant de la collection de M. Gustave Cohen (Paris, 1929).

Champfleury (Jules Fleury), *Henry Monnier, sa vie, son oeuvre* (Paris: Dentu, 1879). Considered definitive until Wolfrum and Marie. Chief source for later studies, in spite of poorly organized material and errors in scholarship. Bibliography of M.'s literary and artistic work is incomplete but fairly reliable. No list of source material used in text. Footnotes incomplete and unsatisfactory.

Courrier des théâtres (Paris, 1831, 1832, 1834). M. as actor.

Daudet, Alphonse, "Henry Monnier," *Trente ans de Paris* (Paris, 1888).

Degouy, Paul, "Henry Monnier et Monsieur Prudhomme," *La Grande revue* (September 1920).

Deval, Jacques, "A travers les théâtres," *Revue des deux mondes* (December 15, 1931).

Doutrepont, Georges, *Les Types populaires de la littérature française* (Bruxelles, 1926). Interesting brief bibliography of works by M. and others in which Prudhomme appears.

Fierens, Paul, "Henry Monnier," *Journal des débats* (July 24, 1931). Review of Marie.

Fleuret, Fernand, "Notice," *Henry Monnier, collection des plus belles pages* (Paris: Mercure de France, 1939).

Fournel, François Victor, *Figures d'hier et d'aujourd'hui* (Paris, 1883).

Gautier, Théophile, "Henry Monnier," *Portraits contemporains* (Paris, 1874). Published as preface to M.'s *Paris et la province*, 1866.

Gide, André, "Henry Monnier," *Marianne* (October 9, 1935).

——— *Nouvelles pages de Journal (1932–35)*, 7th ed. (Paris: Gallimard, 1936).

"Henri Monnier," *Temple Bar, a London magazine for town and country readers* (March 1878).

Henriot, Emile, "Le Centenaire de Joseph Prudhomme," *Le Temps* (February 26, 1929).

"Henry Monnier," *Nouvelle galerie des artistes dramatiques vivants* (Paris: Librairie théâtrale, 1855). Geoffroy, ed. Only autobiography of M. Used by Champfleury, who repeats without verification incorrect date of birth, and quotes rather unreliable statements about early years. Marie is more critical about this material.

Journal des débats, articles on M. (July 8, 1831; June 4, 1832; February 26, 1848; August 13, 1849; November 29, 1852; February 19, 1855; January 7, 1856).

Lazareff, Pierre, "Joseph Prudhomme a aujourd'hui cent ans!" *Paris-Midi* (July 5, 1931).

Marie, Aristide, *L'Art et la vie romantiques: Henry Monnier (1799–1877)* (Paris: Floury, 1931). Last half of M.'s life more fully presented than by Champfleury; unpublished letters, especially after 1850. Passages taken almost verbatim from Champfleury, without acknowledgment. General organization better than Champfleury's, but many bibliographical errors. Fullest published catalogue of M.'s artistic work. Excellent illustrations. See Fierens, above.

——— "Balzac et Monnier," *Nouvelles littéraires* (March 7, 1931).

Melcher, Edith, "Flaubert and Henry Monnier," *Modern Language Notes* (March 1933).

Mirecourt, Eugène de, "Henry Monnier," *Les Contemporains*, no. 76 (Paris, 1857). Amusingly anecdotal but factually inaccurate.

"Monnier mort," *Revue politique et littéraire* (January 13, 20, 1877).

Monselet, Charles, "Monnier, Henry," *Lorgnette littéraire* (Paris, 1857). Biography often used by later writers.

Morienval, Jean, "La Fortune de Joseph Prudhomme," *De Pathelin à Ubu* (Paris: Bloud & Gay, 1929).

Morin, Louis, *Le Triomphe de Joseph Prudhomme* (Paris, 1904).

Reitlinger, Henry S., "Monnier and Lami," *The Print Collector's Quarterly* (January 1930).

Spoelberch de Lovenjoul, Charles, "Henri Monnier et ses épaves," *Les Lundis d'un chercheur* (Paris: Calmann Lévy, 1894). Indispensable to a complete bibliography of M.'s literary work.

Wolfrum, Hildegard, *Das literarische Werk Henri Monnier's* (Lauf a.d. Pegn, Bachmann, 1930). Fullest and most scholarly attempt to evaluate M.'s literary significance. Some confusion of thought. Excellent bibliography.

Woodruff, Sara, "Henry Monnier" (MS, Middlebury College, 1938). Valuable dissertation, emphasizing M.'s influence on Balzac. Excellent bibliography of M.'s literary and dramatic work.

——— "Henry Monnier: Artist, Author, Actor (1799–1877)," *The Furman Bulletin* (Greenville, N.C., April 1939). Abstract of preceding work.

C. WORKS CITED OR MENTIONED IN THIS BOOK

Abancourt (F.-J. Willemain) d', *Proverbes dramatiques* (Berlin & Paris, 1781).

Alexandre, Arsène, "L'Esprit français: Les Caricaturistes," *Pages d'histoire 1914–1916*, ser. 8 (Paris & Nancy, 1916).

Allard, Louis, *Esquisses parisiennes en des temps heureux: 1830–1848* (Montreal: Variétés, 1943).

Alméras, Henri d', *La Vie parisienne sous le règne de Louis-Philippe* (Paris: Michel, n.d.).

Althon-Shée, Edmond d', *Mes mémoires* (Paris, 1869).

Ancelot, Marguérite L.–V., *Les Salons de Paris–Foyers éteints* (Paris, 1858).

Arrigon, Louis-Jules, *Les Années romantiques de Balzac* (Paris, 1927).

Ashbee, Charles R., *Caricature* (London, 1928).

Audebrand, Philibert, *Derniers jours de la Bohême: Souvenirs de la vie littéraire* (Paris: Calmann Lévy, n.d.).

Augier, Emile, *La Contagion, Théâtre complet,* vol. V (Paris, 1890).

——— and Sandeau, Jules, *Le Gendre de M. Poirier, Théâtre complet,* vol. III (Paris, 1890).

Balzac, Honoré de, *Oeuvres complètes* (Paris: Conard, 1912–1938).

——— *Correspondance, 1819–1850* (Paris: Calmann Lévy, 1876).

——— *Lettres à l'étrangère* (Paris: Calmann Lévy, 1906–1930).

——— *Pensées, sujets, fragments* (Paris: Blaizot, 1910). Jacques Crepet, ed.

Baudelaire, Charles, *Curiosités esthétiques, Oeuvres complètes,* vol. V (Paris, 1925).

Berl, Emmanuel, *Frère bourgeois mourez-vous? ding! ding! dong!* (Paris: Grasset, 1938).

——— *Mort de la pensée bourgeoise* (Paris: Grasset, 1929).

Berthet, Elie, *Histoires des uns et des autres* (Paris, 1878).

——— "Silhouettes et anecdotes littéraires," *Revue de France* (May 1, 1877).

Boulenger, J.-R., *Sous Louis-Philippe: les dandys* (Paris: Ollendorff, n.d.), "nouvelle édition augmentée."

"Le Bourgeois poli," *Variétés historiques et littéraires; recueil de pièces volantes, rares et curieuses*, vol. IX (Paris, 1859). Fournier, ed.

Boutet de Monvel, Roger, *Les Variétés 1850–1870* (Paris: Plon-Nourrit, n.d.).

Bouvier, Emile, *La Bataille réaliste (1844–1857)* (Paris: Fontemoing, n.d.).

Calvet, Jean, *Les Types universels dans la littérature française*, ser. 1 and 2 (Paris, 1928).

La Caricature (Paris, 1830–).

Carmontelle (Louis Carrogis), *Proverbes dramatiques* (Paris, 1822).

——— *Proverbes et comédies posthumes* (Paris, 1825).

Cavé, E.-L. Auguste. See Dittmer and Cavé.

Champfleury (Jules Fleury), *Histoire de la caricature moderne* (Paris: Dentu, n.d.).

——— *Histoire de la caricature sous la réforme et la ligue–Louis XIII à Louis XIV* (Paris: Dentu, n.d.).

——— *Histoire de la caricature sous la république, l'empire et la restauration* (Paris: Dentu, n.d.).

——— *Le Réalisme* (Paris, 1857).

——— *Souvenirs et portraits de jeunesse* (Paris, 1872).

——— *Les Vignettes romantiques: Histoire de la littérature et de l'art 1825–1840* (Paris, 1883).

Le Charivari (Paris, 1832–).

Cim, Albert (Cimochowski), *Mystifications littéraires et théâtrales* (Paris, 1913).

Collé, Charles, *Théâtre de société*, "nouvelle édition" (La Haye & Paris, 1777).

Courboin, François, *Histoire illustrée de la gravure en France, 3e partie, XIXe siècle* (Paris, 1926).

Daumier, Honoré, *Les Cent Robert-Macaire* (Paris: Bureau du *Journal pour rire*, n.d.).

Dayot, Armand, *Les Vernet, Joseph–Carle–Horace* (Paris, 1898).

Deberdt, Raoul, *La Caricature et l'humour français au XIXe siècle*, 2nd ed. (Paris: Larousse, n.d.).

Delacroix, Eugène, *Journal* (Paris: Plon, 1932). A. Joubin, ed.

——— *Lettres 1815 à 1863* (Paris, 1878). P. Burty, ed.

Delécluze, Etienne-Jean, *Souvenirs de soixante années (1789–1849)* (Paris, 1862).

Delvau, Alfred, *Les Lions du jour, physionomies parisiennes* (Paris, 1867).

——— *Le Théâtre érotique sous le bas-empire français* (Paris: Pincebourse, n.d.).

Desfeuilles, Paul, *La Vie littéraire sous le second empire: Charles Monselet, 1825–1888, et la critique anecdotique* (Paris, 1927).

Le Diable à Paris–Paris et les Parisiens: Moeurs et coutumes, caractères et portraits des habitants de Paris . . . etc. (Paris, 1845–1846).

Dickinson, Goldsworthy Lowes, *Revolution and reaction in modern France* (New York, 1927).

Dittmer, Adolphe, and E.-L.-A. Cavé, *Les Soirées de Neuilly, esquisses dramatiques et historiques publiées par M. de Fongeray* (Paris, 1827–1828).

DuCamp, Maxime, *Souvenirs littéraires* (Paris, 1892).

Dumas, Alexandre, *Mes mémoires* (Paris, 1897–1900).

Dumesnil, René, "Le Bourgeois à l'ombre d'Hernani," *Formes et couleurs,* vols. III–IV (Lausanne, 1945).

Duvert, Brazier, and Dupeuty, *La Famille improvisée,* in Félix Auguste Duvert, *Théâtre choisi,* vol. I (Paris, 1879).

Escholier, Raymond, *Daumier peintre et lithographe* (Paris, 1923).

Flaubert, Gustave, *Oeuvres complètes* (Paris: Conard, 1910–1936).

Les Français peints par eux-mêmes (Paris: Philippart, n.d.). See *Pictures of the French.*

Friedell, Egon, *A Cultural history of the modern age: the crisis of the European soul from the black death to the world war,* translated by C. F. Atkinson (New York: Knopf, 1930–1932).

Gaultier, Paul, *Le Rire et la caricature,* 3rd ed. (Paris, 1911).

Gautier, Théophile, *Histoire du romantisme* (Paris, 1877).

—— *Les Jeune-France, romans goguenards, suivis de contes humoristiques* (Paris, 1885).

—— *Portraits et souvenirs littéraires* (Paris, 1885).

Gazette anecdotique, littéraire, artistique et bibliographique (Paris, 1876–). Georges d'Heylli (Edmond Poinsot) & D. Jouast, ed.

Gigoux, Jean, *Causeries sur les artistes de mon temps* (Paris, 1885).

Girardin, Delphine Gay de, *Le Vicomte de Launay (Lettres choisies)* (Paris, 1913). F. Roger-Cornaz, ed.

Giraudoux, Jean, "Sur la caricature," *Arts et métiers graphiques* (September 15, 1932).

Goncourt, Edmond & Jules de, *Gavarni, l'homme et l'oeuvre* (Paris, 1912), "nouvelle édition."

—— *The Goncourt Journals,* transl. by Lewis Galantière (New York: Doubleday Doran, 1937).

—— *Mystères des théâtres, 1852* (Paris, 1853).

—— *Quelques créatures de ce temps* (Paris, 1878), "nouvelle édition."

Grand-Carteret, John, *Les Moeurs et la caricature en France* (Paris: Librairie illustrée, n.d.).

Guéchot, M., *Types populaires créés par les grands écrivains* (Paris, 1907).

Guex, Jules, *Le Théâtre et la société française de 1815 à 1848* (Vevey, 1900).

Halévy, Ludovic, *La Famille Cardinal* (Paris, 1883).

—— *Madame et monsieur Cardinal* (Paris, 1882).

—— *Les Petites Cardinal* (Paris, 1894).

Hédiard, Germain, *Les Lithographies de Bonington* (no place, n.d.).

Intermédiaire des chercheurs et curieux (Paris, 1864–).

Jal, Auguste, *Esquisses, croquis, pochades, ou tout ce qu'on voudra, sur le salon de 1827* (Paris, 1828).

—— "La Gaîté et les comiques de Paris," *Nouveau tableau de Paris au XIXe siècle,* vol. II (Paris, 1834).

—— *Souvenirs d'un homme de lettres (1795–1873)* (Paris, 1877).

Jarry, Alfred, "Questions de théâtre," *La Revue blanche* (Paris: January 1897).

——— *Ubu roi ou les Polonais* (Paris: Fasqualle, n.d.).

Jerrold, William Blanchard, *The Life of George Cruikshank in Two Epochs* (London, 1882).

Kock, Ch.-Paul de, *La Grande ville ou Paris il y a vingt-cinq ans* (Paris: Degorce-Cadot, n.d.).

——— *Mémoires écrits par lui-même* (Paris, 1873).

——— *Moeurs parisiennes* (Paris, 1839–1840).

Labédollière, Emile de, *Les Industriels; métiers et professions en France, avec cent dessins par Henry Monnier* (Paris, 1842).

Labiche, Eugène and Edouard Martin, *Le Voyage de monsieur Perrichon*, in Labiche, *Théâtre complet*, vol. II (Paris, 1881).

Labretonnière, Emile, *Macédoine: Souvenirs du quartier latin dédiés à la jeunesse des écoles; Paris à la chute de l'empire et pendant les cent jours; Correspondance avec Béranger* (Paris, 1863).

Lafond, Paul, *L'Aube romantique: Jules de Rességuier et ses amis*, 2nd ed. (Paris, 1910).

Langlé, Ferdinand, *Les Contes du gay sçavoir: Ballades, fabliaux et traditions du moyen âge* (Paris, 1828).

Latouche, H. de, *La Reine d'Espagne* (Paris, 1928). F. Ségu, ed.

LeBreton, André, *Balzac, l'homme et l'oeuvre: origines du roman balzacien* (Paris, 1905).

Leclercq, Théodore, *Oeuvres complètes, proverbes dramatiques* (Paris: Lebigre-Duquesne, n.d.), "nouvelle édition."

——— *Proverbes dramatiques* (Paris, 1835).

Lemercier de Neuville, Louis, *Histoire anecdotique des marionnettes modernes* (Paris, 1892).

——— *Souvenirs d'un montreur de marionnettes* (Paris, 1911).

Lemoisne, Paul-André, *Eugène Lami 1800–1890* (Paris, 1912).

Lhomme, Marie-François, *Charlet* (Paris, 1892).

Loève-Weimars, Adolphe, Emile Vanderburch, and Auguste Romieu, *Scènes contemporaines laissées par madame la vicomtesse de Chamilly* (Paris, 1828–1830).

Lytton, Edward Bulwer, *The Parisians* (Boston: Dana Estes, n.d.).

Maillard, Firmin, *La Cité des intellectuels, scènes cruelles et plaisantes de la vie littéraire des gens de lettres au XIXe siècle* (Paris: Daragon, n.d.).

——— *Les Derniers bohêmes: Henri Murger et son temps* (Paris, 1874).

Marnay, A.-J. de, *Mémoires secrets et témoignages authentiques; chute de Charles X, royauté de juillet, 24 février 1848* (Paris, 1875).

Martino, Pierre, *Le Naturalisme français (1870–1895)* (Paris, 1923).

——— *Le Roman réaliste sous le second empire* (Paris, 1913).

Maynial, Edouard, *La Jeunesse de Flaubert* (Paris, 1913).

Melcher, Edith, *Stage Realism in France Between Diderot and Antoine* (Bryn Mawr College, 1928).

Mérimée, Prosper, *Portraits historiques et littéraires* (Paris, 1874).

Méry, Joseph, "Les Forçats–Aly et Soliman," *Revue de Paris*, vol. XIII (1835).

Mespoulet, Marguerite, *Images et romans: parenté des estampes et du roman réaliste de 1815 à 1865* (Paris: Les Belles-lettres, 1939).

Monnet, Jean, "Les Mystifications de sieur P. . . . ," *Supplément au roman comique, ou Mémoires pour servir à la vie de Jean Monnet . . .* , vol. II (Londres, 1772).

Monselet, Charles, *Théâtre du Figaro* (Paris, 1861).

Morgan, Lady Sydney Owenson, *France in 1829–30* (London, 1830).

Morienval, Jean, *Les Créatures de la grande presse en France: Emile de Girardin, H. de Villemessant, Moïse Millaud* (Paris: Spes, n.d.).

Musset, Alfred de, "Lettres de Dupuis et Cotonet," *Oeuvres choisies* (Paris: Hatier, 1932). Thomas & Berveiller, ed.

Ourliac, Edouard, *Proverbes et scènes bourgeoises* (Paris, 1868).

Petite biographie des acteurs et actrices des théâtres de Paris, avec l'âge de ces dames (Paris, 1831–1832).

Picard, Roger, *Artifices et mystifications littéraires* (Montreal: Variétés, 1945).

Pictures of the French (London: W. S. Orr, 1840; T. Tegg, 1842). Translation of *Les Français peints par eux-mêmes.*

Refort, Lucien, *La Caricature littéraire* (Paris: Colin, 1932).

Renard, Georges, *Les Etapes de la société française au 19e siècle, 1812–1837–1862–1887* (Paris, 1913).

Reybaud, Louis, *Jérôme Paturot à la recherche d'une position sociale* (Paris, 1842).

——— *Jérôme Paturot à la recherche d'une position sociale et politique* (Paris, 1843).

——— *Jérôme Paturot à la recherche de la meilleure des républiques* (Paris, 1848).

Romieu, Auguste, *Proverbes romantiques* (Paris, 1827).

——— *Scènes contemporaines.* See Loève-Weimars.

Roqueplan, Nestor, *La Vie parisienne* (Paris, 1869).

Rousseau, James (Pierre Joseph Rousseau), "Physiologie de la portière," *Physiologies parisiennes* (Paris: Aubert, Lavigne, n.d.).

Saint-Amand, J. A. L., Benjamin Antier, and Frédéric Lemaître, *Robert Macaire* (Paris, 1835).

Scribe, Eugène and Dupin, "L'Intérieur de l'étude, ou Le Procureur et l'avoué," *Fin du répertoire du Théâtre-Français*, vol. XXXVI (Paris, 1824).

——— Imbert, and Varner, "L'Intérieur d'un bureau, ou La Chanson," *Fin du répertoire du Théâtre-Français*, vol. XXXVIII (Paris, 1824).

——— "La Loge du portier," *Fin du répertoire du Théâtre-Français,* vol. XXXVIII (Paris, 1824).

Séché, Léon, *Le Cénacle de Joseph Delorme (1827–1830)* (Paris, 1912).

Ségu, Frédéric, *Un Romantique républicain: H. de Latouche, 1785–1851* (Paris: Les Belles-lettres, 1931).

La Silhouette (Paris, 1830–).

Stendhal (M.-H. Beyle), *Correspondance inédite* (Paris, 1855).

—— *Souvenirs d'égotisme* (Paris, 1892). C. Stryienski, ed.

Stigand, William, *The Life, Work and Opinions of Heinrich Heine*, vol. II (London, 1875).

Thackeray, William M., *The Paris Sketch Book, Works*, vol. XXII (London, 1910–1911).

Thierry, Augustin, *Les Grandes mystifications littéraires*, 2nd. ed. (Paris, 1911).

Tousez, Alcide, "Vie de Napoléon racontée dans une fête de village," *Magasin théâtral*, vol. IV (Paris, 1834).

Trahard, Pierre, *La Jeunesse de Prosper Mérimée (1803–1834)* (Paris, 1925).

Trotain, Marthe, *Les Scènes historiques: Etude du théâtre livresque à la veille du drame romantique* (Paris, 1923).

Vanderburch, Emile. See Loève-Weimars.

Véron, Louis, *Mémoires d'un bourgeois de Paris, comprenant la fin de l'empire, la restauration, la monarchie de juillet, la république jusqu'au rétablissement de l'empire* (Paris, 1856).

Veuillot, Louis, *Les Odeurs de Paris, 3rd. ed.* (Paris, 1867).

La Vie parisienne à travers le XIXe siècle; Paris de 1800 à 1900, d'après les estampes et les mémoires du temps (Paris, 1900–1901). Ch. Simond, ed.

Villiers de l'Isle-Adam, Auguste de, *Tribulat Bonhomet* (Paris, 1896).

Waxman, Samuel M., *Antoine and the Théâtre-Libre* (Cambridge: Harvard University Press, 1926).

Weinberg, Bernard, *French Realism: The Critical Reaction, 1830–1870* (dissertation University of Chicago, 1936; New York: MLAA General Series, 1937).

Young, Arthur Henry, *Thomas Rowlandson* (New York: Willey Book Co., 1938).

Yriarte, Ch.-E., *Paris grotesque; les célébrités de la rue; Paris (1815 à 1863)* (Paris, 1864).

—— *Les Cercles de Paris 1828–1864* (Paris, 1864).

D. SELECTED LIST OF OTHER WORKS CONSULTED

Standard bibliographies, histories of literature and art, critical works, and works of general reference are omitted; also books examined only for illustrations by artists other than Monnier.

Adeline, Jules, *Hippolyte Bellangé et son oeuvre* (Paris, 1880).

Alexandre, Roger, *Le Musée de la conversation: répertoire de citations françaises, dictons modernes, curiosités littéraires, historiques et anecdotiques* (Paris, 1892).

Alhoy, Maurice, "Physiologie de la lorette," *Physiologies parisiennes* (Paris: Aubert, Lavigne, n.d.).

Balzac, H. de, "Etudes sur M. Beyle. (Frédéric Stendalh [*sic*])," *Revue parisienne* (September 25, 1840).

Bergerat, Emile, *Souvenirs d'un enfant de Paris* (Paris, 1911).

Brenner, Clarence D., *Le Développement du proverbe dramatique en France et sa vogue au XVIIIe siècle, avec un proverbe inédit de Carmontelle* (Berkeley: University of California Press, 1937).

Challamel, Augustin, *Souvenirs d'un hugolâtre: La Génération de 1830* (Paris, 1885).

Chaumeix, André, "La Comédie-proverbe," *Revue des deux mondes* (August 1, 1927).

Cordier, Henri, *Stendhal et ses amis: Notes d'un curieux* (Evreux, 1890).

Dayot, Armand, *Les Maîtres de la caricature française au XIXe siècle* (Paris: Quantin, n.d.).

——— *Raffet et son oeuvre* (Paris: Quantin, n.d.).

Désaugiers, M.-A.-M., *Théâtre* (Paris, 1887).

De Tolnay, Charles, *Pierre Brueghel l'ancien* (Bruxelles: Nouvelle société d'éditions, 1935).

Dumersan, Th.-M., *Mme. Gibou et Mme. Pochet, ou Le Thé chez la ravaudeuse* (Paris, 1867).

——— and Gabriel, *Mémoires de Mlle. Flore, artiste du Théâtre des Variétés* (Paris, 1845).

——— and Sewrin. See Sewrin.

Duranty, Louis E.-E., *Réalisme* (Paris, 1856–1857).

Farcy, Ch.-François, *Les Commis, ou L'Intérieur d'un bureau* (Paris, 1818).

Flamand, Albert, "Tableau de Paris–Gros," *Revue de Paris* (July 1, 1936).

Forgues, Eugène, *Gavarni* (Paris: Rouam, n.d.).

Gavarni (Chevallier, G.-S.), *Manières de voir et façons de penser* (Paris, 1869).

Gérard de Nerval (Labrunie, Gérard), *La Bohême galante* (Paris, 1866).

Gillot, Hubert, *E. Delacroix; l'homme, ses idées, son oeuvre* (Paris, 1928).

Gilman, Margaret, *Baudelaire the Critic* (New York: Columbia University Press, 1943).

Green, Frederic C., *Stendhal* (Cambridge, Eng.: Cambridge University Press, 1939).

Haussonville, G. P. Othenin de Cléron d', "Prosper Mérimée, à propos de lettres inédites," *Revue des deux mondes* (August 15, 1879).

Houssaye, Arsène, *Histoire de la peinture flamande et hollandaise*, 2nd. ed. (Paris, 1848).

Huart, Louis, "Physiologie de la grisette," "Physiologie de l'étudiant," *Physiologies parisiennes* (Paris: Aubert, Lavigne, n.d.).

Janin, Jules, *The American in Paris, or Heath's picturesque annual for 1843* (London, 1843).

——— *L'Eté à Paris* (Paris: Curmer, n.d.).

——— *Un Hiver à Paris* (Paris, 1843).

Kahn, Gustave, "Le Salon d'automne–Rétrospectives," *Mercure de France* (December 1, 1931).

Labédollière, Emile de, *Histoire de la mode en France* (Paris, 1858).

—— *Histoire illustrée de Paris depuis les temps les plus reculés jusqu'à nos jours* (Paris, 1879).
Legouvé, Ernest, *Soixante ans de souvenirs* (Paris, 1886).
Lemercier de Neuville, Louis, *Nouveau théâtre des pupazzi* (Paris, 1882).
—— *I Pupazzi* (Paris, 1866).
Longfellow, Henry W., *Manuel de proverbes dramatiques: Selections from the Proverbes dramatiques published at Paris in 8 volumes 1768–1782*, 3rd. ed. (Boston, 1840).
Maigron, Louis, *Le Romantisme et la mode* (Paris, 1911).
—— *Le Romantisme et les moeurs* (Paris, 1910).
Der Maler Daumier (New York: E. Weyhe, n.d.). E. Fuchs, ed.
Marie, Aristide, *Alfred et Tony Johannot, peintres, graveurs et vignettistes* (Paris, 1925).
Mendès, Catulle, *La Légende du parnasse contemporain*, 2nd. ed. (Bruxelles, 1884).
Milatchitch, Douchan Z., *Le Théâtre de Honoré de Balzac* (Paris: Hachette, 1930).
Parfait, Noël, *Première philippique au roi*, 2nd. ed. (Paris, 1833).
Parton, James, *Caricature and other comic art in all times and many lands* (New York, 1877).
Pavie, Victor, *Souvenirs de jeunesse et revenants, Oeuvres choisies*, vol. II (Paris, 1887).
Petits albums pour rire (Paris: Philipon fils, n.d.).
Pietsch, Ludwig, *Horace-Vernet-Album* (Berlin: G. Schauer, n.d.).
Praz, Mario, *The Romantic Agony*, transl. by Angus Davidson (Oxford: Oxford University Press, 1933).
Réal, P.-F. de, *Indiscrétions 1798–1830: Souvenirs anecdotiques et politiques tirés du portefeuille d'un fonctionnaire de l'empire* (Paris, 1835). Musnier-Desclozeaux, ed.
Reybaud, Louis, *César Falempin* (Paris, 1861).
Rhodes, Henry J., *The Art of Lithography* (London, 1924).
Rocheblave, Samuel, *L'Art et le goût en France de 1600 à 1900* (Paris, 1923).
Le Romantisme et l'art (Paris, 1928).
Saintsbury, George, "Désaugiers," *Miscellaneous Essays* (London, 1892).
Salomon, Michel, *Charles Nodier et le groupe romantique* (Paris, 1908).
Sewrin, Ch.-A. & Dumersan, *Les Anglaises pour rire, ou La Table et le logement*, 2nd. ed. (Paris: Huet-Masson, n.d.).
Soixante ans dans les ateliers des artistes, C. A. Dubosc modèle (Paris: Calmann Lévy, n.d.).
Stendhal raconté par ceux qui l'ont vu: souvenirs, lettres, documents réunis, annotés et accompagnés de résumés biographiques (Paris: Stock, 1931). P. Jourda, ed.
Tourneux, Maurice, *L'Age du romantisme–Gérard de Nerval, prosateur et poète* (Paris, 1887).

Truc, Gonzague, *Scènes et tableaux du règne de Louis-Philippe et de la IIe république* (Paris: Gautier-Languereau, 1935).

Veth, Cornelis, *Comic Art in England* (Amsterdam: M. Hertzberger, 1930).

Vigny, Alfred de, *Journal d'un poète* (Paris, 1926). L. Ratisbonne, ed.

Vitet, Louis, *Etudes sur les beaux arts et sur la littérature–De la caricature* (Paris, 1846).

Weitenkampf, Frank, *The Illustrated Book* (Cambridge: Harvard University Press, 1938).

Wood, Henry T. W., *Modern Methods of Illustrating Books* (London, 1887).

Wright, Charles H. C., *Background of Modern French Literature* (Boston, 1926).

Wright, Thomas, *A History of Caricature and The Grotesque in Literature and Art* (London: Virtue Bros., n.d.).

GENERAL INDEX
AND
INDEX OF WORKS

GENERAL INDEX

INDEX OF MONNIER'S WORKS

ARTISTIC

BOOK ILLUSTRATIONS

POLITICAL AND LITERARY CARTOONS

PORTRAITS

SCENES OF MANNERS

SOCIAL SATIRE

LITERARY